Theorising heterosexuality

Theorising heterosexuality
Telling it straight

Edited by
Diane Richardson

OPEN UNIVERSITY PRESS
Buckingham · Philadelphia

Open University Press
Celtic Court
22 Ballmoor
Buckingham   MK18 1XW

email: enquiries@openup.co.uk
world wide web: http://www.openup.co.uk

and
325 Chestnut Street
Philadelphia, PA 19106, USA

First Published 1996
Reprinted 1998

A catalogue record of this book is available from the British Library

ISBN 0 335 19503 2 (pb)   0 335 19504 0 (hb)

Library of Congress Cataloging-in-Publication Data
Theorising heterosexuality : telling it straight / edited by Diane Richardson
        p.   cm.
    Includes bibliographical references and index.
    ISBN 0-335-19504-0 (hardcover). – ISBN 0-335-19503-2 (pbk.)
    1. Heterosexuality.   2. Gender identity.   I. Richardson, Diane.   1953–
HQ23.T52   1996
    306.76'4–dc20   96-12682
                                                                                   CIP

Typeset by Type Study, Scarborough
Printed in Great Britain by Biddles Ltd, Guildford and King's Lynn

For Ann

Contents

Acknowledgements

First of all I would like to thank my editor Jacinta Evans for her positive and swift response to the idea for this book, and for her perseverance in pursuing a working relationship that has at last borne fruit! I must also thank the production staff at Open University Press and the administrative staff in the Department of Sociological Studies at Sheffield for their practical support, especially Joanne Crossland who worked on the Bibliography. I would also like to take this opportunity to thank all the contributors to the book. I have enjoyed working with them and have been impressed with both their professionalism and their contributions. For part of the time spent working on the book I was Visiting Scholar in Women's Studies at Harvard University. Various people there made my experience of Harvard a stimulating and enjoyable one and I would especially like to thank staff of the Committee on Degrees in Women's Studies in the faculty, as well as Pirjo Ahokas, Margaret Morganroth Gullette, Jillian Roe, Ann Schofield and Sabina Sielke. Last, but most certainly not least, my thanks to my family and friends who have continued to provide me with love and support this year, in particular Sarah Bishop, Wendy Bolton, Jean Carabine, Carol Standish, Helen Thompson, and Ann Watkinson.

Diane Richardson

Notes on the contributors

Jean Carabine lectures in social policy at the University of Loughborough. Her research interests are in the areas of women, sexuality and social policy; sexual risk and social policy; feminist campaigning; and local and national politics. She is currently working on a book, *Women, Sexuality and Social Policy*, to be published by Macmillan. She is also a member of the Critical Social Policy Editorial Collective.

Janet Holland is reader in sociology and Director of the Social Science Research Centre, South Bank University, and lecturer in education at the Open University. Her publications include: (coeditor with J. Weeks) *Sexual Cultures: Communities, Values and Intimacy* (Macmillan 1996); (coeditor with L. Adkins) *Sex, Sensibility and the Gendered Body* (Macmillan 1996); and (with C. Ramazanoglu) 'Coming to conclusions: power and interpretation in researching young women's sexuality' in J. Purvis and M. Maynard (eds) *Researching Women's Lives from a Feminist Perspective* (Falmer 1994).

Wendy Hollway is reader in gender relations in the Department of Psychology, University of Leeds. She has researched and published on questions of subjectivity, gender and sexuality, the history of work psychology and gender relations in organizations. Among her published books are *Subjectivity and Method in Psychology: Gender, Meaning and Science* (Sage 1989), *Changing the Subject*, with Henriques, Urwin, Venn and Walkerdine (Methuen 1984) and, as coeditor, *Mothering and Ambivalence* (Routledge 1997). She is working on an edited collection, with Brid Featherstone, on mothering.

Stevi Jackson is Professor in Sociology and Women's Studies at the University of York. She is author of a book on Christine Delphy in the 'Women of Ideas' series (Sage 1996). She has coedited *Women's Studies: A Reader* (Harvester Wheatsheaf 1993), *The Politics of Domestic Consumption: Critical Readings* (Prentice Hall/Harvester Wheatsheaf 1995) and *Feminism and Sexuality* (Edinburgh University Press 1996). She has also published a number of articles on romance, sexuality and family relationships.

Sheila Jeffreys is the author of three books on the history and politics of sexuality; she teaches sexual politics and lesbian and gay politics at the University of Melbourne. She has been a feminist activist since 1973, campaigning against sexual violence and for lesbian liberation.

Caroline Ramazanoglu is a reader in sociology at Goldsmiths College, University of London. Her publications include *Feminism and the Contradictions of Oppression* (Routledge 1989); (as editor) *Up Against Foucault: Explorations of Some Tensions between Foucault and Feminism* (Routledge 1993); 'Back to basics: heterosexuality, biology and why men stay on top' in M. Maynard and J. Purvis (eds) *(Hetero)sexual Politics* (Taylor and Francis 1995).

Diane Richardson is Professor of Sociology in the Department of Social Policy at the University of Newcastle. Her works include *Women and the AIDS Crisis* (Pandora 1989), *Safer Sex* (Pandora 1990), *Women, Motherhood and Childrearing* (Macmillan 1993) and, as coeditor, *Introducing Women's Studies: Feminist Theory and Practice* (Macmillan 1997 Second Edition). She is currently writing a book on sexuality, social theory and social change to be published by Sage.

Victoria Robinson lectures in women's studies at the University of Sheffield and has recently published articles on heterosexuality, non-monogamy and developments in women's studies. She has coedited, with Diane Richardson, *Introducing Women's Studies: Feminist Theory and Practice* (Macmillan 1997 Second Edition).

Carol Smart is Professor of Sociology at the University of Leeds where she teaches sociology and women's studies. She is currently researching marital and relationship breakdown. She is author of *Feminism and the Power of Law* (Routledge 1989) and *Law, Crime and Sexuality* (Sage 1995).

Rachel Thomson is senior research fellow in the Social Science Research Centre, South Bank University. Recent publications include: (with J. Holland, C. Ramazanoglu and S. Sharpe) 'Pleasure, pressure and power: some contradictions of gendered sexuality' *Sociological Review* 40(4): 645–74, 1992;

'Power and desire: the embodiment of female sexuality' *Feminist Review* 46: 22–38, 1994; (with J. Holland, C. Ramazanoglu and S. Scott) 'Desire, risk and control: the body as a site of contestation'; (with J. Holland, C. Ramazanoglu and S. Sharpe) 'Achieving masculine sexuality: young men's strategies for managing vulnerability', both in L. Doyal, J. Naidoo, T. Wilton (eds) *AIDS: Setting a Feminist Agenda* (Taylor and Francis 1994); 'Moral rhetoric and public health pragmatism: the recent politics of sex education' *Feminist Review* 48: 40–60, 1994.

Jo VanEvery teaches sociology in the Department of Cultural Studies, University of Birmingham and is the author of *Heterosexual Women Changing the Family: Refusing to be a 'Wife'!* (Taylor and Francis 1995). Her research and teaching interests are in feminism, families and sexualities. She is currently developing research focusing on housework as a set of practices which constitute identities (including gender, sexuality and kinship).

Tamsin Wilton is reader in health and policy studies at the University of the West of England at Bristol, where she also teaches women's studies and lesbian studies. She has published widely in the areas of lesbian studies and HIV/AIDS. Her books include (with Lesley Doyal and Jennie Naidoo) *AIDS: Setting a Feminist Agenda* (Taylor and Francis 1994); *Immortal, Invisible: Lesbians and the Moving Image* (Routledge 1995); *Lesbian Studies: Setting an Agenda* (Routledge 1995); and En*gendering AIDS: Deconstructing Sex, Text, Epidemic* (Sage 1997).

Heterosexuality and social theory

Diane Richardson

...an understanding of virtually any aspect of modern Western culture must be, not merely incomplete, but damaged in its central substance to the degree that it does not incorporate a critical analysis of modern homo/heterosexual definition.

(Sedgwick 1990: 1)

Introduction

Within social and political theory little attention has traditionally been given to theorising heterosexuality. Although it is deeply embedded in accounts of social and political participation, and our understandings of ourselves and the worlds we inhabit, heterosexuality is rarely acknowledged or, even less likely, problematised. Instead, most of the conceptual frameworks we use to theorise human relations rely implicitly upon a naturalised heterosexuality, where (hetero-)sexuality tends either to be ignored in the analysis or is hidden from view, being treated as an unquestioned paradigm. Where sexuality is acknowledged as a significant category for social analysis it has been primarily in the context of theorising the 'sexual other', defined in relation to a normative heterosexuality. Perhaps more surprisingly is the failure of a great deal of feminist work, even when writing about the family, to question a naturalised heterosexuality. Monique Wittig (1981) and Susan Cavin (1985), for example, have criticised feminist theories which attempt to explain the origins of women's oppression for assuming the universality and normality of heterosexuality.

More recently there have been significant attempts by both feminists and proponents of queer theory to interrogate the way that heterosexuality encodes and structures everyday life, and to recognise the impact that ignoring or excluding heterosexuality has had on the development of social theory. In this chapter and in those that follow we shall be exploring and furthering these debates. Ultimately, this requires not only a commitment to theorising heterosexuality, but also a recognition of the challenge posed by this new theorisation of heterosexuality in so far as it invites a radical rethinking of many of the concepts we use to theorise social relations.

Heteronormativity

Heterosexuality is institutionalised as a particular form of practice and relationships, of family structure, and identity. It is constructed as a coherent, natural, fixed and stable category; as universal and monolithic. Despite being commonly represented in this way, there actually exists a diversity of meanings and social arrangements within the category 'heterosexuality', rather than a unitary heterosexual subject and a unified, distinct heterosexual community. However, whereas there is a growing albeit largely North American literature documenting how race, class and ethnicity interacts with sexuality in the case of lesbians and gay men (Moraga and Anzaldua 1981; Torton Beck 1982; Beam 1986; Ramos 1987; Roscoe 1988; Penelope 1994), there is, so far, relatively little in the case of heterosexuality. Where there is a substantial literature, it is on the interaction of heterosexuality and gender.

Heterosexuality is a category divided by gender and which also depends for its meaning on gender divisions. For women it is an identity defined primarily in relation to desire for men and/or the social and economic privileges associated with being the partner of a man, in particular the traditional roles of wife and mother. How the construction of heterosexuality both privileges and disempowers women, and the relationship between heterosexuality and feminism, are important themes of this book and are taken up in more detail in the following chapter by Stevi Jackson, as well as by others in subsequent chapters. The meanings of heterosexuality for men, and its interconnections with masculinity, are also explored in Janet Holland, Caroline Ramazanoglu and Rachel Thomson's chapter, as well as by Victoria Robinson in her critique of new developments in theorising masculinities.

The experience of institutionalised heterosexuality is also informed by, and informs, constructions of race and class. Yet, as bell hooks (1989) has pointed out, there has been relatively little public discussion of the connections between race and sexuality. This is despite the fact that dominant discourses of sexuality refer primarily to a white, as well as male and heterosexual subject. That is, we tend to assume that ' "whiteness" figures the normative center of political and theoretical discussions about sexuality and identity' (Goldsby 1993: 116). When black sexuality is represented in debates about sexuality, it has historically been as a form of hypersexuality. Most commonly, black women and men are portrayed as oversexed – as oversexed heterosexuals, that is. It is, moreover, a black especially male heterosexuality that has been perceived as posing a threat to especially white womanhood (Harper 1993). By implication the concepts lesbian and gay are also racialised, as race is (hetero-)sexualised. The image of a gay man and, perhaps to a lesser extent, a lesbian is characteristically white and, increasingly, middle class.

There is also a need to examine further the ways in which class position intersects with sexuality (see, for example, earlier work by D'Emilio 1984; Weeks 1986, 1990). This is true not only in terms of asking how might a person's class position affect the formation of sexual identities and practices, but also in terms of how notions of class are informed by the assumption of heterosexuality and how, consequently, our analysis of class may be changed by a questioning of this. Very often, in traditional left discourse, the working class is not only a masculinised but also, implicitly, a heterosexualised concept. Thus, lesbian and gay political struggles have often been dismissed as bourgeois.

The privileging of heterosexual relations as the assumed bedrock of social relations without which, it is posited, society would no longer function nor exist, reinforces the idea that heterosexuality is the original blueprint for interpersonal relations. According to Michael Warner, following Wittig (1992), 'Western political thought has taken the heterosexual couple to represent the principle of social union itself' (Warner 1993: xxi). This serves to delimit interpretations of both heterosexuality (as stable, necessary, universal) and the social (as naturalised heterosexuality). It also structures and organises understandings of individuals, as well as sexual and familial relationships, that are not included within the construction of the category 'heterosexual'.

In what is often described as the first major study of female homosexuality, Frank Caprio claims that:

> Many lesbian relationships between two women become the equivalent of a husband-wife relationship. The mannish or overt lesbian likes to take on the role of the 'husband' and generally attaches herself to a female partner who is feminine in physique and personality. She regards her mate as her 'wife'.
>
> (Caprio 1954: 18)

The point is not that butch/femme relationships did not exist among lesbians in the 1950s, clearly they did (Nestle 1988), nor that lesbians did not incorporate into their lives meanings drawn from the model of the heterosexual married couple: rather, that this view is constituted as scientific truth. Of course a great deal has changed since Caprio wrote this, both in terms of lesbian and heterosexual lifestyles, and such crude characterisations of lesbian relationships as copycat 'marriages' are nowadays relatively rare. However, this is not to say that heterosexuality has relinquished its hegemonic hold on conceptualisations of both the sexual and the intimate. For example, recent debates about gay marriages and the right of lesbians and gay men to have legally recognised 'domestic partnerships' have overwhelmingly been framed in a political language of inclusion. In assimilating lesbians and gay men, the dominant discourse of understanding familial forms is hardly undermined. Another example of this is the linking of parenting to gendered difference constituted through a heterosexual relationship. Hence, the tendency to see lesbian and gay parenting as confusing: 'I can't help but wonder what a child would do whose parents are two males; are they both referred to as "Daddy"? Or does the child learn to refer to one of the men as "Mom?"' (Grover, quoted in Weston 1993: 164). Behind such questions is the belief that if one man is the father, the only identity available to his partner is mother. Similarly, to ask of lesbian parents 'What will a child call the mother's lover?' seems to invoke the idea that there must be two distinct and differentiated parental roles rather than two mothers.

Related to this is the question of identity. As I have already indicated, historically lesbians have been portrayed as virtual men trapped in the space of women's bodies: 'mannish' in appearance and masculine in their thoughts, feelings and desires, rendering their existence compatible with the logic of gender and heteronormativity. Although she is necessary to this logic, the complementary femme 'type' of lesbian is mentioned much less frequently in representations of lesbians in scientific discourses and popular culture – perhaps not unsurprisingly as she is more problematic.

In the 1970s, both lesbian feminist and gay liberation movements challenged dominant scientific constructions of homosexuals and women as oppressive, claiming the power to name for themselves through the political process of 'coming out'. One might caricature this as a time of the politics of self-discovery and personal authenticity; a politics of the reformation of the self and an attempt at a new construction of both the female body and the homosexual body. The female body was constituted as no longer sexually passive and 'disciplined'/ordered; the homosexual body as no longer diseased and sexually dis-ordered; the lesbian body as no longer non-reproductive.

Lesbian feminists also critiqued heterosexuality as both an institution oppressive to women, and as practice. In doing so they rejected definitions of lesbian identity, desire and practice that were seen as derived from a patriarchal and heterosexual model of society. The establishment of new lesbian identities, such as lesbian feminist, radicalesbian, political lesbian and woman-identified woman, represented something new: an attempt at the establishment of a definition of lesbianism as a political alternative to, rather than derivative of, heterosexuality.

Viewed from the postmodern 1990s many writers now regard such struggles over lesbian (and gay) identity as just another example of 'identity politics', reinforcing an essentialism which does little to threaten the sexual *status quo* (Wiegman 1994). A new politics of identity, emphasising the fragmentation and fluidity of identity, has arisen in the 1990s, alongside new political movements such as, for example, ACT UP, Outrage, Lesbian Avengers and, in the United States, Queer Nation. In part, this owed something to the shift in the

1980s to a politics of difference, which within feminism was very much prompted by debates about race and class as much as sexuality. Related to this 'the lesbian subject' and 'the gay subject' were increasingly seen as untenable categories, as awareness of diversity and difference increased, aided by a new gay and, to a lesser extent, lesbian commercialism. The postmodern influence on social and political theory was also a key factor in encouraging the deconstruction of sexual and gender categories.

The term most often used to encapsulate this shift in the politics of identity is 'queer', which displaces the categories 'lesbian' and 'gay' *and* heterosexual. According to some writers, queer represents a form of sexual politics which sees 'the labels gay and lesbian as proscriptive, as having become as oppressive as heterosexuality in restrictiveness'(Woods 1995: 31).

The postmodern critique of earlier feminist and lesbian/gay thinking as essentialist and universalist is, I would argue, overly simplistic. The theoretical emphasis within gay liberation and feminism was on understanding sexuality as 'mediated by society, rather than as biologically given' (Segal 1994: 178). The notion of 'choice' featured strongly, especially in feminist accounts which, in many respects, represented a massive shift away from essentialist accounts of sexuality.[1] For example, long before queer theory was ever heard of, concepts such as political lesbianism (Leeds Revolutionary Feminist Group 1981), the woman-identified woman (Radicalesbians 1970) and the lesbian continuum (Rich 1980) challenged the heterosexual/homosexual binary, blurring the boundaries between straight and lesbian. Similarly, Adrienne Rich's (1980) groundbreaking work on 'compulsory heterosexuality', in highlighting the socially and economically constructed nature of heterosexuality, represented an early attempt to denaturalise heterosexual society, an aim which queer theory has more recently claimed.

Judith Butler's work (1990a, 1993a) represents a sophisticated postmodern attempt to theorise heterosexuality and its relationship to lesbian identity. Butler argues, as does Foucault, that we can never escape hegemonic discourses so that even a lesbian feminist identity is produced within hegemonic heterosexual norms. However, she goes on to argue that this is also true of heterosexuality. That is to say, far from being a natural expression of gender and sexuality, heterosexuality is always in the process of being produced. There is, in other words, no original of which homosexuality is an (inferior) copy. Heterosexuality is itself always in the process of being constructed, according to Butler, through repeated performances that imitate its own idealisations and norms and thereby produce the effect of being natural.

If our understandings of the structure of intimate relations is typically mediated through dominant heterosexual and gender norms, it is also the case that conceptualisations of desire and of 'sex' as a specific set of practices are similarly encoded. As Wendy Hollway and Carol Smart point out in their chapters, central to the theorisation of desire in 'sexual' relationships has been the notion of desire as desire for 'the other'. Typically, desire is conceptualised in terms of attraction to difference, where gender is the key marker of difference. Female sexuality has traditionally been defined as different from, yet complementary to, male sexuality. It is this difference, constructed as gendered power difference, that is assumed to be both natural and necessary to sexual arousal and pleasure. This approach suggests that desire is the 'province and the privilege of heterosexuals' (Fuss 1993: 63) or at least that to achieve desire one must identify with and mimic this reading of (heterosexual) desire. Historically, this is evident in theoretical constructions of sex between women as either involving role-playing, with one woman playing the part of the man and the other the part of the woman, or as primarily acts of affection and not really 'sex' at all (see Richardson 1992). Even within the feminist literature, where theorists might have been expected to take a different view, some writers have echoed this model in claiming that unless some kind of tension, difference, power discrepancy is introduced lesbians are unlikely to experience sexual desire. For example, lesbian feminist writer Margaret Nichols suggests that: 'Two women together, each primed to respond sexually only to a request from another, may rarely even experience desire, much less engage in sexual activity' (Nichols 1987: 103).

In this sense, homosexual desire – what Jeffreys (1994 and in this volume) has termed 'eroticised equality' – is not properly desire at all. The eroticisation of sameness is, in short, written out of the picture, as is the possibility of understanding difference, and its relation to desire, in terms other than gender. In this sense heterosexuality inscribes difference; it is a construction of 'otherness' in gendered terms. Clearly, as I have indicated, this has implications for our understanding of the desires of lesbians and gay men; but equally significantly it also shapes the ways in which heterosexual desires are constructed as relations between 'others' or even 'opposites'. In their chapters, both Stevi Jackson and Wendy Hollway take up this point in examining the possibilities of forms of non-oppressive heterosexuality. Elsewhere, Tamsin Wilton powerfully examines the concept of homosexual and heterosexual desire and its implications for understanding sexual difference.

Ideas about what is 'normal' and 'acceptable' sexual behaviour, indeed what is regarded as sexual practice, also reflect dominant constructions of sexuality as heterosexual (vaginal) intercourse. If we do not engage in such activity we are not recognised as sexual beings, we are still virgins even after a lifetime of 'foreplay'. Not only does this affect how forms of sexual activity are evaluated as sexually satisfying or arousing or even as counting as 'sex' at all, it also serves to 'discipline' the body (Bartky 1988), marking out the boundaries which represent our private and public zones,[2] and distinguishing the potentially sexual from the non-sexual bodily surfaces and actions.

For instance, both men and women have an anus. Yet the anus as a part of the sexualised body is predominantly encoded as a gay male body. This has led some to ask if the anus is a homologue of the vagina (Bersani 1987), allowing a heterosexualised understanding of penetrative sex between men which, at the same time, denies visibility to female anality and anal intercourse as a heterosexual practice. Indeed the very use of the terms heterosexual — meaning vaginal – intercourse and homosexual – meaning anal – intercourse are revealing in this respect. Similarly, our understanding of bodies has been bounded within a 'heterosexual matrix', which operates through naturalising a heterosexual morphology (Butler 1993a). That is, heterosexuality depends on a view of differently gendered individuals who complement each other, right down to their bodies and body parts fitting together; like 'a lock and key' the penis and vagina are assumed to be a natural fit. What happens, then, when the lock or the key is missing?

As I have already indicated, lesbians have frequently been portrayed as masculine and feminine types who complement each other. In many accounts the lesbian body too is heterosexualised; for instance through the production of lesbian bodies with spectacular clitorises which can penetrate vaginas or in the characterisation of lesbians as 'boyish' with narrow hips and flat chests. The marking of lesbian bodies as non-procreative is another example of the lesbian body as only rudimentarily female. The conceptualisation of male homosexuals as feminised men with a particular body build and chemistry was also characteristic of early investigations of homosexuality. More recent work has focused on the idea that gay men have 'feminised brains' (see Byne 1995 for a critical review of studies). Another common assumption, which has not altogether disappeared (for a review of studies see Banks and Gartrell 1995), was that male homosexuals had reduced levels of testosterone compared to heterosexual men, resulting in the appearance of 'cross-sexed' physical characteristics such as wider hips, reduced hairiness and small-sized genitalia. In this sense dominant discourses of heterosexuality organise the physical and social space of our bodies.

At an individual level, this may have a significant influence on the way we experience our own bodies and those of others, discouraging us from engaging in certain kinds of bodily activities, whilst at the same time encouraging others. For instance, if a lesbian says 'If I do that I might as well go with a man', what might she mean? Her remark could be interpreted as an example of the depth to which certain conceptions of both the body and the sexual are heterosexualised (and the extent to which heterosexual and lesbian identities are bounded). Thus, certain activities may be seen by some as an imitation of heterosexuality rather than as authentically lesbian. Related to this, an alternative interpretation would be that this statement represents a rejection of heterosexual norms and/or a politicisation of certain activities as patriarchal practices. Sheila Jeffreys, for instance, believes that the emergence of the new lesbian sex industry, with porn videos, sex phone lines, and the marketing of 'sex toys' (but more especially dildos) institutionalises and commodifies the eroticised subordination of women and dominance of men (Jeffreys 1994).

Such inscriptions of the (sexual) body are highly contested. The increasing dominance of deconstructive, postmodern accounts in feminist theory, as well as in social theory more generally, has emphasised the unstable, fragmented nature of categories like heterosexual/homosexual, man/woman, masculine/feminine. In aiming to disrupt and denaturalise such conventional binary divisions, writers have foregrounded parody (as distinct from imitation) and the possibilities of 'playing with gender', in particular through butch, femme and drag. In her chapter, Sheila Jeffreys takes up this theme, providing a critical examination of such developments.

One form this politics of signification has taken is in relation to the phallus. Traditionally the phallus is understood to symbolise masculine authority and through its assumed absence or lack it is argued that women are constituted as a subjugated class. In accepting this, various writers have argued that instead of rejecting phallic signifiers, as does Jeffreys and others, we should recognise that there is no escape from the phallus because in Western culture it is central to the culturally constructed meanings of gender and sexuality. Thus, it is suggested that 'reclaiming the phallus' is an important strategy for challenging ('displacing') current sexual and gender relations; a way of challenging male authority and thereby empowering women.

What does this mean in practice? Recent cultural productions of lesbian bodies by lesbians themselves have emphasised the postmodern lesbian body as phallic. It is claimed that the effect of appropriating the phallus, through packing/wearing dildos (or 'phallic body prostheses' as some would have it) is to expose the assumed linkage between the phallus and the penis as artificial (Butler 1993a; Griggers 1993). Also, as Judith Butler (1993a) has argued, if the penis is only one phallus and not *the* phallus then it does not 'belong' to men: women can have it too and in their own right, not as copycats. This denaturalisation of the penis as phallus, it is claimed, also undermines heterosexual as well as male power and privilege. Since the phallus as penis symbolises desire – hence lesbians get asked 'What do you do?' as when there is no penis it is assumed there can be no 'real' sex – the lesbian phallus, it is argued, is potentially disruptive and can show how the naturalisation of heterosexuality is imaginary (p. 91).

Whilst I can follow the above argument, I would question its political significance. I am extremely sceptical of the extent to which 'parodic replication' of heterosexual constructs such as, for instance, understanding the 'lesbian cock', or chicks with dicks, as a parody of the phallus/penis, will challenge heterosexuality as a social institution. For, as Davina Cooper points out, 'not only does hegemony operate through exclusion, but also by making visible failed attempts to attain the status of the real' (Cooper 1995, though I would prefer to use 'real'). In other words, to suggest that we can effect social change through (queer) performances, however transgressive, provocative or challenging, would seem to assume, amongst other things, that such performances will have a revolutionary effect on (straight) audiences, rather than being interpreted as imitating and reproducing heterosexuality.

(Paradoxically, the latter would suggest that the norms of heterosexuality are being constituted through such performances, thus confirming the effect of heterosexuality as natural.)

As Colleen Lamos remarks: 'Alas, the dildo-bedecked lesbian may be disappointed that her parody of the phallus is interpreted differently by others, especially by heterosexuals who take the dildo or butch/femme straight, so to speak' (Lamos 1994: 95).

Indeed, the possibilities of a queer reading would seem to be significantly constrained by the fact that historically the dominant (hetero-)sexual discourse has positioned lesbians as butch or, to a much lesser extent, femme types who are, albeit in different ways, suffering from penile deprivation, thereby needing to use dildos as a 'penis substitute'.

There are, in any case, other considerations which go beyond the currently fashionable concern with subversive performance as political strategy and social method. Whilst this may indeed be valuable in highlighting some of the contradictory meanings embedded in discourses of gender and sexuality, and the socially constructed and potentially unstable nature of identities and practices, I would argue that we also need to ground this in the context of the material conditions of people's lives at local, national and global levels. If we are to develop social theory which can adequately theorise and challenge the ways in which our everyday lives are structured by heterosexual practices, within a variety of institutional domains such as families, religion, the economy and so forth, we require more than a queerying of the sexual. Much more significantly, we need to rethink the social.

Sexual/social worlds

Having made the above comment, I immediately want to disown it. How can the sexual be separate from the social? What does it mean to attempt, as some have done, to theorise these as separate if related spheres? How, within social theory, are conceptual categories such as, for example, the private/public distinction, mediated through distinguishing the sexual from the social?

Part of the difficulty in discussing concepts such as 'society' and 'sexual', not to mention 'public' and 'private', is the tendency to assume that we each know what these concepts represent. Indeed, we very often use these concepts in a taken-for-granted way, as if their meanings were uncontested. Yet, as we shall see, it is clear that such concepts *are* contested; that there are different discourses which produce different understandings of 'the social' and 'the sexual' and their presumed relationship to each other.

According to some writers, the social realm is a relatively new phenomenon, 'whose origin coincided with the emergence of the modern age and which found its political form in the nation-state' (Arendt 1958: 28, quoted in Warner 1993). Similarly, the emergence of the sexual as a new theoretical object, as a distinct field of knowledge and experience, is also claimed to be a relatively recent historical and cultural production (Foucault 1981; Weeks 1985). As a result, the sexual and the social have been conceptualised as bounded, though interconnected, realms. Thus writers can theorise heterosexuality as sexual practices and as social practices (VanEvery 1995b and in this volume); work on human identity can treat sexual and social identities as distinct; and theories of social and political change can explore questions of sexuality impacting on social relations or of the possibility of transforming sexual relations through social change (see Cooper 1995).

The problem of separating the sexual and the social, it seems to me, is how can we have a distinct sexual experience which is not interpreted and constructed through social meanings and interactions? The conventional approach sidesteps this by inventing the sexual as something individuals possess more or less independently of their involvement in the social. Nor am I satisfied by the view that, as Connell (1995) suggests, the social is already a part of the sexual domain, and vice versa, as this still seems to imply separate, if dynamically interconnected domains. Much as Butler and others (for example, Nicholson 1994) have argued in relation to the concepts sex and gender, I would argue for a much more sophisticated analysis which examines how the production of the sexual/social is achieved. If we accept that 'the sexual' is always seen through social interpretation, then the sexual is not something that can be separated from the social but is rather that which is produced by it; it is the social organisation of knowledge that establishes meanings for the sexual. However, even this is not enough, for it almost suggests a determinacy of the social as productive of the sexual, when the notion of the social is itself a complex construction. Although I do not have the space here, I intend to develop this analysis further in Richardson (forthcoming).

Most commonly, the relationship between the sexual and the social has been theorised in terms of a distinction between 'the public' and 'the private'. The 'social' realm, at least in Western contexts, is usually equated with 'issues affecting daily life ... issues like equitable distribution of resources ("poverty"), the environment, and "lifestyle"' (Patton 1993: 172). This has the effect of disassociating sexuality, conceptually at least, from many aspects of everyday life and relationships, a belief that it lies outside the sphere of political and economic, and therefore State, influence. (In her chapter, Jean Carabine develops this theme through an examination of the relationship between sexuality and social policy.) The sexual, by contrast, is generally associated with the individual, personal aspects of our lives, as well as with the idea of nature, more especially that sexuality is grounded in the body, in our individual, essential natures. Related to this is the belief in sexuality as the basis for human identity, prior to other cultural or social affiliations (Kotz 1993). In this sense, to examine the relationship between the sexual and the social is to raise questions about the relationship between human beings and nature; between the body and social membership; between the social and the natural – what was often referred to in the past as the nature/nurture debate.

What is often presupposed in this connection of the sexual with the natural is that the social sphere acts upon the sexual as a mediating or modifying influence; social institutions having the effect of both liberating and repressing different sexualities at different times. At the same time, the sexual is also conceptualised as outside of the social. It is, in this respect, constitutive of the social, rather than produced by it. Thus, as Diana Fuss comments, 'the natural provides the raw material and determinative starting point for the practices and laws of the social' (Fuss 1990: 3). In so far as this naturalised sexuality is interpreted as heterosexuality, albeit in particular forms of practice, it becomes a central and determining feature of our understanding of social life. The heterosexual couple are the raw material through which society may interpret and imagine itself.

To give a concrete example, in countries such as China, where due to the government's policies on population control there is a policy of one child per family, there is concern that reproductive technologies such as ultrasound and amniocentesis, followed by selective abortion, are currently being used to ensure that the only child is a son. As a result, new laws have been proposed to ban the use of such techniques to determine the sex of the foetus. The main concerns that have prompted this situation are the real and imagined social consequences of demographic change, as more males are being born than females. In particular, there is concern over the state of marriage, with fears that the growing number of single unmarried men within Chinese society will threaten the stability of marriages and lead to rising divorce figures. What this example and most other population control measures elsewhere demonstrate is the assumed natural, heterosexual basis of society. Society must reproduce itself as male and female in more or less equal amounts because heterosexuality, in its institutionalised form as marriage, requires one man for each woman, and vice versa. If we abandon that principle, and the assumption that social stability depends upon it, then there would be no obvious gender basis of society which needs to be regulated in this way by public policy.

If the social is interpreted through heterosexuality, it is also the case that understandings of heterosexuality are informed by definitions of the relationship between the sexual and the social. For example, the (naturalised) split between the social and the sexual means that writers can divorce analyses of sexual practices and relations from those about social relations: such as, for instance, analyses of the 'family', the workplace, and domestic living arrangements. Jo VanEvery examines this possibility in more detail in her chapter on heterosexuality and domestic labour.

The construction of the sexual as relatively autonomous, occupying its own terrain, is also relevant to debates about heterosexuality and social change. One interpretation of this is that the sexual (here, heterosexuality) will not necessarily be transformed by changes in wider social relations. A less essentialist reading of the sexual/social split assumes a sexual which is to a greater or lesser extent modified by the social; thus allowing for the possibility that if society changed, then so might (hetero-)sexualities. Campaigners on the 'moral right', for example, have argued for stronger controls over sexuality, such as restrictions on sex education and a ban on access to contraception for young people, as part of an attempt to restore and constrain heterosexuality to married monogamous relationships.

For some, including many on the 'moral right', the sexual/social relationship is also understood to be a two-way process, with the social mediated through the sexual. The latter would seem to assume a direct link between the social and the sexual, with sexual practices presumed capable of generating social change. In the case of the 'moral right' this might be envisaged in terms of sexual immorality in the form of, for example, 'promiscuity', adultery and prostitution leading to moral and social decay. The discourse of sexual liberation, on the other hand, has traditionally seen sexual freedom as a force for social change, as a means for achieving social freedom. More recently, albeit with a different, postmodern conceptualisation of sexuality, queer politics and sex radicalism has also claimed the power to disrupt the dominance of heterosexuality and the hegemony of particular desires and practices through 'transgressive' sexual practices such as butch/femme; S/M; and the (queer) use of dildos (see my earlier comments, Jeffreys in this volume, and Cooper 1995).

Many feminists in the early 1970s also saw a connection between the 'repression' of female sexuality and social powerlessness; believing that 'discovering' one's sexuality, largely conceptualised as heterosexuality, would empower women. With hindsight, many feminists have questioned this association and there has been considerable debate and argument between feminists over the relationship between sexuality and social change. In the context of heterosexuality the tension has primarily been around the extent to which sexual relations are determined by, or are determing of, other social relations. For some, especially radical feminists the main concern is not so much how women's sex lives are affected by gender inequalities but, more generally, how heterosexuality as it is currently institutionalised constrains women in most aspects of their lives. Here, then, the emphasis is primarily upon how the social is constructed and maintained as oppressive to women through the sexual realm, itself a construction, of course. For others, there is a much greater emphasis on how sexual relations are determined through inequalities in the social sphere, limiting personal pleasures (and pains) and desires. For example, Lynne Segal, in her book *Straight Sex: Rethinking the Politics of Pleasure* concluded by saying: 'Straight feminists, like gay men and lesbians, have everything to gain from asserting our non-coercive desire to fuck if, when, how and as we choose' (Segal 1994: 318).[3]

The sexual/social distinction is also significant in the construction of boundaries between heterosexual/lesbian/gay. Or, to put it another way, the sexual/social split is also part of the means by which divisions between heterosexuals and sexual 'others' are produced. As I have suggested above, heterosexuality infuses the social realm; it represents the idea of normal behaviour which is central to the concept of the social and the process of socialisation into the social realm. Consequently, heterosexuality is defined primarily in terms of social identification, for instance identities such as 'wife'/'husband'; 'girlfriend'/'boyfriend'; 'mother'/'father' are rooted in heterosexuality. (Although, as feminist writers have pointed out, this is gendered: heterosexuality is more of a principal site of identity construction for women than it is for men; which is not to say that heterosexuality is unimportant in the production of conventional masculinities, as Janet Holland, Caroline Ramazanoglu and Rachel Thompson demonstrate in their chapter on heterosexual practice.)

Indeed, heterosexuality's naturalisation means that it is rarely acknowledged as a sexuality, as a sexual category or identification. By contrast, historically lesbians and gay men have been defined primarily as sexual beings, placed outside (the underworld) or at the margins (the twilight zone) of the normative boundaries of the social realm. As a result, homosexuality is defined primarily in terms of sexual identification and very rarely are the social relations within which lesbians and gay men are embedded acknowledged. Once named as lesbians and gays we are at risk of the vast complexity of our lives – even our claim to a certain race, religion, ethnicity, nationality, or even in some cases humanity itself – disappearing under the dominant sexual marker: non-heterosexual. In this sense, the notion of the social/sexual split is a sexualised notion, establishing heterosexuals as a socially inscribed class and lesbians and gay men as a sexually inscribed grouping. It is also a gendered and racialised concept. Thus, for instance, the category 'gay man' is a more sexualised concept than 'lesbian'; as is black heterosexuality compared to white heterosexuality.

Defining public and private boundaries

As I mentioned above, the relationship between the social and the sexual has often been understood in terms of the public/private distinction, itself a cultural construction, with the social associated with the public and the sexual with the private. Yet, this division can immediately be questioned: social relations occur in the domestic, increasingly private sphere; and there is public expression of sexual relations, what many refer to as a sexualisation of society. Similarly, feminist theory has critiqued this separation of the public and the private in ways that have illuminated understandings of, for example, women's position in the labour market, the sexual division of labour, as well as violence against women (Walby 1990). The claim that 'the personal is the political', a feminist catchphrase of the 1970s and 80s, also reflects the emphasis placed within feminism on disrupting the public/private binary. In this context, however, I wish to draw attention to the ways in which the private/public distinction serves to influence the process of the production of sexualities.

The association of sexuality with the private as distinct from the public sphere is institutionalised. In the UK, for example, it is part of the current legal constitution and the definition of the role of the State in individuals' lives. The Wolfenden Report (1957), which led to the liberalisation of laws on prostitution in 1959 and male homosexuality in 1967, concluded that it was not the role of the law to interfere in the private lives of citizens, but rather it was the law's duty to preserve public order and decency. Issues like homosexuality and prostitution (and later pornography) were thus defined as matters of individual conscience, acceptable as private actions of the individual, as long as they did not encroach into the public arena. Thus, whilst homosexuality may have been defined as a matter for individual conscience, the 1967 changes to the law pertaining to sexual acts between men nevertheless maintained legal limitations that did not apply to heterosexuality on the grounds that 'homosexual' acts in public might cause offence to others. By implication, public decency and public order – indeed the public sphere as it is defined in legal terms – is identified with heterosexuality.[4]

More recently, there has been a shift towards understanding the construction of public space in terms of modes of cultural production, as well as through social institutions such as the law. Once again there is an identification of the public sphere (as cultural space) with heterosexuality. To give a concrete example taken from a letter to the (liberal) British newspaper, the *Guardian*: 'Why are homosexual/lesbian issues occupying so many column inches in your publication when these people form a minute sub-culture?' (29 July 1995).

These examples serve to highlight how heterosexuality, more especially within a married relationship, is normally granted both more privacy and more public recognition than other sexualities. In other words, not only can the public be understood as characterised by heterosexual norms, but so too can the private in so far as it is traditionally associated with domestic and (heterosexual) family life. Some have related this to the notion of a 'homosexual diaspora' (Mort 1994), crossing nation-states and linking lesbian and gay communities. However, I wonder whether this term is appropriate for the sense of cultural and spatial exclusion lesbians and gay men frequently experience. Rather than an original 'homeland' from which homosexuals were dispersed, I would argue that any sense of loss/exclusion is largely connected with the heterosexualisation of the private and the public, rather than a loss of country or nation-state. It is from the domestic homeland, their families, that lesbians and gay men are often estranged: 'Citizens who inhabit the same country may live worlds apart. Queer youth often feel homeless in their own homes even before some of them are thrown out onto the streets' (Tucker 1995: 25). Similarly, to become homosexual is to be *en route* from the public as well as the private. It may be that lesbians and gay men do not get told to 'get back from where you came from' on the grounds of their sexuality (although they may in so far as it intersects with their racial and ethnic identifications), but they can be told to get back to the private if they are seen as challenging the boundaries of public 'tolerance'.

The private/public distinction is, then, a sexualised notion: it has a different meaning depending on whether one is applying it to a heterosexual or homosexual context. For lesbians and gays the private has been institutionalised as the border of social tolerance, as the place where you are 'allowed' to live relatively safely as long as one does not attempt to occupy the public. In some instances that might even mean feeling comfortable about talking about lesbian or gay issues in one's own garden or backyard. For heterosexuals not only is the construction of private space likely to be very different, but the public is also likely to be a far less contested or constrained space than for most homosexuals. Although, once again, we need to relate this to race and gender; various forms of oppressive practice most notably racial and/or sexual violence also render the public a contested space and the private/public distinction a gendered and racialised construction.[5]

Much of feminist theory, as I have already mentioned, has focused on how the separation of the public and the private is a patriarchal construction (Nicholson 1984; Walby 1990). Queer theory has also challenged the public/private distinction within its more general critique of the heterosexual/homosexual binary and its resistance to a normalised and naturalised heterosexuality. There is an emphasis on occupying space, both culturally and socially; increased public visibility is one of the stated goals of queer politics. 'Our refusal to live in a closet is one way of "just saying no" to a world, a nation, and a regional culture intent on closing borders to those who are "different"' (Geltmaker 1992: 650).

Being queer is not about seeking the democratic right to privacy, the right to do what one wants in private, it is concerned with establishing safe space for public sexualities that are currently bounded by straight tolerance (for example: lesbians and gays are fine by me, just as long as they don't flaunt themselves) – or not as the case may be (most obviously lesbian and gay bashing). In the United States, for example, one of the stated aims of Queer Nation was to expose the straightness of public spaces and to 'reterritorialise' them (Berlant and Freeman 1993). In this sense queer shares with certain strands of feminism a concern to 'reterritorialise' public space and, in so doing, disrupt the ways in which certain issues as well as subjects (woman/man; heterosexual/homosexual) are constituted in the public or the private sphere.[6]

In the following section I want to relate this discussion to the concept of citizenship, which has often been defined in terms of the right to privacy, the right to private acts and private opinions if not always public identities.

Citizenship

'Citizenship may be defined as that set of practices (juridical, political, economic and cultural) which define a person as a competent member of society, and which as a consequence shape the flow of resources to persons and social groups' (Turner 1993: 2).

Although we increasingly hear talk about citizenship, whether treating it as a set of civil, political and social rights (Marshall 1977) or, as above, using the concept in the broader sense, as a set of socially and culturally specific practices which define the nature of social membership (Turner 1993), it is important to recognise that it is a contested concept. That is to say that, in addition to its contested meaning, 'all attempts to clarify the concept of citizenship . . . are themselves a part of practical politics' (Shotter 1993: 115).

So far, the tradition of thinking behind the idea of citizenship, which has become a key concept of modern social theory, has given insufficient attention to either gender or sexuality (for a discussion see Lister 1990; Evans 1993; Walby 1994). For example, in *Citizenship and Social Theory*, although passing reference is made to the fact that many of the new issues of citizenship 'appear to centre around gender politics' and that 'interesting and radical developments appear to be centred around . . . the struggle for homosexual rights' (Turner 1993: 13), none of the contributors elucidate how the study of such social movements might change notions of citizenship and, more significantly, its presumed relation to social theory.[7]

There is therefore a need to broaden the analysis of citizenship to include debates around sexuality and, still, gender. All the more so given that, as David Evans points out in his introduction to *Sexual Citizenship*:

> The history of citizenship is a history of fundamental formal heterosexist patriarchal principles and practices ostensibly progressively 'liberalised' towards and through the rhetoric of 'equality' but in practice to effect unequal differentiation.
>
> (Evans 1993: 9)

This is to imply that claims to citizenship status, at least in the West, are closely associated with the institutionalisation of heterosexual as well as male privilege. That this is the case is made abundantly clear when the association of heterosexuality with a certain form of citizenship status is threatened or challenged. If we take citizenship to mean national identity, for example, it would appear that in many if not most nation-states this form of citizenship is equated with a naturalised heterosexuality. For example, a representative of the Romanian Ministry of Justice (Cojocaru Octavian) speaking at the

CEPES-UNESCO conference in Bucharest on 'Homosexuality: A Human Right?' (31 May 1995) declared: 'the nature of the Romanian does not admit this prose of unnatural law [homosexuality], this immorality'.

Although the State may act to construct the nation as heterosexual,[8] this does not necessarily mean that all forms of heterosexuality are regarded equally. It is heterosexuality as marriage and 'the family' which is associated with the nation and, moreover, seen as necessary for ensuring its survival, its strength and well-being. By implication, it would seem that other forms of heterosexuality, for instance young women who are single mothers, imperil the nation. The association of heterosexuality and nation also intersects with race; it is a white heterosexuality which has historically been privileged, with black heterosexual relationships invoked as a supposed threat to the nation (Williams 1989).

Related to this, it would seem that very often nationality is not merely connected to being heterosexual, but also to a heterosexuality that is markedly anti-lesbian and anti-gay.[9] Speaking of nationalisms in the United States, Henry Louis Gates Jr. claims that 'national identity became sexualized in the 1960s, in such a way as to engender a curious subterraneous connection between homophobia and nationalism' (Gates 1993: 234). Similarly, in the UK homosexuality, but more especially homosexual family relationships, has been perceived as a threat to the nation-state (Reinhold 1994). Thus, for example, David Wiltshire (the member of Parliament responsible for introducing the anti-homosexual section 28 of the Local Government Act 1988) justified the need to oppose homosexuality: 'My actions were motivated wholly by the principle of supporting normality ... Homosexuality is being promoted at the ratepayers' expense, and the traditional family as we know it is under attack' (*Guardian*, 12 December 1987).

The exclusion of lesbians and gay men from the meaning of 'family', thus reinscribing it as a heterosexualised concept, is evidenced in the government's definition of homosexuality as a 'pretended family relationship' in section 28. The discussion around section 28 also raised other issues of citizenship and its relationship to heterosexuality, where citizenship can be interpreted as social rights expressed through social policy. Although the linking of social rights to welfare policy has been critiqued by feminists and others, it is nevertheless important to recognise the suggestion in what David Wiltshire and others were arguing in support of section 28: not only are lesbians and gay men presumably not ratepayers, but that they are not deserving of social services funded by local authorities. Jean Carabine returns to this issue in her chapter, where she examines in more detail the relationship between sexuality and access to and eligibility for welfare.

Definitions of citizenship as national identity have been brought into question in recent years as a result of social and political changes which have challenged traditional boundaries of nation-states, in particular the process of 'globalisation'. In part, this has encouraged discussion of whether citizenship might develop within the context of larger forms of social membership than nation-states, such as humanity itself. If we take citizenship to mean human identity, belonging to what is called the human race, even then it is still possible to argue that citizenship continues to be premised within heterosexuality.

A documentary shown on British television, entitled *Better Dead Than Gay*, described how a young man killed himself because he couldn't reconcile his Christian beliefs with the fact that he was gay. In an interview, his father stated that learning his son was gay was as bad as losing him (*Guardian*, 26 July 1995).

The assumption that heterosexuality and humanity are synonymous, that being human is being straight, is reflected in those who would question the right to life of lesbians and gay men. In some parts of the world such views are institutionalised through laws which recommend the death penalty for homosexuality; in countries where homosexuality is legally 'tolerated', violent attacks on lesbians and gay men have led to killings (for example killings in Plymouth reported in the *Guardian*, 9 November 1995).

More recently, there has been a shift towards defining citizenship in terms of consumerism. It is in this framework that non-heterosexuals seem to be most acceptable as citizens, as consumers with identities and lifestyles which are expressed through purchasing the appropriate products. The awareness of the commercial 'power' of lesbians and gay men is seen by some as important in promoting other forms of citizenship, such as the development of social rights and entitlements. As David Evans states:

> Sexual minorities have progressively become distinct, formal though not necessarily formally clear, participants within the citizenship of developed capitalism, whilst simultaneously becoming, not surprisingly for of course the two are closely connected, legitimate consumers of sexual and sexualized commodities marketed specifically for their use and enjoyment.
>
> (Evans 1993: 2)

For others, however, the impact of the increasing commercialisation and commodification of homosexuality is viewed much more critically, not to say cynically (Woods 1995).

Finally, what if we were to regard citizenship as a set of social practices which 'define social membership in a society which is highly differentiated both in its culture and social institutions, and where social solidarity can only be based upon general and universalistic standards' (Turner 1993: 5)? This raises the question of the power of heterosexuality, conceptualised as universal, natural and normal, as a unifying principle; a means of achieving social solidarity among differentiated groups.

Certainly, implicit in the right to many forms of (public) social membership based on ethnic, religious and racial identifications is a presumed heterosexuality. To give two concrete examples:

Last month Brian Gordon, a member of the Board of Jewish Deputies, attacked a fellow member for addressing the World Congress of Gay and Lesbian Jewish Organisations in Brussels: 'Their [gays and lesbians] activities have no more legitimacy under a Jewish banner than, say, pork-eating.'

(*Guardian*, 8 July 1995: 7)

In 1995 the organisers of the annual Irish Day Parade in Boston successfully sought a court order banning Irish/American lesbians and gay men from marching in the parade. Similarly, writing about the (hetero-)sexualization of black identities Goldsby claims that:

This ideology [of American slavery] privileged and enforced heterosexuality as authentically 'black' because the regulation of black reproductive rights demanded this definition . . . No wonder, then, that black homophobes characteristically malign homosexuality as a 'white thing', as a relationship that, by definition, re-enacts slavery itself.

(Goldsby 1993: 122–3)

What these examples and the various forms of citizenship I have examined serve to illustrate is the significance of heterosexuality for shaping Western social and political thought, in ways that dramatically affect all of our lives.

Notes

1 It is possible, though, to identify a certain essentialism in feminist thinking about sexuality in the early years of the women's liberation movement, in the emphasis on 'discovering' or 'reclaiming' an authentic female sexuality which had been denied women.

2 The use of the term 'privates' to refer to the genitalia is a useful example of such bodily zoning.

3 I do not have the space here to develop the analysis of the ways in which different feminist writers have theorised the sexual/social, but would merely point out that insufficient attention has been given exploring this aspect of feminist thinking on sexuality.

4 There are, of course, parallels and interrelationships with the identification of public space as heterosexualised and feminism's identification and critique of the construction of the public sphere as masculine and the private sphere as feminine.

5 In some cases, the private may also be a site of violence, as is evidenced, for example, by attacks on gay and black people's homes.

6 For example, one might make some interesting comparisons between feminist actions such as Take Back the Night campaigns and, in the United States, Queer Nation's shopping mall 'visibility actions', whose aim is to challenge the heterosexualised family environment of shopping malls through public performances of being 'lesbian' and 'gay'.

7 Ken Plummer (1995b) makes a similar point in discussing the way in which social

theorists have ignored and/or marginalised sociological work on lesbian and gay lives, highlighting 'mainstream texts' on the study of social movements and the study of identities as classic examples. What determines the right, for example, to lesbian citizenship? Are lesbians who have relationships with men 'hasbians', as some have suggested? (see Stein 1993). How does raising questions such as these inform notions of citizenship and social theory?

8 I acknowledge that there are different 'nationalisms', for example, cultural, economic, political, but do not have the space here to elaborate on how these different aspects of nationality may be differently theorised in relation to sexuality.

9 Political contestation of (American) nationality has been apparent within feminism and, more recently, queer politics. Lesbian Nation (Johnson 1973) Bitch Nation (quoted in Berlant and Freeman 1993) and Queer Nation (Berube and Escoffier, and other articles in *Out/Look* 1991) suggested a new nationality.

2

Heterosexuality and feminist theory

Stevi Jackson

The resurgence of interest in heterosexuality among feminists has occurred in the context of more than two decades in which the theory and politics of sexuality have been fiercely contested. While discussions on heterosexuality are currently less acrimonious than they have been in the past, there is still a gulf between its radical lesbian feminist critics (Jeffreys 1990; Kitzinger and Wilkinson 1993b, 1994a; Kitzinger 1994) and heterosexual feminists seeking to defend their sexual practices (Hollway 1993; Segal 1994). Like many heterosexual feminists,[1] I find myself uneasily located between these two positions. I am convinced of the need to analyse heterosexuality critically, to explore the ways in which it is implicated in the subordination of women, but without conflating heterosexuality as an institution with heterosexual practice, experience and identity. This chapter is in part a response to these recent debates, but also addresses some broader theoretical issues. What I have to say derives from my attempts, over several years, to deal theoretically with issues of sexuality and to deal personally with my own heterosexuality.

The difficulties of theorising the relationship between institutionalised heterosexuality as a system of male domination and individual women's heterosexual practice and experience are, in my view, part of a wider problem: that we have yet to find satisfactory ways of conceptualising sexuality as fully social. While most feminists agree that sexuality is socially constructed, there is no consensus on precisely what we mean by social construction, nor on how it should be analysed, nor on what it is about sexuality as currently constituted that needs to be challenged. In the early years of the modern feminist movement we at least had a common point of departure: that the current ordering of heterosexual relations was detrimental to women and implicated in our subordination. Viewing sexuality as socially constructed followed from politicising it, from seeing it as changeable rather than fixed by nature. From this starting point feminist theory has taken diverse directions and the divisions among us have subsequently deepened and hardened. Adherents of particular positions have pursued their own theoretical and political agendas with little constructive dialogue across the 'sex wars' battle lines.

Given this history, taking a radical feminist perspective poses its own problems – not least the necessity of correcting the misapprehensions currently in circulation about what radical feminism is (see Cameron 1993). For example, it is widely believed that radical feminism is essentialist and ahistorical, that it views male and female sexuality as fixed and sexual relations between men and women as inherently oppressive. This, as I hope to demonstrate, is a gross misrepresentation. It is also often assumed, as it is by Lynne Segal (1994), that radical feminism and political lesbianism are inseparable, and that the only opposition to the latter has come from socialist feminists. In fact there has always been a current within radical feminism which is critical of attempts to establish political lesbianism as feminist orthodoxy, which regards the oppression of lesbians and of heterosexual women as 'two sides of the same coin' (Trouble and Strife Collective 1983). In keeping with this tradition, I want to develop a perspective on heterosexuality derived from French materialist radical feminism, in particular the work of Christine Delphy (1984, 1993). In so doing I will argue that gender – as a socially constructed product of patriarchal hierarchies – is fundamental to an analysis of sexuality.

Feminist perspectives on sexuality

Within current feminist thinking on sexuality three main strands of analysis have developed. None of these is necessarily limited to any one theoretical or political position but each has, in practice, become associated with a particular variant of feminism. What is distinctive about these tendencies is the object of their analysis: in other words, precisely what they see as being socially constructed. Each foregrounds a specific aspect of sexuality: the centrality of male domination, the variability and plasticity of sexuality and the construction of our individual desires. Since particular theorists have tended to concentrate on one aspect of sexuality to the exclusion of others, the ways in which these issues have been conceptualised have given rise to serious differences among those who have analysed sexuality in relation to patriarchal structures, those who have emphasised its historical construction as an object of discourse and those primarily concerned with its constitution at the level of individual subjectivity.

It is my contention that each of these strands of social construction theory is essential to an adequate feminist perspective on sexuality, and that a critique of heterosexuality should find a means of weaving them together. All three are necessary if we are to transcend the difficulties we have in maintaining a critical perspective on heterosexuality without implicitly or explicitly condemning individual heterosexual women. This is not a plea for compromise, for some disinterested middle ground, but for a more rigorous radical feminist theorisation of sexuality.

The first tendency I have identified, which sees sexuality as a site of male power, had its roots in feminist political activism, in efforts to challenge men's sexual appropriation and abuse of women. This has brought us analyses of sexual violence and pornography and, more generally, of the ways in which sexuality had been defined and constructed from a masculine perspective. The social construction of sexuality is here seen as patriarchal, as serving the interests of men, as coercing women into compulsory heterosexuality (Rich 1980). It is therefore linked to a structural analysis of patriarchy (for example, MacKinnon 1982). Moreover, the erotic itself is understood as culturally constituted, so that currently prevailing definitions of eroticism are themselves the product of gendered patterns of domination and submission intrinsic to patriarchal societies and written into their cultural representations (Kappeler 1986; Cameron and Frazer 1987; Jeffreys 1990). It is this form of analysis which is most closely associated with radical feminism (and also with revolutionary feminism).[2]

From this perspective heterosexuality has always, implicitly or explicitly, been problematised. For example, those writing on sexual violence – where male sexual power is starkly evident – have stressed the continuities between apparently 'deviant' acts and the 'normal' expression of (socially constructed) masculinity (Jackson 1978a; Kelly 1988; Scully 1990). Work on diverse aspects of heterosexuality – from the analysis of sex manuals to research on young women's sexual relationships – has sensitised us to the complexity and ubiquity of power relations within sexuality. These accounts of heterosexuality have played an important role in anchoring critiques of a range of sexual practices, both heterosexual and non-heterosexual, particularly from anti-libertarian positions within the 'sex wars' debates. This is most explicit in the work of Sheila Jeffreys (1990), for whom all practices which eroticise power, whatever the gender of those engaging in them, are 'heterosexual'.

Whether or not one endorses such conclusions, it is clear that a serious social constructionist position must accept that there is no total escape from the heterosexual framing of desire within a social order where heterosexuality is so privileged. We all learn to be sexual within a society in which 'real sex' is defined as a quintessentially heterosexual act, vaginal intercourse, and in which sexual activity is thought of in terms of an active subject and passive object. As many feminists have pointed out, this has also had an impact on lesbian and gay sexuality (Cameron and Frazer 1987; Jeffreys 1990). Even those who do not practice sado-masochism or take on butch and femme identities may find the cultural opposition between active/dominant and passive/subordinate sexuality intruding into their fantasies or practices. While feminists, both lesbian and heterosexual, are challenging the construction of sexuality in terms of active masculinity and passive femininity, our creativity in developing alternative forms of eroticism is necessarily limited by the social conditions which have shaped our desires. This implies that a critique of heterosexuality needs to underpin all theorising about sexuality.

Curiously, such radical feminist arguments are often misread as essentialist, as implying that men are naturally sexually violent and predatory and that women are innately loving and egalitarian (see, for example, Weedon 1987). It is indeed odd that a perspective dedicated to challenging and changing both male and female sexuality, and to transforming radically our ideas about what is erotic, should be seen as biologically determinist. The emphasis on coercive aspects of sexuality and on the interconnections between sexuality and women's oppression has also led to the charge that radical feminists cannot deal with sexual pleasure and are simply anti-sex. This caricature both ignores the diversity of opinion among radical feminists and equates opposition to specific sexual practices with an anti-erotic stance. What is the case is that radical feminists have problematised desire and pleasure and have suggested that they might be reconstituted (see, for example, Cameron and Frazer 1987).

There are, however, aspects of sexuality which are undertheorised within radical feminism. We do need to think further about the possibility of engaging with the positive aspects of pleasure while remaining critical of current sexual desires and practices. Moreover, the focus on power raises further questions about how we trace the connections between the structural bases of patriarchal power and the ways in which power is exercised and resisted at the level of personal sexual relations (Ramazanoglu and Holland 1993). Finally, radical feminists have not devoted much attention to the ways in which sexuality is constructed in our individual subjectivities. While constantly asserting that specific sexual desires and preferences are learnt, little has been said from this perspective about how this happens beyond a few attempts to adapt models of socialisation for this purpose (see, for example, Jackson 1982a).

Radical feminists share with other feminists the idea that human sexuality is historically and culturally variable, a premiss which is fundamental to all forms of social constructionism. It challenges biologistic notions of the fixity of human sexuality and enables us to envisage future transformations of sexual relations as a political goal. This has provided the impetus for historical work on sexuality from a range of perspectives.[3] Radical feminist contributions have included work on the pathologising of lesbian relations

(Jeffreys 1985) and the constructions of sexuality within sexology (M. Jackson 1987, 1994). The idea that radical feminists regard sexual relations as fixed and unchanging is another false stereotype (Walby 1990; Richardson 1993). The agenda for much academic work in this area, however, has been set by Foucauldian perspectives. The appeal of Foucault to feminists lies in his radical anti-essentialism and his view of power as constitutive of sexuality, rather than merely repressive (Foucault 1981).[4] Feminists have, however, found fault with Foucault's acute gender blindness and the difficulty of linking his conception of socially diffuse power to structural analyses of inequality (see, for example, Ramazanoglu 1993). Most feminists working within a Foucauldian framework have sought to bring gender back in, to explore constructions of female sexuality as an object of regulatory discourses and practices (see, for example, Smart 1992). Often, however, such historical analyses are too obsessed with disjunctions, in particular with the Victorian 'discursive explosion', at the expense of continuities. Hence the persistence and restructuring of patriarchal domination under changing historical conditions tends to be played down or ignored.

Sexuality is also subject to synchronic variability. This is certainly an issue which should be addressed since we need to consider the intersections of gender and sexuality with class, ethnicity and other social divisions. The discourses around sexuality circulating within modern Western culture have been framed from a predominately white and middle-class, as well as male and heterosexual, perspective. Moreover, we each live our sexuality from different locations within social structures. Although some attention has been given to these issues, particularly to the racism embedded in Western sexual discourses and practices, Foucauldian-inspired perspectives tend to focus on sexual diversity *per se*, on 'sexualities'. With this pluralisation of sexuality the lack of attention to structural bases of power can become acutely problematic, especially when coupled with the denial of the importance of gender – as in Gayle Rubin's (1984) work. There is then no way of establishing regularities underpinning diverse 'sexualities', of relating them to dominant modes of heterosexual practice or of locating them within power hierarchies. Instead attention is directed to the 'outlaw' status of various 'sexual minorities', each judged from a libertarian perspective as equally worthy of protection from oppression and opprobrium. Rubin apparently does not see that there is a world of difference between a street prostitute and a millionaire pornographer, or between a man who has sex with a child and that child.[5]

What is missing from much libertarian theory is a critique of heterosexuality. In defending sexual 'pluralism' it is often forgotten that feminist theories of sexuality began by questioning the relations of dominance and submission inscribed in conventional heterosexual practice, suggesting that such relations were neither natural nor inevitable but resulted from the hierarchical ordering of gender. Many of the 'sexualities' currently being defended or promoted reproduce these hierarchies whether in the form of sado-masochism or 'cross-generational relations' – Rubin's euphemism for paedophilia. [6] There is no questioning of where such desires come from: 'the analysis begins from existing desires and thereby takes them to be "natural", immutable and ultimately valid' (Cameron and Frazer 1987: 173). Hence such arguments are at root essentialist, as some erstwhile defenders of libertarianism are beginning to admit (see Seidman 1992).

Libertarian arguments draw on Foucault only selectively, emphasising that aspect of his work which sees 'bodies and pleasures' as the point of resistance to power while losing sight of the constitutive effects of power as creating desire (see Foucault 1981: 156–7). The danger lies in treating bodies and pleasures as unproblematic. As Nancy Fraser (1989: 63) has commented, it is difficult to see 'what resistance to the deployment of sexuality . . . in the name of bodies and pleasures would be like', given that 'the disciplinary deployment of sexuality has, according to Foucault, produced its own panoply of bodily pleasures' and that 'disciplinary power has thoroughly marked the only bodies that we potential protesters have'. Hence diverse forms of sexuality are taken as given, already there to be outlawed, bringing us back to the repressive hypothesis which Foucault so effectively critiqued. The false equation of the transgressive with the progressive is in fact framed from within the very discourse of repression it seeks to subvert: one which gives undue privilege to sexuality either as the route to personal fulfilment and social liberation or as leading to individual degradation and social disintegration.

Where it does not lead to libertarian conclusions, I find Foucauldian analyses interesting in sensitising us to the multiplicity of often contradictory ways in which sexuality has been constructed and regulated. However, its inability to deal with the regularity and pervasiveness of patriarchal power, with the ways in which what counts as sexual has been constructed in terms of gender hierarchy, is problematic. The idea that our sense of what is sexual, including our desires and practices, is discursively constituted is potentially productive. But, whereas Foucault (1980) sees the concept of discourse as antithetical to ideology, I would argue that we should view discourses as ideological – in that they can serve to obscure or legitimate relations of domination and subordination. Discursive constructions of sexuality have produced very particular 'truths' which have defined hierarchically ordered heterosexual relations as natural and inevitable. Discourses do not, therefore, float free from the structural inequalities characterising the societies in which they are produced.

This still leaves us with the problem of the relationship between our individual desires and the discourses circulating within society, of how sexuality is socially constructed at the level of our individual subjectivities. Some feminists have applied Foucault to the problem of subjectivity by analysing how we locate or position ourselves within discourses (Hollway 1984a; Weedon 1987), or have suggested that Foucault's later work on technologies of self might be productive (McNay 1992). In neither case, however, has this led to any consistent theorisation of the processes by which we become gendered, sexual subjects. Indeed, when it comes to this question, Foucault is frequently abandoned in favour of psychoanalysis. Wendy Hollway (1984a), for example, has attempted the most systematic application of Foucault to the issue of how we make sense of sexual desires and relationships, yet elsewhere she resorts to psychoanalysis in order to explain how such desires come into being (1989, 1993). Indeed much of poststructuralist and postmodernist thinking is premised on the assumption that it is possible to draw simultaneously on both Foucault and Lacan, despite Foucault's contention that psychoanalysis is just another discursive formation producing its own disciplinary regime of truth.

Psychoanalysis has established a virtual monopoly on theorising the construction of sexuality at the level of subjectivity, despite the numerous cogent critiques of it. Many feminists agree that psychoanalysis is ahistorical, that it rests on essentialist premises. While the Lacanian version suggests that sexed, desiring subjects are constituted through their entry into language and culture, this refers not to a historically specific language and culture but to the very process of becoming a 'speaking subject'. Moreover, psychoanalysis depends upon interpreting infantile emotions through a filter of adult assumptions and then makes incredible conceptual leaps from presumed infantile frustrations and gratifications to adult sexual desires and practices. Importantly, psychoanalysis makes no distinction between gender and sexuality: the two are conflated and ultimately reduced to the gender of our 'object choice'. 'One either identifies with a sex or desires it, but only these two relations are possible' (Butler 1990b: 333). Hence, while psychoanalysis calls the normality of heterosexuality into question by insisting that it is not innate, it reinstates it as a norm through this linkage between gender and desire.

Although it is hardly a promising perspective for feminism, psychoanalysis retains its tenacious hold in part because of the lack of viable alternatives. It is not that there are no other theories, but that they are either inadequate or underdeveloped. Most of us have long since abandoned conventional models of socialisation, indeed the concept of socialisation itself, as far too simplistic and mechanistic to reveal much about subjectivity at all. Gagnon and Simon's (1974) work on sexual scripts, although flawed by its lack of attention to structural inequalities, could still prove productive if used critically – but few of us have bothered to try.[7] Foucauldian perspectives on discourses and technologies of self could be applied to the problem, but this too has not been attempted in any consistent way. These two perspectives still seem to offer the best way forward, in that they allow for active agency in the construction of individual sexualities, but remarkably little progress has been made in this area over the last 20 years. While we are engaging in ever more sophisticated modes of theorising about gender, sexuality and subjectivity, we still have no satisfactory way of approaching the very basic question: How did I get this way? For those who are sceptical of psycho-analysis the lack of a convincing theory of subjectivity is a major gap in femin-ist and sociological theory.

In theorising sexuality we need a means of understanding how we become gendered and how we become sexual without conflating gender and sexu-ality, without assuming that particular forms of desire are automatically con-sequent upon acquiring feminine or masculine gender and without reducing the complexity of desire to the gender of its object. Furthermore, we require an analysis of how this process is related to discourses on sexuality circulat-ing within our culture and how these in turn are related to structural inequal-ities, particularly gender inequality. We should also be able to tie these strands together in such a way as to recognise the force of cultural and ideological constructions of sexuality and the constraints of social structure, but which does not deny human agency and therefore the possibility of challenging and resisting dominant constructions of sexuality. This enterprise, in my view, requires that we do not overprivilege sexuality. Part of the problem we have in thinking about sex derives from the weight we make it carry, the way we view it as qualitatively different from other aspects of social life. This is one of the few points on which I am in agreement with Rubin (1984). Running through much feminist thought as well as some interactionist and Fou-cauldian work (Gagnon and Simon 1974; Heath 1982), is the idea that we should question the way in which sexuality is singled out as a special area of existence, as fundamental to individual and social well-being, as defining who and what we are. We should recognise that the 'specialness' of sexuality derives not from its intrinsic 'nature', but from the social meanings it has his-torically acquired.

If we are to understand sexuality in context, neither giving it causal pri-ority nor treating it in isolation, then a feminist analysis should consider its interlinkages with other aspects of women's subordination. Hence, while I am convinced of the continuing necessity of relating sexuality to gender, I regard the latter as more important than the former. Here I would argue, following Delphy (1984, 1993), that gender – the existence of 'men' and 'women' as social categories – is a product of hierarchy. Gender is not ordered by anatomical sex nor by sex in the sense of the erotic/reproductive, as in Rubin's (1975) conceptualisation of the sex/gender system. Rather, hierarchy precedes division in that the existence of gender as a socially meaningful system of classification depends on the dominance of men over women (Delphy 1993). Sexuality, in particular institutionalised heterosexuality, is woven into this hierarchy.

This perspective entails a radical questioning of gender categories them-selves, a position which is often associated with postmodernist and queer theory (Riley 1988; Butler 1990a, 1993a; Fuss 1991a). Materialist radical feminists differ from poststructuralists and postmodernists in two crucial respects. Firstly, the latter see the meaning of social categories as fluid and shifting, constantly being contested and renegotiated, while materialists see them as rooted in social practices and structural inequalities which are built into the fabric of society – although they accept that these categories can and must be challenged. 'Men' and 'women' are not, then, simply discursive constructs, but are materially existing social groups founded upon unequal, exploitative relationships. Secondly, whereas postmodernists and queer theorists posit heterosexuality as a normative construction of cross-sex desire – Butler's (1990a) sex-gender-desire matrix – materialist feminists see it primarily as a gendered hierarchy involving not just sexual desire but also the appropriation of women's bodies and labour.

The complexity of heterosexuality

Feminist discussions of heterosexuality frequently distinguish between heterosexuality as institution and as practice or experience (Richardson 1993; Robinson 1993a). These separate aspects of heterosexuality are, of course, interlinked, but such distinctions enable us to avoid critiques of heterosexuality which implicitly attack heterosexual women. They are also necessary in order to deal with the complexities of heterosexuality. Whereas differences among lesbians have been foregrounded in recent debates, heterosexuality is often represented as monolithic from both libertarian and anti-libertarian positions.

In celebrating diversity libertarian theorists frequently appear to regard heterosexuality as unproblematic, as the accepted singular norm against which sexual pluralism must be defended, as merely conventional. Quite simply heterosexual sex is boring – unless it is redefined by virtue of the ambiguity of its participants or practices as 'queer'.[8] Lying inside Rubin's (1984) 'charmed circle' of acceptable sexual practice, heterosexual sex escapes scrutiny. The effect of this erasure is that heterosexuality can appear to be surprisingly monolithic, although Rubin does at one point note that 'moral complexity' is conventionally admitted for those inside the charmed circle or on the righteous side of the moral divide. A similar thing happens in some postmodernist arguments which seem, at first sight, to be questioning and deconstructing all gender and sexual categories – a point Mary Evans has recently made about Judith Butler's work (Butler 1990a, 1993a; Evans 1994). While Butler aims to destabilise the 'regulatory fiction' of gender and the heterosexual ordering of desire it gives rise to, heterosexuality itself is denied the possibility of being anything other than an unexamined norm.

Heterosexuality is frequently constructed as equally monolithic in the writings of its radical lesbian feminist critics (for example, Jeffreys 1990; Kitzinger 1994). These feminists do not allow the conventional 'moral complexity' of heterosexuality to go unchallenged and would certainly not place it on the 'good' side of any moral or political divide. In the process, however, they frequently deny it any complexity at all: it is simply eroticised power. This is something I, along with many other heterosexual feminists, find problematic. This position emphasises the structural inequalities which the libertarians ignore, but views practice and experience as directly determined by structure. It thus leaves no space for the contestation of patriarchal power within heterosexual relations nor for exploring the interconnections between gender, sexuality and other power relations (see Kanneh 1993).

In terms of meeting the needs I have identified above in thinking about sexuality at the level of social structure and culturally constituted discourses, as well as at the level of individual agency and subjectivity, I would suggest that we need to consider four aspects of heterosexuality: its institutionalisation within society and culture, the social and political identities associated with it, the practices it entails and the experience of it. These are, of course, analytical distinctions which, as heterosexuality is lived, intersect and interrelate. I have also argued that we should not overprivilege sexuality in relation to other aspects of social life. While here I am concentrating on the specifically sexual aspects of heterosexuality, I should make it clear that as institution, practice, experience and identity heterosexuality is not merely sexual. Moreover, while heterosexuality's central institution is marriage, the assumption of normative heterosexuality operates throughout society and even its specifically sexual practice is by no means confined to the private sphere (see, for example, Hearn *et al.* 1989); nor is such practice, consensual or otherwise, limited to heterosexuals.

Heterosexuality: institution and identity

As it is institutionalised within society and culture, heterosexuality is founded upon gender hierarchy: men's appropriation of women's bodies and labour underpins the marriage contract (Delphy and Leonard 1992). The benefits men gain through their dominant position in the gender order are by no means reducible to the sexual and reproductive use of women's bodies. Men may say that 'women are only good for one thing' but, as Delphy (1992) points out, this is no reason why we should accept this at face value. In marriage, for example, the home comforts produced by a wife's domestic labour are probably far more important to a man's well-being and his ability to maintain his position as a man than the sexual servicing he receives. None the less, a man does acquire sexual rights in a woman by virtue of marriage and a woman who is not visibly under the protection of a man can be regarded as fair sexual game by others (Guillaumin 1981). Fear of sexual violence and harassment is also one means by which women are policed and police themselves through a range of disciplinary practices: for example, restricting their own access to public space, where they choose to sit on a bus or train, how they sit and who they avoid eye contact with (Bartky 1990).

Here the macro level of power intersects with its micro practices. The institutionalisation of heterosexuality also works ideologically, through the discourses and forms of representation which define sex in phallocentric terms, which position men as sexual subjects and women as sexual objects.

The question of sexual identity, in particular lesbianism as a political identity, has been much debated by feminists. Heterosexuality, however, is still infrequently thought of in these terms and the vast majority of heterosexual women probably do not define themselves as such. None the less many of the identities available to women derive from their location within heterosexual relations – as wife, girlfriend, daughter or mother. Attachment to these identities affects the ways in which women experience the institution and practice of heterosexuality. For example, women's ambivalent feelings about housework – their unwillingness to be critical of the appropriation of their labour, even when they are aware of the inequity of their situation – very often springs from their feelings about those they work for and from their desire to be good wives and mothers (Oakley 1984; Westwood 1984). In sexual terms, too, women's identities may be shaped by heterosexual imperatives – by the need to attract and please a man. The desire to be sexually attractive appears to be profoundly important to women's sense of self-worth and closely bound up with the gendered disciplinary practices through which docile, feminine bodies are produced (Bartky 1990). Hence heterosexuality, while uninterrogated, is pivotal to conventional feminine identities.

To name oneself as heterosexual is to make visible an identity which is generally taken for granted as a normal fact of life. This can be a means of bringing heterosexuality into question and challenging its privileged status, but for women being heterosexual is by no means a situation of unproblematic privilege. Heterosexual feminists may benefit from appearing 'normal' and unthreatening, but heterosexuality as an institution entails a hierarchical relation between (social) men and (social) women. It is women's subordination within institutionalised heterosexuality which is the starting point for feminist analysis. It is resistance to this subordination which is the foundation of feminist politics. It is hardly surprising, then, that heterosexual feminists prefer to be defined in terms of their feminism – their resistance – rather than their heterosexuality, their relation to men (Swindells 1993). Resisting the label 'heterosexual', though, has its problems. It can imply a refusal to question and challenge both the institution and one's own practice; it can serve to invalidate lesbianism as a form of resistance to patriarchy and to deny the specific forms of oppression that lesbians face. For these reasons Celia Kitzinger and Sue Wilkinson (1993b) are sceptical about those who 'call for the dissolution of the dichotomous categories "lesbian" and "heterosexual"' (p. 7).

Questioning this binary opposition, however, need not be a way of avoiding the politics of lesbianism or getting heterosexual feminists off the hook, but can represent an honest attempt to problematise heterosexuality (see

Gergen 1993; Young 1993). Nor is it only heterosexual feminists who are engaged in this deconstructive enterprise, but also lesbian queer theorists such as Diana Fuss (1991a) and Judith Butler (1990a, 1991). When such arguments are framed from a postmodernist stance, this does make it difficult to account for the systematic structural bases of any form of oppression (see Jackson 1992). None the less, treating the categories 'lesbian' and 'heterosexual' as problematic is by no means antithetical to radical feminism: indeed, I would argue that it is essential. This is not merely a matter of competing identities, but is fundamental to an appreciation of the social construction of gender and sexual categories.

The categories 'heterosexual', 'homosexual' and 'lesbian' are rooted in gender[9] – they presuppose gender divisions and could not exist without our being able to define ourselves and others by gender. If we take Delphy's (1984, 1993) argument that 'men' and 'women' are not biologically given entities but social groups defined by the hierarchical and exploitative relationship between them, then the division between hetero- and homosexualities is, by extension, also a product of this relation. Within this perspective it is possible to see gender and sexual categories as both social constructs and material realities. 'Women' are a social rather than natural category defined by their relation to men. Lesbianism by virtue of its location in relation to patriarchal heterosexuality also has a real social existence. This does not mean, as Wittig (1992) would have it, that lesbians are not women – they may be fugitives from womanhood, but there is no ultimate escape from the gender categories which define and oppress us. This does not, however, preclude resistance to patriarchal relations on the part of both lesbians and heterosexual women.

Heterosexual eroticism: practice and experience

At the level of heterosexual practice the structural and cultural ordering of gender hierarchy can be reinforced or contested. Complicity in and resistance to heterosexual practice is not just about what does or does not happen between the sheets, but about who cleans the bathroom or who performs emotional labour on whom. In the specifically sexual sense it is here that phallocentricity, the privileging of male pleasure and eroticised power relations involve our material bodies, where male sexual privilege is acted out or where we try to negotiate activities and forms of pleasure which challenge it.

Experience and practice are perhaps too closely linked to be easily disentangled, but the distinction is intended to signal experience as what is felt both sensually and emotionally and what is thought, while practice refers to what we do and how we do it. Specifically sexual experience encompasses our desires, our pleasure and displeasure. Sexual experience, although felt in its impact on our physical bodies, is not simply accessible to us in raw form as bodily sensation: it is actively worked over and made sense of. How we make sense of it depends on the discourses, narratives and scripts available to us, and it is through these interpretative processes that we link our experience and practice. The way we narratively construct our experience will depend on our location within our society and culture – whether, for instance, we have access to feminist discourses that might challenge dominant, patriarchal ones and thus enhance our ability, in practice, to resist.

Recent analyses of heterosexuality, whether attacking it (Kitzinger and Wilkinson 1993b; Kitzinger 1994) or defending it (Hollway 1993; Segal 1994), have tended to focus on sexual experience and practice, particularly on desire and pleasure. It is these issues which I will concentrate on in this final section, while acknowledging that heterosexual experience and practice encompasses more than its erotic dimension. These debates have been centrally concerned with power – its structural underpinnings and its micropractices and the degree to which women can subvert or challenge it within heterosexual relations. The battle lines are drawn between those arguing that heterosexual sex is inescapably oppressive for women and those who claim that the power relation it entails is vulnerable to subversion. Both arguments are problematic. Mirroring the conflicts between proponents and opponents of libertarianism, we have on one side those with an overly deterministic view of the operation of power, while on the other are those who play down its structural underpinnings and overestimate its instability. In seeking an alternative to these irreconcilable positions, I will consider the potential of materialist feminism for furthering our understanding of desire, pleasure and displeasure in heterosexual sex.

I will begin from the premiss that gender is fundamental, that as desiring subjects we are gendered, as are the objects of our desire. This is as true of lesbian sexuality as it is of heterosexuality. To desire the 'other sex' or indeed to desire the 'same sex' presupposes the prior existence of 'men' and 'women' as socially – and erotically – meaningful categories. What is specific to heterosexual desire is that it is premised on gender *difference*, on the sexual 'otherness' of the desired object. From a materialist feminist perspective this difference is not an anatomical one but a social one: it is the hierarchy of gender which 'transforms an anatomical difference (which is itself devoid of social implications) into a relevant distinction for social practice' (Delphy 1984: 144). Since it is gender hierarchy which renders these anatomical differences socially and erotically significant, it is hardly surprising that heterosexual eroticism is infused with power. However, this eroticisation of power is not reducible to the mere juxtaposition of certain body parts. There is nothing intrinsic to male and female anatomy which positions women as passive or privileges certain sexual practices above others. There is no absolute reason why the conjunction of a penis and a vagina has to be thought of as penetration, or as a process in which only one of those organs is active.

The coercive equation of sex = coitus = something men do to women is not an inevitable consequence of an anatomical female relating sexually to an anatomical male, but the product of the social relations under which those bodies meet. Those social relations can be challenged. Even the most tren-chant critics of heterosexuality and penetrative sex such as Jeffreys (1990) and Dworkin (1987) recognise that it is not male and female anatomy nor even, in Dworkin's case, the act of intercourse itself which constitute the problem, but rather the way in which heterosexuality is institutionalised and practised under patriarchy.

Conventional (patriarchal) wisdom tells us that sexual attraction and excitement depend upon the difference between men and women and, by implication, the power relation this entails. There are also some lesbians and feminists who, like Amber Hollibaugh, argue that desire and pleasure depend upon power and who 'don't want to do away with power in sex' (Hollibaugh 1989: 408). For other feminists anatomical difference, or indeed any form of difference between lovers, is seen as a potential source of power imbalance. Hence they strive to 'eroticize sameness and equality' (Jeffreys 1990: 315). But is 'sameness' necessary for equality? And if what we understand by desire does presuppose some degree of difference, does this inevitably entail hier-archy? From a materialist feminist perspective it is not difference which pro-duces hierarchy, but hierarchy which gives rise to socially significant differences. All of us are 'different' from each other: no two human beings are 'the same' and a lover is always someone 'other'. The point is that there are some differences which are of little social relevance – such as the colour of our hair – and others which are constructed as socially significant by virtue of hierarchy – such as the configuration of our genitals or our skin pigmen-tation.[10] Given that gender difference remains a material fact of social life, does this mean that power is an inescapable feature of heterosexual eroticism?

To argue that the power hierarchy of gender is structural does not mean that it is exercised uniformly and evenly at the level of interpersonal sexual relations, nor that our practice and experience is wholly determined by patri-archal structures and ideologies. There is some room for manoeuvre within these constraints. To deny this is to deny heterosexual women any agency, to see us as doomed to submit to men's desires whether as unwilling victims or misguided dupes. Once again, it assumes a monolithic experience of heterosexuality and denies differences among women who relate sexually to men. Heterosexual feminists, here as elsewhere in their lives, have struggled against men's dominance. We have asserted our right to define our own pleasure, questioned phallocentric models of sexuality, tried to deprioritise penetration or reconceptualise it in ways which did not position us as passive objects (Campbell 1980; Jackson 1982b; Robinson 1993a). More recently some have admitted – cautiously or defiantly – that even penetrative sex with men can be enjoyable and that its pleasure is not merely eroticised submis-sion (Hollway 1993; Robinson 1993a; Rowland 1993; Segal 1994).

Critics of heterosexuality are unimpressed by such claims. Kitzinger and Wilkinson (1993b), for example, are scathing about heterosexual feminists' attempts to develop egalitarian sexual practices and to change the meaning of penetration. Such strategies, they say, 'obscure the problem of the *institutionalization* of penile penetration under heteropatriarchy' (p. 21). They see the institution as totally determining practice so that each and every instance of penetration is an enactment of men's power. While it is the case that penetration within patriarchy is loaded with symbolic meanings which encode male power and is often in fact coercive, it cannot be assumed that it invariably carries this singular meaning. To argue that it does is to treat the physical act as meaningful in itself, as magically embodying male power without any intervening processes. It is here assumed that the micro processes of power can simply be read off from the structural level. It certainly cannot be assumed that if women like heterosexual sex we must all be wallowing in a masochistic eroticisation of our subordination – the consistent message of the revolutionary lesbian feminist position (Jeffreys 1990; Kitzinger and Wilkinson 1993b; Kitzinger 1994).

We need to retain a critical perspective on heterosexual pleasure, but one which is more subtle and less condemnatory. Even if we imagine some archetypal ultrafeminine woman who longs to be mastered and penetrated by a powerful man, she may not be straightforwardly eroticising her subordination. What we know about the appeal of romance for women suggests that it holds out the promise of gaining power over a man through love (Modleski 1984; Radway 1987). Even coercive sex can be seen this way, as in the interpretation of Rhett Butler's rape of Scarlett offered by fans of *Gone with the Wind* (Taylor 1989). The sense of power women derive from such interpretations of male desire is of course illusory, but it is indicative of the complexity and contradictions of heterosexual experience. We certainly cannot take such fantasies of power, as Lynne Segal (1994) does, as evidence of an underlying symmetry in heterosexual relations. Men and women may, as she says, both feel powerful on being desired and powerless as a result of desire, but they do not experience these feelings from comparable social locations. Even if, as Segal (1994) suggests, 'sex places "manhood" in jeopardy', threatening the 'masculine ideal of autonomous selfhood' (p. 255), the hierarchical ordering of gender and sexuality is not as easy to subvert as she implies. Wendy Hollway's (1984b) claim that women can produce discourses which contest 'the power of the penis' is similarly flawed by its failure to take account of material sexual power accruing to men as social group. Whatever discourses we produce, whatever fantasies we have, they offer us no protection against the coercive power of the penis enacted as rape.

Hence, while we should not damn heterosexual pleasure as irredeemably masochistic, we should not underestimate the pervasiveness of male power. Power operates at a variety of levels. Although we can contest it at the level of individual practice (and enhance our sexual pleasure in the process), this may have little effect elsewhere. Moreover, as Caroline Ramazanoglu (1994) reminds us, there are very real material constraints on seeking heterosexual pleasure and for many women it remains elusive. As she says, we 'need to distinguish between the undoubted possibilities of heterosexual pleasure, and the extremely powerful social forces which constrain these possibilities from being more widely realised' (p. 321). Women often still discipline themselves to fit a model of sexuality which prioritises male desires and defines women's fulfilment in terms of 'love' and the giving of pleasure (Holland *et al.* 1994a). This attribute of femininity is hardly confined to sexuality: the ethic of service to men is fundamental to other aspects of gender relations, to men's appropriation of women's labour as well as their bodies.

In the final analysis, it is difficult to imagine a truly egalitarian form of heterosexuality while gender division persists; and if that division were eradicated neither heterosexuality nor lesbianism could exist in any meaningful sense, since both are products of it. Sexuality is one site of feminist struggle, but it is by no means the only one. Nor is sexuality the sole basis of women's oppression. Heterosexuality itself is not merely a sexual institution: it is founded as much on men's access to women's unpaid work as on their sexual access to our bodies. In exploring issues of sexual desire, practice and identity we should not forget the myriad other ways in which male domination is colluded with and resisted and the many other means by which women's subordination is perpetuated and challenged.

Notes

1 The term 'heterosexual feminist' is in some ways problematic in that it defines our feminism by our heterosexuality (see Rowland 1993). None the less, given that there is no easy alternative term ('feminist heterosexual' would be worse!) I have used it throughout this chapter.
2 The term 'radical feminism' is now often used to include revolutionary feminism although the distinction between them was once, in the early 1980s, a politically important one. Both analysed patriarchy as a system of male domination and were critical of heterosexuality. Revolutionary feminists, however, gave far greater causal priority to sexuality in explaining women's subordination. While radical feminists saw lesbianism as a potential form of resistance to patriarchy, it was only revolutionary feminists who felt that political lesbianism was a *necessary* strategy for feminists. Hence it was the latter who were critical of those feminists who remained heterosexual (see Onlywomen Press 1981). The boundaries between them may have blurred, but the two separate perspectives are still discernible. Sheila Jeffreys, for example, comes from a revolutionary feminist background and I would see Celia Kitzinger and Sue Wilkinson as continuing in this tradition. Others I cite, such as Debbie Cameron, Liz Frazer, Liz Kelly and Suzanne Kappeler have been associated with a form of radical feminism opposed to the revolutionary feminist position on political lesbianism.

3 To a lesser extent it has also given rise to anthropological work on the cultural variability of gender, sexual practices and the meanings associated with them.

4 It is worth remembering that some of Foucault's ideas, hailed as radically innovative, were current in less fashionable areas of social theory well before the publication of first volume of *The History of Sexuality*. For example Gagnon and Simon (1974) had already critiqued the concept of repression and questioned the privileged place accorded to sexuality within modern culture. There were also analogous ideas circulating among feminists concerning how the 'truth' of sex was produced, particularly with regard to the sexualisation of women. These ideas are difficult to pin down in terms of published sources, but they were fed by such work as Anne Koedt's (1972) questioning of penetrative sex. In one of my own earliest articles (Jackson 1978b) I argued that sexual knowledge was socially constructed. I did not arrive at this conclusion in isolation: it was the product of many hours of discussion with other feminists.

5 I have taken Rubin's work as my main example of libertarianism, since she provides the most sophisticated theorisation of this tendency from a feminist perspective. Hollibaugh (1989) could also be placed firmly in this camp, as of course could Pat Califia whose defence of sado-masochism, published in the controversial 'sex' issue of *Heresies* (1981) has achieved considerable notoriety.

6 Of course such practices are generally defended in the context of gay and lesbian sexualities rather than within heterosexual relationships. Part of the defence is that sado-masochism does not have the same meaning where it is not part of the institutionalised hierarchy of heterosexuality, and that roles enacted in a gay or lesbian S/M scenario need not have anything to do with the balance of power elsewhere in the relationship (see, for example, Califia 1981).

7 I used this approach in my early work (Jackson 1978a, b, 1982a) and Ken Plummer (1975) applied it to the construction of gay male identities. More recently both of us have extended this perspective, in rather different ways, to encompass narratives of self (Jackson 1993a; Plummer 1995b). Plummer's concern in this recent work is with the proliferation of sexual storytelling in contemporary societies, how the narratives available to us enable us to construct stories about our sexuality and how we come to be able to tell some stories and not others. I am interested in how we invest in such stories in such a way that they shape our subjectivities.

8 I am not implying here that queer theory is inevitably libertarian. Rather I am thinking of the ways in which sexual transgression is sometimes equated with the progressive and how, in this context, some heterosexual practices are identified as 'queer' and transgressive. An example is Clare Hemmings's (1993) quotation of the following:

> Heterosexual behaviour does not always equal 'straight'. When I strap on a dildo and fuck my male partner, we are engaged in 'heterosexual' behaviour, but I can tell you that it feels altogether queer, and I'm sure my grandmother and Jesse Helms would say the same.
>
> (Carol Queen, quoted in Hemmings 1993: 132)

Hemmings argues that, in the context of bisexuality, such performances may serve to destabilise the hierarchical ordering of heterosexuality. I prefer Elizabeth Wilson's interpretation of the same passage. She suggests that such acts are not necessarily transgressive, that they are perfectly capable of being incorporated into a conventional, albeit 'kinky', heterosexual couple's repertoire without having any such destabilising consequences (Wilson 1993: 113).

9 Equally, the category 'bisexual' is rooted in gender. As such bisexuality in itself does not challenge gender or sexual categories or hierarchies. A full discussion of this issue is beyond the scope of this chapter.

10 The salience of these features cannot be assumed to be universal. Recent anthropological work suggests that not all cultures think in terms of rigid gender categories and not all define maleness and femaleness exclusively in terms of genital difference (see, for example, Meigs 1990). Skin colour, too, takes on differing significance in different cultures. In Western societies its importance derives from racism while elsewhere, as in the Indian subcontinent, it may be a marker of status because dark skin is associated with the peasantry.

3

Heterosexuality and domestic life

Jo VanEvery

My interest in the study of sexualities has grown out of my work in the areas of feminism and the family. A recently completed project on anti-sexist living arrangements (VanEvery 1995a) was motivated by a desire to find out how individual women put the feminist critique of 'the family' into practice in their daily lives. When I began the project I considered the debate about 'political lesbianism' to be part of the critique of the family. As it happened, I interviewed mainly heterosexual women. However, due to my awareness of heterosexism in sociological research, I tried to problematise hetero-sexuality in the analysis. The special issue of *Feminism and Psychology* (Wilkinson and Kitzinger 1993) on heterosexuality and feminism came out around the time I was completing that analysis. I decided to look at the question of heterosexuality and feminism more explicitly.

What I discovered when I came to look at what was being published, was that the current debate about heterosexuality and feminism seemed to be happening in a vacuum. There is much discussion of sexual practices and sexual identities, most of it couched (sometimes explicitly, but more often implicitly) in terms of choice. The following extract from the *Feminism and Psychology Reader* (which is an expanded version of the special issue) on heterosexuality and feminism is illustrative of the general tone of the debate:

> The felt impossibility of changing one's sexual orientation is not an argument for the desirability of this orientation; indeed, I have often wished that I could love women erotically, but I can't. An appeal to the feminist psychologist readers: invent a therapeutic technique of

releasing the heterosexual woman 'who always knew what she was' from the prison house of necessity into the free space of choice.

(Bartky 1993: 41)

The focus on choice and desire has led to a theoretical emphasis on psycho-analytic and psychological theories. There is relatively little discussion of the fact that heterosexual relationships encompass much more than sex. At the same time, there is a vast sociological literature on households, family and marriage (some of it feminist or influenced by feminism) which rarely explicitly problematises heterosexuality, despite the fact that most research in these areas is on heterosexual couples.[1] In this chapter I will bring these two areas of investigation together, arguing that theories of heterosexuality need to consider more than the sexual and that analyses of domestic life need to problematise heterosexuality.

Hegemonic heterosexuality

My argument rests on the assertion that while heterosexuality has no essen-tial character, it does have a hegemonic form in late twentieth-century Western societies (i.e. in Europe, North America, Australia and New Zealand). I draw on R.W. Connell's use of the term 'hegemony' in his book *Gender and Power*:

'hegemony' means . . . a social ascendance achieved in a play of social forces that extends beyond contests of brute power into the organiz-ation of private life and cultural processes . . . though 'hegemony' does not refer to ascendancy based on force, it is not incompatible with ascendancy based on force . . . 'hegemony' does not mean total cultural dominance, the obliteration of alternatives.

(Connell 1987: 184)

The hegemonic form of heterosexuality is marriage. While it is difficult to find systematic evidence for this, there are several indications. Stevi Jackson (1993b: 42) points out that 'the ideology of heterosexual romance tells us that falling in love is the prelude to a lasting, secure and stable conjugal union.' Sue Lees (1993: 106) reports that girls in North London see no alternative to marriage, despite recognising the inequality and subordination they can expect from it. There has been public anxiety (in the US and the UK), reflected in the pronouncements of political parties, churches, and others, about declining marriage rates and rising numbers of single parents. Government policies in most Western countries privilege marriage over other types of relationships (including heterosexual cohabitation) through tax relief and eligibility for various benefits.

In addition, despite recent public anxiety about declining marriage rates and increasing numbers of out-of-wedlock births, the vast majority of the population do marry, and the majority of such births are registered to both parents (usually giving the same address). In England and Wales, in 1992, 77.2 per cent of women aged 16 and over were reported to have been married at least once. For women aged 24 and over the figure was 87.6 per cent (*Population Trends* 77 (1994)). When the figures are broken down by birth cohort it becomes obvious that age at first marriage is increasing (OPCS 1993: Table 3.12). Thus there may be a significant proportion of the 24–35 age group who will marry but have not yet done so. Furthermore, the 1991 General Household Survey reports that 23 per cent of unmarried women aged 16–49 in Britain were cohabiting (Capron 1994).[2] David Clark and Douglas Haldane (1990: 24) have pointed out that despite higher than ever rates of divorce, about two-thirds of marriages will be 'for life'. A similar pattern is evident in the US statistics: in 1989 only 18.9 per cent of women were single (never married) with a similar difference between younger and older age groups (US Bureau of the Census 1991: 44, Table 52). Thus marriage is not only culturally dominant, it is an overwhelmingly common experience for women.

While theorising heterosexuality seems to be a relatively new or marginal pursuit, mainly undertaken by radical feminists, theorising marriage and the family is a major topic of sociological research. If we accept that 'marriage and the family' is the hegemonic form of heterosexuality in late twentieth-century Western societies, then theorising heterosexuality encompasses theorising marriage and the family. I will, therefore, examine sociological theories of marriage and the family in order to theorise heterosexuality as an 'institution' which encompasses much more than sexual desire or sexual acts. The implications of this theorising for feminist political practice will be drawn out in the conclusion.

Influential theories of marriage and the family

Most sociological research on marriage and the family has been influenced by two main bodies of theory, Parsonian structural-functionalism and Marxism. This influence has been both through the acceptance and development of the theories of Parsons and Marx, and through critique and the development of new theories. Feminists have been particularly prominent in the latter process.

The work of Talcott Parsons has been so influential (particularly in North America) that David Cheal (1991) has called it the 'Standard Theory of the Family' (p. 3). Talcott Parsons's theory of the family refers to the nuclear family household: a relatively isolated, small unit consisting of a married heterosexual couple and their own children, and specialising in the functions of socialisation of children and personality stabilisation of adults (Parsons and Bales 1955: 16). According to Parsons, as society evolves the division of labour becomes more specialised. The increased specialisation of roles includes a split between the public and the private spheres, which is paralleled by the gendered specialisation of what Parsons calls instrumental and expressive tasks. The structural isolation of the nuclear family from the wider kin group is organised to free the man in the instrumental role for geographical mobility, which may be demanded by the occupational system. Men go out to work and provide for the family; women stay in the home socialising children and providing emotional support for the whole family. The two roles were seen as incompatible and the instrumental nature of much of women's role was played down even when recognised. Parsons's explanation of the assignment of roles by gender is based on the biological fact of childbirth which establishes 'a strong presumptive primacy of the relation of mother to the small child and this in turn establishes a presumption that the man, who is exempted from these biological functions, should specialize in the alternative instrumental direction' (Parsons and Bales 1955: 23).

More recent work in this tradition attempts to explain changes in family forms (for example the rise in divorce and single motherhood) as a consequence of women's entry into the labour market. David Popenoe (1988) argues that while the evolution that Parsons explained was largely beneficial to society, it has now gone too far. While some changes in the 'traditional nuclear family' are to be lauded, Popenoe feels that the weakening of the nuclear family unit is much more problematic:

> It is not difficult to argue that the functions that have already been taken from the family – government, formal education, and so on – can in fact be better performed by other institutions. It is far more debatable, however, whether the same applies to childrearing and the provision of affection and companionship. There is strong reason to believe, in fact, that the family is by far the best institution to carry out these functions, and that insofar as these functions are shifted to other institutions, they will not be carried out as well.
>
> (Popenoe 1993: 539)

Although vociferously contested, particularly by feminists, his views are being taken seriously in American family sociology as well as in more public debates about the family.

Miriam Johnson (1989) has a less apocalyptic Parsonian interpretation of the same demographic changes. She agrees that women's entry into the labour market has indeed led to profound changes in the structure of the family (as Parsons himself understood). From a feminist perspective, this allows for greater understanding of gender inequality:

> While some of these phenomena may be experienced now as dislocations, they may also presage new and better modes of articulating

family and work – modes that may bring about greater gender equality and transform definitions of both family and work in ways that
could erase the partially false distinctions between private and public
spheres.

(Johnson 1989: 115)

I will return to Johnson's work below.

Marxist theory has also been influential, particularly in Britain. However,
Marx wrote little about women and the family and there is no systematic
analysis of gender divisions in society in his work. What was written in this
tradition suffered from many of the same problems as Parsonian theory.
Marx (1970: 44) also conceived of the sexual division of labour in the family
as 'natural' and made a distinction between the public and the private. The
most notable feminist attempt to use Marxist theory to understand households and families was the 'domestic labour debate'.[3] The major achievement of this debate was the recognition of household work as work.
However, many of the assumptions of Marxist theory – the separation of
production (public) and reproduction (private), the devaluing of the domestic as less social – were not challenged or, at least, the challenges were not
widely accepted. Women's liberation was seen mainly in terms of entry into
the public (productive) sphere.

Recent economic theories seem to shift away from an explicit naturalising
explanation to one which is based on rational choice. The most influential
of these is Gary Becker's New Home Economics,[4] in which the allocation of
household members' time to household and market activities is explained in
terms of utility maximisation. The value of an individual's time is determined
by actual or foregone market wages. This approach has been criticised for
reinforcing discriminatory processes in the market. However, for my
purposes, there is another problem: a 'natural' division of labour underlies
all these social/economic decisions: 'Although the sharp sexual division of
labor in all societies between the household and market sectors is partly due
to the gain from specialized investments, it is also partly due to intrinsic
differences between the sexes' (Becker, quoted in Morris 1990: 17 and Berk
1985: 33).

It could be argued that these theories have been widely criticised and no
longer have the influence they once did. To a certain extent I would agree.
Few people directly refer to Parsons or Marx when researching or theorising the family. However, many of the underlying assumptions of these positions have become accepted tenets of modern social theory. Lydia Morris
(1990) has argued that the recent renewal of interest in the household is
related to the restructuring of the labour market; particularly the decline of
lifelong full-time employment for men and the rise in married women's
employment. The implicit influence of Parsons's theory is not difficult to see.
The separation of the public and private, and the relegation of the 'natural'

to the private sphere, are perhaps the assumptions most commonly found in research on gender and households.

> It is generally assumed, and indeed widely the case, that the way people live together is structured around the immediately physical needs of the human organism – food, sleep, cleanliness, clothing. Since these needs derive directly from physiology, it has been easy to separate off the servicing of the human organism in this way as a distinct kind of labour.
> (Harris 1984: 148)

This has important consequences for theorising heterosexuality. Is heterosexuality largely invisible in theories of households and families because it is assumed to be the 'natural' precondition of the 'natural' process of childbearing? How is this linked to gender? I will consider these issues in more detail before turning to the feminist debates about heterosexuality.

Conceptualising gender in household/family research

Early feminist critics of Parsonian and Marxian theories emphasised the non-social explanation lurking in predominantly social theories. They also pointed out that it was not simply difference that resulted from this 'natural' division of labour but inequality and oppression. While Parsons, Marx and other theorists recognised the negative aspects of this inequality, the basis of their explanations in nature allowed them to focus their theories on more 'social' forms of inequality (usually those between men, for example class). Feminists directed attention to women's oppression and to the social character of the apparently natural division of labour in the home.

In the past 20 years, major advances have been made in the way sociologists (and others) theorise about sexual difference and the relationship between the 'natural' and the social. In Western societies, gender is constructed in a way that refers to biological characteristics which 'are used to reinforce the "essentialness" of gender' (West and Zimmerman 1987: 137). Social differences between these two categories can then be explained (at least partly) with reference to these biological differences. The ability to bear children is the 'biological characteristic' most commonly referred to in theories of the family and is often the basis for explanations of social differences (for example the division of labour). Most research on households and families has focused on women as mothers in its explanation of continuing inequalities. Although the process is often obscured by the fact that samples are composed of (married) heterosexual couples with children, the implicit naturalising of gender inequality (through motherhood) can happen in studies of childless heterosexual couples. Penny Mansfield and Jean Collard's explanation of the division of labour in newly wed couples provides an example:

The examination of 'who keeps house' took place at a time when the majority of husbands and wives were both working full-time outside the home, so that in this respect, there was equality between husband and wife. However, this symmetry in working roles was not mirrored in the home. Inequality between spouses in the home was only rarely recognised by the couples and few attempts were made to redress the balance of domestic responsibility. It seems that the first phase of marriage for these newly-weds was overshadowed by the event which would bring it to a close – the birth of the first child. The main impact of childbearing is usually perceived to be the loss of the wife's full-time employment and, in anticipation of this, these newly-wed spouses regard the first phase of married life as temporary. *Thus both the current domestic role of the brides and their working role are already influenced by their future perceptions of themselves as mothers.*
(Mansfield and Collard 1988: 135; emphasis added)

A recent empirical study of the division of domestic labour in households in the United States points to a different interpretation of the gendered division of labour in the family. Sarah F. Berk (1985) set out to test Gary Becker's rational-choice model of the domestic division of labour. Using diaries and structured interviews, Berk collected data on time spent on various domestic tasks and on the types of tasks performed by men and women in married couple households with children. In her conclusion she argues that the New Home Economics is flawed because housework is conceptualised as work which produces *only* household goods and services. Gender is conceptualised as a property of individuals wholly separable from the social practices (i.e. the division of labour) which the theory is trying to explain. As Judith Stacey and Barrie Thorne (1985) have pointed out, this is a common problem in quantitative research using gender as a variable. Relating evidence from her interviews to the quantitative analysis of both time and task measures of the division of domestic labour, Berk proposes:

if we retain the assumption that the lopsided arrangements surrounding the allocation of household work are optimal for *some* production process, we must again ask the simple question, What is being produced?
At least metaphorically, the division of household labor facilitates *two* production processes: the production of goods and services and what we might call the production of gender.
(Berk 1985: 201)

Although other studies have highlighted the importance of gender identity to the domestic division of labour (for example Gregson and Lowe 1993), and the importance of local gender norms (for example Morris 1985a, b), Berk's suggestion implies an important conceptual shift. For Berk, gender is not culturally produced elsewhere and influential on the domestic division of labour (as in Morris's model) but is culturally produced (at least partly) *through* the domestic division of labour.

Berk draws on the work of Candace West and Don Zimmerman to develop this point. West and Zimmerman (1987) argue that gender is always relevant in social interaction and use the notion of 'accountability' to understand the way that gender affects all social interaction:

> a person engaged in virtually any activity may be held accountable for performance of that activity as a *woman* or a *man*, and their incumbency in one or the other sex category can be used to legitimate or discredit their other activities ... to 'do' gender is not always to live up to normative conceptions of femininity or masculinity; it is to engage in behaviour *at the risk of gender assessment*.
>
> (p. 136; original emphasis)

Thinking about gender in this way allows us to denaturalise gender. Gender is no longer something that pre-dates a social division of labour (as it is in the theories of Marx, Parsons and Becker) but is constructed through the division of labour (among other things).[5]

This conceptualisation of gender requires a shift of empirical focus in research on families and households. As we have already seen, gender is frequently naturalised through motherhood which is considered to be a natural/biological process with social consequences: women bear children, therefore it is logical that the social process of caring for them (especially in the early stages) will build on this 'biological fact'. Anthropologists have begun to question the use of the 'natural' in kinship theory. This rethinking also raises interesting questions for sociological theory:

> When, for example, we call into question the assignment of 'motherhood' to the domain of 'kinship' defined as rooted in sexual reproduction, we deny neither the existence of physiological processes of human reproduction nor the importance of studying ideas and practices of motherhood. Rather, by questioning the assumption that motherhood in our society as well as in others is fundamentally structured by these physiological processes, we suggest paths of inquiry that will lead us to the productive analysis of other social processes and cultural meaning that are inscribed in motherhood.
>
> (Yanagisako and Delaney 1995b: 12)

In Western societies the hegemonic construction of 'natural' motherhood includes a heterosexual relationship. This is evident in Macintyre's (1976) analysis of abortion provision and the social construction of 'wanted' babies. Roseneil and Mann (1994) have argued that the recent public concern about lone mothers could be interpreted as an attempt to reinforce the hegemony of this notion in the face of feminist contestation of it.[6] However, the relationship between motherhood and (hetero-)sexuality is not widely problematised in sociological research on families and households, including feminist sociology. Heterosexism is beginning to be recognised in 'family studies' but, so far, as a problem of the exclusion of 'the families of lesbians and gay men' (Allen and Demo 1995). The existence of (hetero-)sexuality in families is widely recognised in the literature on domestic violence and child sexual abuse, but is only beginning to be examined in 'normal' families. When heterosexuality is recognised it is in terms of sexual practice and 'pleasure' (see O'Connor 1995).

While these avenues of inquiry are all interesting and important, I want to pose some more fundamental questions. Could mothering, like housework, be a process *through which* gender is constituted? If so, how does this work? To return to Mansfield and Collard's explanation, how does 'the main impact of childbearing' become 'the loss of the wife's full-time employment'? Is this related to heterosexuality and, if so, how?

Heterosexuality and the social construction of gender

The oppressive features of heterosexuality for women are not found only in sexual practices or sexual desire itself: a common interpretation of arguments for 'political lesbianism'. Several authors, particularly lesbian separatists (for example Frye 1983, 1992; Wittig 1992), have pointed out that gender is constructed as heterosexual:

> The category of sex is the political category that founds society as heterosexual. As such it does not concern being but relationships (for women and men are the result of relationships), although the two aspects are always confused when they are discussed. The category of sex is the one that rules as 'natural' the relation that is at the base of (heterosexual) society and through which half of the population, women, are 'heterosexualized' (the making of women is like the making of eunuchs, the breeding of slaves, of animals) and submitted to a heterosexual economy. For the category of sex is the product of a heterosexual society which imposes on women the rigid obligation of the reproduction of the 'species', that is, the reproduction of heterosexual society.
>
> (Wittig 1992: 5–6)

Recently, male sociologist R.W. Connell (1987) has developed an analysis of gender which rests on a similar observation. This is not simply a 'complementary' heterosexuality. As Hester Eisenstein (1991: 111) points out, 'Theories of gender are fundamentally about relations of domination and subordination and about how these are perpetuated or contested.' In addition, it is not solely the (hetero-)sexual act of fucking that constitutes gender as domination and subordination, as has been argued by Catherine MacKinnon (1987) and others (for example Kitzinger and Wilkinson 1994b:

444).[7] I would argue that the analyses of the role of penetrative heterosexual sex in constituting women as (subordinated) women is but one aspect of the hegemonic construction of women as wives (female partners in heterosexual relationships). While being sexually available to (particular) men is one aspect of being a wife, it is not the only one. An adequate feminist theory of heterosexuality must, therefore, take other aspects of (hegemonic) hetero-sexuality into account. Some feminist theories of marriage and the family provide a useful basis for theorising heterosexuality in this way.

Marriage and family in feminist theory

Some recent feminist theories of the family have offered social explanations of women's position in the family which provide the basis for developing this link between gender and heterosexuality. For example, in her book *Strong Mothers, Weak Wives* Miriam Johnson (1988) argues that to understand the oppression of women we need to separate the role of mother from that of wife. In other words, we need to shift our analytic focus from the parent-child relationship to the heterosexual couple relationship. Johnson locates women's oppression in the role of wife, which is by definition subordinate and under which the role of mother has been subsumed. Christine Delphy and Diana Leonard's (1992) theory of the economic nature of male power in the family household provides a deeper understanding of the content of the role of wife and the way that it subsumes mothering within it.

In these theories 'wife' is not defined simply as 'a married woman' (Oxford Concise English Dictionary) although most such women would come within its scope. Rather, it refers to the particular social position of women as sub-ordinates of individual men. For Johnson (1988), the characteristics central to the definition of 'wife' are subordinate status, economic dependence and the accompanying psychological characteristics such as deference. Delphy and Leonard (1992) specify the economic characteristics of wife further to include the appropriation of labour, paid and unpaid, by the (male) head of household, including the work involved in raising his children as well as any work done for someone else. They also highlight the fact that unmarried women may be 'wives' in this sense. Women who are not married to a man may also have their labour thus appropriated, either by a resident man, for example a father or a brother, or a non-resident man, such as the father of their children (Delphy and Leonard 1992: 127).

Johnson notes the elision of sexuality and gender in Western societies, heterosexuality being the basis of the definition of femininity and masculin-ity. Carole Pateman's (1988) work on the 'sexual contract', which underlies the 'social contract' of liberal individualism, highlights the fact that hus-bands' rights still include the right to their wives' work and sexual rights, and that relations between men and women include the right of male access to female bodies. Despite recent changes in the laws of many countries to recognise rape within marriage, 'sexual rights' are still an accepted part of marriage. Sally Cline's (1993) study of celibacy provides an example: after 30 years of marriage, Susan decides to be celibate. She says,

> I didn't want to do it any more. I was tired of pretending. Sex had never been good. We could have a much better life without it . . . He asked me why I thought I could *choose* not to do it? Finally he calmed down and said what did I mean by saying I was deciding not to do it? No woman can decide that, certainly not his *wife*. I must be sick in the head. He said I needn't think I had any choice.
> (Cline 1993: 56–7; second emphasis added)

Even those women in Cline's study whose husbands/partners were more accepting of their choice tended not to tell other people and may not even use the term 'celibate' to describe themselves. As Cline says, 'Seeing yourself as celibate comes as a shock to a married or partnered woman. Being a "celibate wife" is almost a contradiction in terms' (Cline 1993: 77).

It is not just within the family that women are constituted as wives. Delphy and Leonard (1992) point out that women's ability to undertake non-domestic work is usually controlled by the male head of household either directly, through the giving or withholding of permission, or indirectly, through the expectation that non-domestic work should not affect the performance of domestic duties. In addition, the social role of wife appears in the occupational sphere, both in the types of segregated work women perform (e.g. secretaries, waitresses) and in the expectations of certain professional jobs. Cynthia Cockburn's (1991) analysis of men's resistance to equal opportunities in the workplace highlights the way that men actively place women in the role of wife in the public sphere by sexualising them and resisting their authority.

In a recent study of women in the tourist industry, Lisa Adkins has highlighted two ways that women appear as wives in the labour market. The first is explicit in the hiring of 'married management teams' in hotels and pubs where wives' labour is contracted through their position as wives. Only husbands have a labour contract with the hotel chain/brewery and husbands decide what wives will do, including covering for their husbands when men get bored with their tasks (Adkins 1995: 78–80). The second is implicit in the job descriptions and conditions of work of waitresses and similar staff. In this case the characteristic sexual availability of wives (emphasised by Carole Pateman) is particularly prominent (Adkins 1995: 93–143).

Choosing heterosexuality?

Although radical feminist analyses of heterosexuality often argue that there are complex links between heterosexuality and the social construction of gender as a relationship of dominance and subordination, the focus of the recent debate, particularly in writings by heterosexual feminists, is on choice. It seems that heterosexual women have started with the political demand that they reject the oppressive institution of heterosexuality. Not surprisingly, given the extent to which heterosexuality is 'imposed, managed, organized, propagandized, and maintained by force' (Rich 1980: 648), they have found this difficult. Their analyses of heterosexuality have focused on the issue of 'choice'.

The radical insight of Adrienne Rich's (1980) article was her characterisation of heterosexuality as 'compulsory'. Rich provides numerous examples which demonstrate that women are physically, economically, emotionally and psychologically *coerced* into heterosexuality. She concludes by saying,

> Within the institution exist, of course, qualitative differences of experience; but the absence of choice remains the great unacknowledged reality, and in the absence of choice, women will remain dependent upon the chance or luck of particular relationships and will have no collective power to determine the meaning and place of sexuality in their lives.
>
> (Rich 1980: 659)

Recent heterosexual contributors to the renewed debate about heterosexuality have turned this argument around to claim that it is possible in the 1990s in the West for a woman to choose 'non-oppressive' heterosexual sex. In the process, heterosexuality is reduced to a desire, the intransigence of which is in need of explanation.

For example, Wendy Hollway (1993: 412) argues that 'The absence of discourses which make sense of the pleasures, desires and satisfactions, for women, of heterosexual relationships is damaging both to feminist theory and feminist politics.' In a similar vein, Lynne Segal (1994: xii) writes: 'If we really cannot offer a response to much of women's sexual experience [i.e. heterosexuality], other than to condemn it as part of a repressive social order, we can only dishearten rather than inspire the majority of women.' Moreover, the examples which Hollway uses of the pleasures, desires and satisfactions of heterosexuality for women – penetration, and the embrace of 'strong arms' – reduce 'heterosexual relationships' to heterosexual sex.

Neither author addresses the issue of coercion. In particular, they sidestep the particular issue which Rich raises about choice: in a society which constructs any woman who prefers not to have relationships with men (whether she be lesbian or celibate) as sick or deviant, can women really be said to *choose* heterosexuality? The focus of these theories of heterosexuality on desire and individual women's (in)ability to change their sexual 'orientation'/identity ignores the fact that gender and heterosexuality, and the family and heterosexuality, are so closely intertwined. This is evident in

Hollway's (1993) article where her particular (privileged) context is ignored in the discussion of the meaning of the (hetero-) sexual acts she describes:

> I love the experience of being wrapped in my partner's 'strong arms' and 'adored' . . . Later I will be out there in the world doing my own thing, on my own (though – I hope – in the knowledge that my partner is there for me). However, for those moments I am safe, protected and loved.
>
> (p. 414)

In using this example (without irony) Hollway ignores feminist research on families. How many women go out there to do their own thing, on their own? Although there has been a massive increase in (married) women's labour market participation in the past 50 years, women's wages are considerably lower than men's and women are much more likely to work part-time. Research on the feminisation of poverty has highlighted the extent of women's economic dependence on men and the considerable difference divorce can make to a woman's standard of living. Arlie Hochschild (1989) points out that this can have a direct impact on women's (negotiating) power within marriage. Hochschild conducted a study of married couples with children, where both partners were in full-time employment, in order to examine the effect on the division of domestic labour. Her study is unique in that she links the activities of each individual to their ideologies and emotions. Using a series of case-studies, Hochschild illustrates the complexities of negotiating the domestic division of labour. Regardless of the actual division arrived at by a couple, there was often a lack of fit with their ideas about how it should be divided. In two cases, women were doing much more domestic work than their husband despite working full-time in demanding jobs. They both believed that their husbands should do more but 'their fear of divorce led them to stop asking for more help in the second shift' (Hochschild 1989: 253). While for many women fear of divorce is related to economic dependence, these two women were in well-paid jobs. One of them even earned more than her husband. This example illustrates the hegemony of marriage as the model for heterosexuality. These women are making decisions about the amount of inequality and oppression they are willing to put up with; *not* that heterosexuality is not oppressive.

Theorising heterosexuality

Feminist theories of heterosexuality would be inadequate if they ignored the points that inspire Hollway's and Segal's analyses. We need to understand the complexity of our desires, and our analyses of sexual acts must not invest them with essential, fixed meanings. I agree with many heterosexual feminist commentators that heterosexuality can afford women many pleasures.

However, heterosexuality is about much more than sexual desire and sexual acts.

Heterosexual acts usually take place within relationships. While they could take place in many different types of relationships, a particular type of heterosexual relationship is hegemonic in Western societies: lifelong, monogamous, cohabiting relationships, legally sanctioned through marriage and producing children. The hegemony of this type of heterosexual relationship is being challenged. Women are marrying later and some women are not marrying or having heterosexual relationships at all. They are bearing fewer children later in life and the number of women who will never have children is rising. Increasing divorce rates mean that some people will not expect their relationships to be lifelong. However, the hegemony of this type of relationship is also being supported by the State, the church, and (negative) public representations of other types of relationships.

Feminists have theorised extensively about this type of relationship, usually called marriage and the family, and continue to do so. However, these theories do not always problematise heterosexuality and often look to motherhood for the explanation of continuing inequalities. As Miriam Johnson (1988, 1989) points out, in order to understand the oppression of women, we must separate (analytically) the heterosexual couple relationship from the mother-child relationship. Along with other theorists she emphasises the extent to which being a wife, the female partner of the hegemonic heterosexual relationship, is central to women's oppression in both the public and the private spheres.

Theorising heterosexuality in this way involves a denaturalising of gender. Although initially a useful way of thinking, we have reached the limits of understanding gender as a social construction based on the biological category of sex. Biology is also socially constructed (Yanagisako and Delaney 1995b). Instead of examining the way that gender affects social interactions, we need to study the ways that gender is constituted in social interaction. I have used the example of housework to illustrate the shift required; gender is not culturally produced elsewhere (through socialisation, for example) and then affects the division of domestic labour, but rather the division of domestic labour is one social practice (among many) which constitutes gender. Heterosexual sex (fucking) is another.[8]

Denaturalising gender releases us from the idea that there are two and only two sexes/genders. This enables us to imagine ways of having sex, cleaning the house, etc. which construct gender in a different way and, perhaps, to attempt to put them into practice. However, despite the possibility of multiple genders, femininities and masculinities are usually constructed as complementary dyads – as heterosexual – and those dyads are usually unequal. Constructing gender differently will not necessarily eradicate dominance and subordination, although the details may look very different.

It seems to me that this way of conceptualising gender is analogous to certain ways of theorising 'race': the (biological) categories called races are socially constructed through racism in order to subordinate particular groups of people (called black), which entails a political process of anti-racism. Feminists are, similarly, involved in a politics of anti-sexism which challenges the social construction of gender as a means to subordinate particular groups of people (called women).

Theorising heterosexuality involves examining the links between hetero-sexualities and the social construction of gender(s). The political impli-cations of this way of theorising heterosexuality are similarly complex. Separatist politics can be understood as one set of attempts to construct women as something other than the subordinates of men. This is what Monique Wittig (1992: 32) means when she says, 'Lesbians are not women.' But it is also possible to imagine other forms of political resistance. The women that I interviewed in my study of anti-sexist living arrangements were all resisting being wives in different ways and with varying degrees of success. This process was often contradictory, in that those women who lived with men were dependent on the men's agreement for their ability to live in an anti-sexist way (VanEvery 1996). Nevertheless, the changes they were able to make, however limited, were still important. I also interviewed women who did not live with men. Some were in long-term monogamous heterosexual relationships, others were not. What their living arrangements told me about the politics of heterosexuality is that it may be possible to identify as heterosexual and/or to engage in heterosexual sex, while still challenging the hegemonic construction of heterosexuality and gender (Van-Every 1995b).

It is also important to address Adrienne Rich's statement about choice, particularly in relation to the way we represent various options in our own research and writing. What are the implications of saying that most women are heterosexual and therefore we need a theory of heterosexuality which accounts for its pleasures? What are the implications of dismissing lesbian separatism as marginal to most women's feminist politics? Do we (implic-itly or explicitly) treat particular types of relationships as 'normal', for example only studying heterosexual couples with children as 'families'? When we theorise heterosexuality do we represent a variety of heterosexu-alities, albeit within an analysis that acknowledges the hegemony of par-ticular forms of heterosexuality? Feminist theories of heterosexuality are firmly located in a political process of contesting (or reinforcing) the hegemony of a particular construction of 'woman'. This construction is a heterosexual one. There is also a hegemonic construction of heterosexuality. If feminist theorists of heterosexuality do not want to reject the possibility of a non-oppressive heterosexuality for women, then they must contribute to the political process of contesting the hegemony of 'marriage and the family' *as* heterosexuality.

Notes

1 There is one area of feminist research on families which does routinely problematise heterosexuality: domestic violence and child abuse. However, this area appears
to be treated separately from other household and family research, if recent books
reviewing the field are an indication (for example Morris 1990; Clark 1991).

2 For an analysis of the trends in the registration of births in the UK see Cooper
(1991).

3 For a review of the domestic labour debate see Molyneux (1979) and Delphy and
Leonard (1992: Chapter 3).

4 Becker's theory is developed in several publications. Sarah F. Berk (1985: 20–35)
provides a critical summary.

5 To say that gender is socially constructed does not mean that it is superficial or 'not
real'. It is, rather, to say that it is not inevitable or inevitably the way it is now,
though it may be very difficult to change.

6 This is an addition to the racist character of much of the 'underclass' debate. This
particular model of heterosexuality is a white, middle-class one and its hegemony
is contested by groups other than feminists.

7 These authors mean 'fucking' when they say 'heterosexuality'. For example, Mac-
Kinnon concludes a short section on whether heterosexuality can be a choice by
saying 'I would like you to address a question that I think few here would apply
to the workplace, to work, or to workers: whether a good fuck is any compensation for getting fucked. And why everyone knows what that means' (MacKinnon 1987: 61).

8 This particular (hetero-)sexual act is not the only one which constitutes gender but
it is the one most often referred to in radical feminist accounts which argue that
sexual acts do so (see, for example, the introduction to Kitzinger and Wilkinson
1994b).

4

Heterosexuality and social policy

Jean Carabine

Introduction

Within the context of social policy, both as a discipline and as practice, sexuality is generally ignored or invisible. Yet, it is evident from only a cursory examination of the media and political issues and debates in the UK and in other countries that sexuality is intimately connected with social policy. For example, recent topics include gays in the military in the UK and USA; single motherhood and teenage pregnancy in the UK, USA and Singapore; laws in China requiring that people with mental illness or disabilities be sterilised or use contraceptives; and more generally, recent debates about sex tourism, HIV and AIDS, population control and sex education.

Social policy has also become a focus for the politics of sexuality; a site where various issues and 'truths' about sexuality are contested, challenged, reformed and transformed. However, little attention has been given to theorising sexuality or heterosexuality as a form of sexuality specifically in relation to social policy. Commonly sexuality tends to be disregarded as a relevant issue for social policy, or there is universal acceptance of it as heterosexual, 'normal', 'natural' and fixed. This has resulted in a tendency in much previous social policy work to reinforce heterosexual norms and relations (Carabine 1992a). Examples of this can be seen in much, particularly mainstream, work on the family which is often presented in an unproblematic and universalistic way.[1] The existence of non-nuclear family forms is often ignored, and where they are acknowledged writers often fail to consider service and welfare provision based on non-universalistic family forms.

One explanation for this omission may be the way in which sexuality and social policy have come to be defined and commonly understood as about private relations and public policy. The public and private are representively seen as being independent and discrete: the public sphere appertaining to the objective, masculine and non-sexual; and the private sphere which is assumed to be inherently feminine, concerned with privacy, and the sexual. Sexuality is also commonly perceived as intimately a personal and private matter. A pervasive belief is that what individuals do sexually whether on their own or with others is primarily their own business provided they do not affect or harm others.[2]

Why, if sexuality is visible as a policy issue, does social policy as a discipline fail to incorporate it theoretically? One possible explanation for this exclusion and lack of explicit acknowledgment of sexuality in social policy critiques and theorising lies in the implicit consensus about what constitutes the important issues and policy concerns in social policy. The discipline of social policy is traditionally concerned with welfare and the provision of welfare to meet individual needs (Marshall 1975: 15). Most definitions of social policy are about achieving welfare objectives in relation to services such as housing, health, education, social care and income maintenance. Similarly, social policy is defined as the establishment of statutory social services for the furtherance of public welfare (Madge and Brown 1982: 277). Even when writers go beyond these definitions and include the consequences of ideology, as in the work of Mishra (1981) and Walker (1983), the impact of heterosexuality is omitted. On the face of it these are all very general definitions and it could be argued that in their non-specificity they include all; but a closer examination reveals this not to be the case (Carabine and Richardson 1995).

This lack of attention is apparent not only in what might be specified traditional mainstream accounts, but perhaps, more surprisingly, in feminist critiques. Feminists have long been concerned with the question of sexuality, both in practice and theory, as in campaigns and analyses of abortion, sexual violence, pornography, reproduction, contraception, lesbianism and sexual definition, but feminist social policy has tended to ignore sexuality. Work on, for instance, informal caring and the family shows that attention has largely focused on heterosexual family forms. For example, *Women's Issues in Social Policy* (Maclean and Groves 1991) is a text written in response to a male-centred *Challenges to Social Policy* (Berthoud 1985) and its 'limited discussion of social policy issues relevant to women' (p. 2). Whilst this text provides an important response to the Berthoud collection, it too makes similar assumptions and omissions with regard to sexuality, that is, the inadvertent reinforcement of the universality of the institution of heterosexuality. For example, Hilary Land in her chapter 'Time to care' highlights the importance of books such as this in raising issues which are 'still inadequately recognized (if recognized at all) by male policy analysts and policy makers' despite the existence of feminist critiques (Land 1991: 7). On the one hand, Land identifies as important the requirement to explore the relationship between women, caring, markets, families and the State together with the 'conceptualization of a dichotomy between public and private which is somehow "natural" and unchanging' (pp. 7–8); and on the other accepts and adopts a model of the family which is both universal and 'natural'. Land uses 'family' uncritically; and whilst the role of women as carers is challenged, there is an inherent assumption that caring takes place within a/the heterosexual family, and that it is undertaken by women who are themselves also heterosexual. Like the use of 'family', the category 'woman' is also applied universalistically: there is no differentiation between the experiences of women carers as black, working and/or middle class, lesbian and/or disabled. The examples given of women's experiences of caring focus on women who are wives, mothers and daughters, and although lesbian women are also mothers and daughters it is clear from the context of the text that lesbian mothers and daughters are not included because of the unquestioning use of 'family'. Further, 'care by the community . . . means care by the family, which largely, although not exclusively, still means care by women' (p. 9).

An examination of the rest of the book reveals similar assumptions, although Peggy Foster (1991: 82) does acknowledge the need for the feminist healthcare to be equally accessible 'to all women regardless of class, race or sexual orientation' this is the only reference to sexuality, despite repeated reference to issues related to healthcare provision for working-class and ethnic minority women.

This tendency to ignore sexuality is prevalent in more up-to-date work. A new text *Women and Social Policy* (Hallet 1995) is heralded as the 'first comprehensive textbook on women and social policy for the 1990s . . . [it] covers all the traditional core areas of social policy provision, but also addresses other social policy issues of relevance to women'. However, sexuality is not highlighted as either a core or other social policy issue in the publicity material.

There are, however, exceptions; some feminist writers acknowledge that diverse sexualities and sexual relations exist (see, for example, Abbott and Wallace 1989; Williams 1989; Dominelli 1991; VanEvery 1991/92; Cosis Brown 1992; and Graham 1993). The form this usually takes is the acknowledgement that there are different family forms and that the 'ideal' family is in fact the minority form. For example, in 'The family' Pamela Abbott and Claire Wallace (1989) provide a review of Thatcherite policies on the family. Abbott and Wallace differ from more mainstream commentators in acknowledging the existence of heterosexuality and different family forms, and also in their analysis of the family as an ideology. Although they acknowledge that policies continue to prioritise the heterosexual nuclear family 'and in some cases to reinforce the view that this is the only morally correct living arrangement', their analysis is not extended beyond the ideology of the family to an analysis of sexuality and social policy more broadly. For example, they do not critique social policy using the ideology of heterosexuality or examine how social policy might be constituted in relation to sexuality. Nor do they consider specifically how lesbian or gay families might be affected by such policies. Examples given in the text tend to use traditional family forms, as in the effects of policies on married men and women (pp. 85–6) or are used in a neutral non-specific way which tends to suggest a universalistic family experience under Thatcherism, although clearly this is not their intention (p. 85).

Whilst acknowledging, to varying degrees, the universalising impact of heterosexuality and the existence, for example, of lesbianism and same-sex relations and parenting, most writers do not, however, extend their analyses further into a critique of social policy as sexually socially constructed or in a way which adequately challenges the taken-for-granted nature of heterosexuality (see, for example, Dale and Foster 1986).

One implication of this is that social policy as a discipline plays a role in constituting heterosexuality as a both 'natural' and 'normal' set of relations. Not only have sexuality issues been marginalised within the discipline of social policy, they have also been treated as a focus of normalisation and regulation in social policy practice. In this way, the reality of many people's experience is denied and people are fixed in a sexed subject position in relation to society and to social policy.

Sexuality issues may be forced to the margins, but activists such as feminists, lesbians and gay men have sought to use social policy as a vehicle for positive change in terms of attitudes, practice and resource allocation.[3] Social policy as practice and as a discipline has been nudged, sometimes willingly, to recognise sexuality and the diversity of sexual behaviours, identities and beliefs. But sexuality itself has failed to be awarded the status of analytic power in social policy. Social policy has failed to engage with discourses of sexuality in the same way that it has been pushed to do so with discourses of resistance focusing on gender, class, 'race' and (to a lesser extent) disability. So while social policy has looked to other knowledges in its development it would appear that it has not so far looked to the knowledges and resistances of sexuality.

The aim of this chapter is not only to argue that a relationship between sexuality – specifically heterosexuality – and social policy should and does exist, but also to explore, define and outline the specific nature of this relationship and its implications for women. In the main, the focus will be on social policy as practice using a Foucauldian-informed feminist approach – because it offers analytical and theoretical insights into not only sexuality – an area where I would imagine readers are more familiar with Foucault's work – but also social policy.

Foucault's ideas offer us a number of useful ways to understand the relationship between sexuality and social policy, through the application of his concepts of power, discourse, the body, disciplinary power, bio-power and normalisation (Foucault 1979, 1990). Applying Foucault's ideas means that we can interrogate sexuality as a discourse which is constituted, amongst others, through social policy. This is a complex relationship because not only are discourses about sexuality 'played' through social policy as an effect of disciplinary power with its normalising effects, but also sexuality discourses interact with and are mediated through other discourses central to welfare and to social policy. These other discourses include femininity, masculinity, gender, 'race', class, disability, childcare, parenting and motherhood, the family, 'rights', citizenship, need, and dependency alongside professional discourses of social work, education, medicine, psychiatry, psychology and law.

In this chapter I draw on these aspects of Foucault's work and suggest that one way to understand the complex, multilayered, dynamic and often contradictory nature of the relationship between sexuality and social policy is to distinguish between three different aspects: normalisation, constitutive and contestation. Normalisation refers to the role of social policy in defining and reaffirming heterosexuality in its composition at any specific moment as acceptable and appropriate sexuality. Constitutive is defined where sexuality as discourse and knowledge – that is, what we know as the 'truth' of sexuality – is constituted through social policy. Contestation reflects how social policy is a focus for political action, a site where the 'truths' of sexuality are contested, challenged and changed.

Normalisation

Foucault (1990) argues that social theorists continue to base their understandings of power using a model based on a concept of 'the sovereign' which is no longer appropriate. Sovereign power is juridico-discursive, final and ultimate, operating through laws and rules which carry with them the threat or practice of torture or punishment, even death. In *The History of Sexuality* (1990) Foucault outlines an alternative and contemporary bipolar mechanism of power – disciplinary and bio-power – neither of which is dependent on sovereign power nor reducible to law. Power is effected through social policy explicitly by being reducible to law, but also implicitly through more subtle and complex means.

The development of disciplinary power with its 'seeing gaze' and 'normalising' techniques meant it was no longer necessary to evoke sovereign power and its power to take life. Disciplinary power shifted the focus of control to individuals and attempted to submit individuals to constant surveillance rather than physical punishment. For Foucault this type of power is most evident in the apparatus of the panopticon. There are three aspects to disciplinary power: the gaze/panopticon, normalisation and examination.[5]

For the purposes of this chapter I shall focus on the effect of normalisation, whereby individuals are compared and differentiated between according to a desired norm. It establishes the measure by which all are judged and deemed to conform or not (Bell 1993: 34–5). Martin Hewitt comments that

> The application of discipline to correct deviations of the body, its timing, speech, sexuality and even thought, required attending to the norm. A 'swarm' of technicians, 'normative judges', namely teachers, psychologists, psychiatrists and social workers, would differentiate, quantify and rank individuals according to the norms of disciplinary technology . . . Normalization becomes one of the main instruments of power in society.
>
> (Hewitt 1992: 156)

For Foucault, a 'norm' was not an aspect of power totally dominant, imposed by one section of society on another. Rather he saw it as a dynamic of knowledge, practised and learnt, which was dispersed around various centres of practice and expertise (Hewitt 1992: 164), such as social policy and sexuality.

Taking sexuality first, in *The History of Sexuality*, Foucault (1990) investigates the ways in which sexuality has come to be seen and spoken of – the development of knowledges about sex – as a means of understanding the operations of power. Foucault's primary concern was the development of a theory of power. For Foucault, not only is sexuality socially constructed and produced by effects of power, but so too are bodies (Ramazanoglu 1993: 6) explicable only in terms of 'truths' which are themselves socially produced. Foucault's interest does not lie in finding, for example, the causes of heterosexuality, or sexual violence or lesbianism, but rather in describing how heterosexuality, or sexual violence, or lesbianism come to be defined and constructed as the operation and effects of power. Foucault (1972, 1990) argues that power is constituted through discourses. The concept of discourse is central to Foucault's work. He identified discourses as historically variable ways of specifying knowledges and truths, whereby knowledges are produced as 'truths', in this case, about sexuality. Discourses function as sets of socially and historically constructed rules designating 'what is' and 'what is not'.

Thus, sexuality not only becomes the focus or object of discourses, the focus of 'experts', of scientific concern and sexologists; sexuality also becomes knowledge itself. Within these 'knowledges', categories or typologies of sexuality such as homosexual, bisexual, invert, and paedophile – which tended to focus on 'abnormal' aspects of sexuality – were identified. By focusing on what was considered abnormal, that which was considered normal was also constituted in 'expert' accounts of sexuality. It is through this normalising effect, which places 'perverse' sexualities under the microscope for examination, categorisation, castigation and regulation, that a knowledge of 'normal' as well as 'abnormal' sexuality is created.

In relation to sexuality and social policy, normalisation can be identified as operating in four main ways:

1 It constitutes appropriate and acceptable sexuality.
2 It operates in a regulatory capacity through which not only is heterosexuality established and secured, but also women's bodies and sexuality are disciplined and controlled. This regulatory function can be seen to operate explicitly through legislation and statutes, and implicitly through assumptions about heterosexuality as 'normal' and natural underpinning and informing social policy. It also links 'rights' and 'access' to welfare to ideas about appropriate and acceptable sexuality.
3 It behaves with differentiating effects and fragmented impacts, being variously regulatory, penalising or affirmative in respect to different groups of women.
4 It has a role in achieving the aims of social policy and welfare.

Appropriate and acceptable sexuality

Normalising judgement compares and contrasts, differentiating between all individuals according to a desired norm. It establishes the measure by which all are judged and deemed to conform or not. The normalising effect is a means by which appropriate and acceptable sexuality – hetero- and homosexuality – is enforced and regulated. The normalising effect is such that sexuality is understood in terms of what is 'natural' and 'normal' and 'unnatural' and 'abnormal'.

In relation to sexuality, the normalising effect means that we commonly believe sexuality to be an inherently natural biological drive and that the natural and normal direction of the drive is heterosexuality. Therefore, it is only 'normal' and 'natural' to want to engage in heterosexual sex. Applying the normalising judgement means that it is commonly felt that it is 'normal' to be heterosexual and that it is 'abnormal' to be lesbian or homosexual; similarly, that it is 'normal' for women and men to get married or to live in a monogamous heterosexual relationship; or that it is 'natural' and 'normal' for women to be mothers, albeit in certain contexts. By the same token, it is considered 'natural' for children to have both a male and female parent – father and mother. A single parent and same-sex parents are usually considered to be deviant and not 'normal'. This results in an expected experience of sexuality as fixed, stable and universal reflected in what are seen as not only 'normal' and 'natural' sex and sexuality for women and for men, but also in terms of acceptable and appropriate sexuality.

Normalising judgements are also made in relation to male and female sexuality. It is generally accepted that 'normal' male sexuality is active, aggressive, dominating and initiating; and that men are 'highly sexed' and in need of regular sexual release. By comparison women's sexuality is commonly believed to be oppositional yet complementary to men's sexuality. Whilst women's sexuality has traditionally been seen as closely linked to their reproductive function and motherhood, this is now changing: love is more likely to be seen to constitute women's sexuality. Women are generally perceived as being sexually passive and submissive (although now being required to learn a new sexual assertiveness with the help of *Cosmopolitan* and other similar magazines), more emotional and nurturant and as having a lesser sexual drive than men. As Stevi Jackson (1994: 6) comments, '[We] all learn to be sexual within a society in which "real sex" is defined as a quintessentially heterosexual act, vaginal intercourse, and in which sexual activity is thought of in terms of an active subject and passive object.' As I outline in the next section, social policy enacts this normalising feature of the active subject and the passive object.

The UK welfare system exemplifies this idea of active subject and passive object. Here social policy is both dependent on the normalising effects of sexuality (as well as gender, masculinity, femininity, the family and mothering) and is a primary vehicle through which they are effected, albeit inconsistently and unevenly. The foundations of the UK welfare state are firmly constructed on the basis of normal heterosexual relations, with the heterosexual family form central to the provision of welfare and women's major role as mothers and carers seen as 'natural' and 'normal'. Implicit in the founding policies of the welfare state and subsequent social policies are the normalising effects of these discourses, which have as their object 'active' men and 'passive' women. For example, ideas are reflected within social policy about men as physically, economically and sexually active (that men go out to work, are the breadwinners and take the lead in sexual relations) and that they are dominant (head of household and sexually dominant). Corresponding ideas which assume women's dependency on men, both financially and sexually, are also evident in social policy and form the basis of not only the welfare state but also the mixed economy of welfare.[6] Women's passive and nurturing femininity is not only incorporated in but central to the public and private provision of welfare and caring as in, for example, community care policies, and women's labour market involvement in welfare as nurses, teachers, cleaners, social workers and auxiliaries.

Social policy (in its widest sense) either implicitly or explicitly conveys messages about appropriate sexuality and acceptable female sexuality. Some sexual arrangements and relations are favoured over others. By and large, these tend to be heterosexual married relations. But there are inconsistencies. Different countries are demonstrably more tolerant of diverse family forms including lesbian and gay relationships; this may be reflected in social policies which accept gay coupling or marriages, or which give immigration rights to gay partners as in The Netherlands (anti-discrimination and equal opportunities legislation and legal parity), parts of Australia (immigration rights), Denmark (anti-discrimination and equal rights legislation, recognition of lesbian and gay couples but no right to adopt) and Sweden (Homosexual Cohabitees Act). However, common to all of these countries is a privileging of heterosexuality. Tolerance of diversity, it could be argued, is no more than another aspect of normalisation. Similarly, ideas about women's sexual passivity and submissiveness coexist alongside newer ideas and expectations that women should be sexually more active, exciting, and initiating sex; but within a carefully balanced exercise that encourages activity whilst still retaining submissiveness. For instance, AIDS education campaigns in the UK – where women are traditionally seen as passive – encourage women to carry condoms and initiate safer sex.

An analysis of social policy also reveals that the normalising process does not apply to all heterosexuals or even all married couples evenly and equally, but to a very narrowly defined 'ideal' of heterosexuality. In this way, all women, including heterosexuals, are compared and differentiated between. The 'ideal' against which all women are measured is white, heterosexual, preferably married or at least in a long-term stable, heterosexual relationship, non-disabled, and if a mother, aged between 18 and 40 years. Women who do not conform to this ideal, such as older, teenage or single mothers, and those who may also be black and/or lesbian, disabled or working class are situated as 'not normal', in need of normalisation.

One example of this is the availability in the UK of fertility 'treatments', particularly where these are provided through the National Health Service. 'Treatment' is usually restricted to heterosexual women within certain age limits who are in stable long-term monogamous relationships. It is also reported (Ham 1992) that treatments are usually restricted to women who are married, white and non-disabled. In Sweden, where homosexuality is viewed more favourably than in most countries, there is no access for lesbians to donor insemination (Ward *et al.* 1992: 121). It would appear from this that discourses about acceptable and appropriate sexuality and motherhood are evoked as a means of determining eligibility or access to limited welfare resources, illustrating the complex and contradictory relationship between sexuality and social policy for women. (The question of eligibility will be considered later.) On the one hand, women's role as mothers is accepted as 'normal' and is central to much of social policy; on the other hand, women are simultaneously differentiated between and against a narrow 'ideal' which at different moments they may or may not conform to. The relatively privileged status of heterosexuality (including heterosexual women) also acts as a disciplinary form of power which affects all women, as policy responses to single mothers in the USA, UK and Singapore reveal below.

As well as defining acceptable and unacceptable sexuality, social policy has a related regulatory function. It is through social policy that acceptable sexuality is regulated, being rewarded or privileged – as in the case of ideal heterosexuality – or penalised, when women fail to conform and fall outside the 'norm'.

Regulatory function

An important aspect of the normalisation process is its regulatory function. This is evident in social policy explicitly and implicitly. First, regulation is operationalised at an explicit level through legislation and statutes. In relation to sexuality the law is a primary mechanism of regulation and social control which specifies what you can and cannot do, who with and where. The normalising effect is such that not only does it inform what is natural and normal sexuality but also the acceptable contexts, behaviours, relationships, ages, and places, etc. In the UK, as in other countries, there are a number of pieces of legislation which stipulate what is legal and illegal sexuality: for example, the Sexual Offences Act 1967, section 28 of the Local Government Act 1988, rape in marriage legislation, control of prostitution, divorce Acts, marriage Acts, and age of consent legislation.

Assumptions about heterosexuality

What are the various normalising effects and messages behind much of the legislation? First, they all, albeit variously, support and set the boundaries for heterosexual relations, whilst confirming the illegality or unacceptability of lesbian and gay sexuality. For example, heterosexuality is taken to be the acceptable 'norm' and legislation, as in section 28[7] makes it illegal for local authorities to promote homosexuality. There is no similar legislation prohibiting the promotion of heterosexuality. Heterosexuality is also reinforced through legislation concerned with marriage and in divorce Acts. Recent amendments to UK divorce legislation have been concerned to maintain heterosexual relationships by making it more difficult to obtain divorces.

Legislation often operates differentially in relation to different kinds of sexuality; different rules apply and different boundaries are set. For example in the UK, until recently, with the introduction of the Rape in Marriage Act 1991, sex within married (or living as married) relations did not have to be consensual. Contrast this to the situation for gay men, who can be sent to prison for having sex they consented to if they are under 18 years of age (recently 21) or if they have sex in a public place. The Sexual Offences Act 1967 allows that sexual acts between consenting male adults over the age of 21 (now 18) years of age are only permissible provided that they do not take place in the presence of others. Under the 1967 Act if two men have sex in a hotel or other public place or where other people are present then this would be considered illegal – a breach of the peace or act of gross indecency, even though both consented and were over 18 years of age. Contrast this with the situation for heterosexuals where it is perfectly acceptable to engage in sex publicly – in hotel bedrooms, at least.

Age of sexual consent legislation also reflects different forms of control and ideas about acceptability concerning heterosexual and non-heterosexual relations. The age of consent for heterosexual sex is younger than for gay men in many countries including Austria, Bulgaria, Finland, Germany, UK and Hungary. For example, in the UK age of sexual consent legislation is applied in different ways reflecting different forms of control and ideas about the acceptability of when heterosexual and gay male sexual relations may legally commence. In the UK the age of consent for heterosexual sexual relations is 16 years of age and for homosexual relations 18 years of age.[8] There is no similar legislation in force for lesbian sexual relations. This does not, however, reflect a support for sexual relations between women, but rather invisibility resulting out of a discourse in which 'real' sex is heterosexual, penetrative and focused on male sexuality, with men as sexual initiators. Thus by definition what lesbians do in bed (or anywhere else for that matter) is not 'real' sex because the male (and penis) is absent.

Regulation is also operationalised through the implicit assumptions about heterosexuality contained in social policy. Bartky (1988: 63–4) uses Foucault's work to account for the 'disciplinary practices that engender the "docile bodies" of women … more docile than men'. She shows how the female body is ordered without the formal constraints of institutional boundaries or structures, through the disciplinary regime of femininity. In many ways women are not explicitly controlled and are even less regulated (p. 80); neither are they restricted to the home nor, she continues, expected to fulfil their maternal destinies. Instead, normative femininity is centred on women's bodies: 'not its duties and obligations or even its capacity to bear children, but its sexuality, more precisely, its presumed heterosexuality and its appearance' (p. 81). In a similar fashion social policy effects disciplinary power on women both explicitly, through legislation and statutes, and implicitly, through the assumptions inherent in social policies about the universal 'normality' and 'naturalness' of heterosexuality. For example, Family Credit claim forms use the neutral term 'partner', defined as 'a person you are married to or a person you live with as if you were married to them'. Clearly a glimmer of hope here, as this could just include same-sex relationships. But in Britain normative values are such that to live in a same-sex relationship would not really be the same as living with someone as though you were married. The following clinches it: 'The woman should claim – even if the man is working' (Family Credit form FC1).

Through these implicit assumptions about heterosexuality it is not always necessary for social policy to operate through 'wielding a big stick' (this is considered in more detail later); sometimes it operates by offering 'carrots' or rewards. Women today are not generally forced through legislation and social policies to form heterosexual relations or to get married. But they do, through the combined disciplinary regimes of femininity and heterosexuality. Recently in the UK, the Archbishop of York, John Habgood, called for tax cuts to support married people and to encourage cohabiting couples to marry. He argued that 'the selfless commitment of marriage needs to be buttressed by social support' and 'the Government could encourage marriage by making it fiscally more attractive' (*Guardian*, 14 February 1995). Currently in the UK marriage is supported through the married couples tax allowance, amongst other things. However, this is not to say that women are not penalised for refusing to conform to heterosexual norms. Lee Kuan Yew, until recently prime minister of Singapore, said in 1986 that 'it was a "possible error" to educate Singaporean women because of their increasing reluctance to perform traditional tasks and be full-time mothers' (*Guardian*, 20 May 1995).

Heterosexuality, however, works in some importantly different ways to the disciplinary effects of femininity. Unlike femininity, heterosexuality tends to be awarded a privileged status position, and this is mirrored, enacted and constituted through social policy. Whilst femininity is measured against masculinity as the 'norm', heterosexuality is itself the 'norm' by which all – heterosexual or not – are measured, differentiated and categorised.

In this way, social policy can be said to 'watch over sexual practices' (Bell 1993: 21). Through legislation (as in the examples cited above) and social policies concerned with, for example, childcare and sex education; through professional responsibilities and codes of practice and conduct for teachers, health and social workers, social policy 'watches over' sexual practices in differentiated ways. All variously delineate and define, implicitly and explicitly, what are acceptable and appropriate sexual relations and behaviours: when and where we can have sex, and with whom.

Access to and eligibility for welfare

Normalising ideas about appropriate sexuality explicitly inform and influence social policy and welfare in other ways. For example, through an explicit relationship between 'appropriate' sexuality and access to and eligibility for welfare. The normalising effect is also a mechanism by which rights and entitlement and, therefore, access to welfare are determined. For example, in 1988, Margaret Thatcher, the then British Prime Minister, spoke of the problem of young single girls who were deliberately getting pregnant in order to jump the housing queue and obtain benefits (*Guardian*, 23 November 1988). These ideas were more forcibly endorsed in the run-up to the 1993 Conservative Party conference with a swingeing attack on single mothers. The message came through loud and clear that welfare benefits and housing should only be available to, by implication, 'respectable' married women. It was also believed that welfare worked as a perverse incentive to young girls to become pregnant. Although the British government backed down, rhetorically at least, as a result of public and media pressure, policies were still introduced which resulted in removing a local authority's responsibility to prioritise single mothers' access to public housing. In Singapore the government has taken steps to maintain traditional family values through making it impossible for single mothers to obtain cheap council housing. Children of single mothers working in the civil service are denied the usual medical insurance benefits, and if a woman divorces she must repay all family allowance payments to the State (*Guardian,* 20 May 1995).

Other examples of the way in which normalising ideas about sexuality influence eligibility for welfare include income maintenance, where a (hetero-)sexual relationship, whether married or cohabiting, is a factor in determining eligibility for benefit. Social policy may also be linked to eligibility as a means of enforcing appropriate and acceptable sexual behaviour. In some states in the USA (for example in Baltimore, Maryland) women are being encouraged to have Norplant contraceptive implants[9] by being offered cash and extra benefits and/or the threat of removal of benefits. Those who refuse to follow the programme or risk having another child will have their benefits cut (World in Action, October 1993, *Children Having Children*). It is also reported that Norplant is being targeted at teenage mothers and poor women from ethnic minorities (*Independent,* 7 October 1993). An important aspect of the debate focusing on single mothers is not only that social policy can be presumed to affect appropriate behaviour, but also that many politicians on the Right believe the increasing numbers of single mothers, teenage pregnancies, divorces and the breakdown of the conventional family to be the result of social policies which encourage dependency (Ginsburg 1992: 119).

The introduction of the Child Support Act in Britain in 1992 also has a number of disciplinary implications for women in that it regulates and penalises women who are seen to be 'promiscuous' and may not know or wish to disclose the name of their children's father through the actual or threat of withdrawal of benefits. The Child Support Act can also have a regulatory effect where single and lesbian women who choose to have a child through donor insemination are forced to name the father or risk suspension of benefits. In this way the 'normal' and heterosexual means of reproduction is reinforced through attempts to restrict women's sexual and social autonomy. Women could be seen to be pushed into a position of dependence on men. One outcome of this is that you may have little choice but than to allow people to assume you are 'normal', for instance married and heterosexual, in order to gain access to certain services and welfare benefits.

Social policy can also have powerful normalising effects without 'wielding a big stick'. For example, social policies and the law do not explicitly identify lesbianism as something requiring to be controlled, as with gay male sexuality. But nevertheless lesbians experience social policies as discriminating and excluding. It is not illegal to be a lesbian, but many lesbians have lost their jobs specifically for being lesbian especially where they work with children or young girls (*Pink Paper*, 26 May 1995). Additionally, lesbian mothers tend to lose child custody cases where usually the 'norm' is for mothers to be given custody (VanEvery 1991/92: 64) – because they are deemed to be 'unfit' mothers because of their sexuality.

Differentiating effects

Discourses of sexuality also interact with and are mediated by, for example, discourses of 'race', disability and class to produce differentiating effects (Bartky 1988: 72; Ramazanoglu and Holland 1993: 240). Ideas about black women being sexually voracious, lacking sexual self-control, Asian women as erotic and passive are reflected in the practice of social policy. Black women have argued that they have always had easier access to abortion, contraception and sterilisation (see Bryan *et al*. 1985: 105). In discourses concerned with women's sexuality, as well as gender, 'race' and disability, there is very often a fusion of women's social characteristics with their biological functions, as with reproduction (McNay 1992: 18). Social policy at one and the same time both defines the social category of women in terms of biological functions – through focusing on discourses of motherhood, family and caring – whilst also being a means through which to challenge these assumptions. These various discourses – of sexuality, gender, 'race', disability, femininity – come together to be mediated and constituted in social policy and become a means of effecting normalisation and of differentiating between women and of establishing eligibility to welfare. For example, women who are disabled are either seen as incapable of sex, and as having no sexuality at all, or as sexually vulnerable. In social policy this is reflected in women with learning disabilities being placed on the contraceptive pill and/or being given no sex education at all, and/or being 'protected' from personal/sexual relations, or being invisible in the recognition of sexual abuse or in the need for education about safer sex (Hayes and Wright 1989).

Within social policy, as well as in society more generally, women's subject position is relative not only to men but also in relation to other women. Thus the relative power of women depends on particular practices which differently favour (or not) 'mothers', 'single women', 'married women'(see McNay 1992: 69), 'black women', 'lesbian women', 'disabled' and 'non-disabled women'. The extent to which women are favoured in social policies is influenced by the extent to which they conform to that which is considered 'normal'. 'Normal' is generally and consistently associated with heterosexuality. The greater the convergence with the 'norm' the narrower the gap to entitlement to welfare services and resources. The greater the divergence away from the 'norm' usually means less entitlement as of a 'right'. For example, I would suggest that lesbians and gay men are often denied citizenship' rights, if not in reality, then often in discursive formation; hence the notion that lesbians and gay men are not taxpayers, are somehow 'outside' and not part of the electorate (Carabine 1992b). In particular circumstances (for example, as with the disability movement) the relationship between 'normalisation' and 'rights' has been reversed.

Achieving the means of welfare (bio-power)

The normalising effect is discernible at another, fourth level as an instrument for achieving the aims of social policy, and welfare specifically. At the core of postwar British welfarism were a series of fundamental and essentially traditional assumptions about the family, motherhood (Weeks 1981: 235) and also appropriate sexuality, whereby heterosexuality was seen, amongst other things, as the means of achieving the aims of welfare. The welfare state was predicated on the heterosexual couple and the traditional nuclear family, both prerequisites if a healthy postwar population was to be established fit to work and to form a new world. Beveridge, who established the welfare state in Britain, expressed a concern about the 'importance of a child being brought up in the proper domestic environment, and was anxious not in any way to encourage illegitimacy, or immorality' (Weeks 1981: 235). The welfare state and social policies were concerned with births, propagation, health, life expectancy and the conditions which affect these. Foucault (1990) identifies this as an aspect of bio-power focused, unlike disciplinary power, on the body social, targeting populations rather than individuals or groups of individuals. Bio-power

> focused on the species body ... serving as the basis of the biological processes: propagation, births and mortality, the level of health, life expectancy and longevity, with all the conditions that cause these to vary. Their supervision was effected through an entire series of interventions and *regulatory controls: a bio-politics of the population.*
> (Foucault 1990: 139; original emphasis)

If sexuality was closely linked to achieving the aims of welfare after the Second World War it is as closely linked today, although not only through meeting welfare through welfare state provision. For example, New Right thinking in the UK has resulted in a shift in Conservative social policies, particularly relating to welfare provision. This shift has been in the direction of private/market provision of welfare, whereby the individual and the heterosexual family have been made primarily responsible. In parallel to this, the Conservative government in Britain has also sought to buttress the traditional family. (This is evident also in welfare approaches in other countries, including the USA and Singapore.)

Constitutive

It is also through social policy that sexuality is produced, but this is not a one-way process because what we understand to be the 'truths' or knowledges of sexuality also constitute social policy in a specific way which reflects the existing power-knowledge relations centred on sexuality, as well as other discourses, such as 'race', gender, politics and welfarism. Despite criticising Foucault for ignoring women and for developing theories which have been gender-blind and androcentric (see, for example, Bartky 1988; Fraser 1989; Braidotti 1991; Sawicki 1991; McNay 1992; Bell 1993; Ramazanoglu 1993), many feminists have none the less found his work useful: specifically, that 'bodies are the effects of power, produced in social relations by discourses of sexuality, medicine, education and so on' (Ramazanoglu and Holland 1993: 242). Gendered body differences are not only produced at the level of discourse but also 'as effects of power in public policies' (p. 251). Bodies – especially women's bodies and sexualities – are produced by, and constituted through, social policy discourses: not only in social policy as a discipline but also in the practice of social policy in policies concerned with health, education, income maintenance, housing, taxation, reproduction, and so on, as will become evident later. What we know sexuality to be is formed, and arises, from these and other discourses, including medicine, psychiatry, psychology, social work, the law, education, and social policy which take sexuality as their concern (Foucault 1990; Bell 1993: 17).

Sexuality is not only a concern of social policy, but also a means by which sexuality is spoken about. Social policy is not just a tool – a 'highway' for carrying discourses – it too is part of the discourse on sexuality: what we know as sexuality is constituted through social policy. For example, section 28 of the Local Government Act 1988 states that a local authority should not promote homosexuality or publish material for the promotion of homosexuality, nor give financial or other assistance to anyone to do so. It is also illegal for a local authority to promote the teaching in maintained schools of homosexuality as pretended family relationship. David Wiltshire, the member of Parliament who was responsible for introducing the section said at the time: 'My actions were motivated wholly by the principle of supporting *normality* . . . homosexuality is being promoted at the taxpayers' expense and the traditional family as we know it is under attack' (*Guardian*, 23 November 1988). The example of section 28 illustrates that as well as sexuality being a concern of policy it also speaks of sexuality, conveying a clear message about the abnormality of homosexuality and with it the implied normality of heterosexuality and of heterosexual family relations.

A further example can be seen in policy relating to sex education. Current policy in the UK makes it clear that sex education will speak of sexuality that is focused on biological reproductive sexuality, and placed within a moral framework (Thomson 1994). In The Netherlands there is a more open and tolerant approach to sexuality and sex education which involves the provision of information about safer sex, emotional and relational aspects, as well as the 'mechanics' of sex. In these two examples we can see that officially in social policy, although not necessarily always in practice, there are two different approaches to sexuality constituted within social policy. One a liberal discourse and the other a more negative discourse. Taking each country's experiences of teenage pregnancy, as this is often the focus of sex education, we can see that the UK has one of the highest levels of teenage pregnancies in the industrialised West. Of every 1,000 pregnancies in Britain, 69 are to young women aged between 16–19 compared with 9 in The Netherlands (*Guardian*, 19 November 1993). It has been variously argued by professionals working in the field of sex education, but also by politicians and policy makers, that The Netherlands has the lowest level because of their approach to sex education, notwithstanding the fact that The Netherlands is popularly believed to be a sexually liberated society and to hold and practice libertarian views in relation to sex and sexuality.

Do the significantly lower teenage pregnancy rates arise as an outcome of specific policies on sex education and/or a more liberal approach to sexuality generally in Dutch society? That is, can they be said to result from the way in which the 'truths' of sexuality are constituted within and mirrored by social policy. What would an examination of the social policy/sexuality dynamic reveal in relation to The Netherlands? It would certainly show that there is not a fixed or universal relationship between the two. It might also reveal the existence of other sexuality discourses, a different power/knowledge network and a different form of disciplinary power. Perhaps such an examination would reveal a different construction of 'normal' and 'natural' sexuality; that the difference in pregnancy rates was due in part to the exercise of different disciplinary techniques; a different power-knowledge network; the interplay of other discourses which affect the way in which gender and sexual relations are both constructed and negotiated; or perhaps even that the different rates are more than the outcomes of particular policies but different gender and sexual relations: a different heterosexuality?

Social policy can be said therefore to contribute to the techniques of power, not only as a discipline and practice, but also to the 'truth' it speaks of sexuality. Knowledges become encapsulated within social policy in naturalised forms as 'truths' about sexuality. When knowledge is accepted as 'truth', and 'naturalised' and 'normalised' as such, it becomes more difficult to question and challenge it. However, social policy is also a site where such 'truths' are contested.

Contestation

I suggested at the beginning that social policy can be a site of contestation, political action and change as well as being a site of confirmation of the *status quo*. Social policy is recognised both for its power to regulate sexuality and compel heterosexuality, and also as a way by which our knowledge about sexuality is conveyed. It is therefore also the site where the 'truths' of sexuality are challenged and contested – as in local, national and international campaigns for access to abortions and contraceptives, for lesbian and gay rights, against sex tourism and about HIV and AIDS. Activists have sought to use social policy as a vehicle for positive change, and have sought to transform social attitudes and social practices and to redirect resources. Social policy, both as a discipline and as practice, has been pushed to recognise not only sexuality and the diversity of sexual behaviours, identities and relationships, but also the power effects and privileging of heterosexuality. Similarly, those designated as 'perverse' sexualities have not always accepted their scientific or clinical categorisations. Thus female and male homosexuality have been transformed, reversed, reclaimed by those defined by it and adopted to represent a positive and sometimes political identity as lesbian and gay (McIntosh 1968; Foucault 1990).

Feminists have also challenged the assumptions in discourses about sexuality which have regarded unequal heterosexual power relations between men and women, based on gender and sex, as 'normal' and 'natural'. Women are not passive; they are also part of resistances to discourses which affect them and which are constituted in social policies, for example, through challenging sexual harassment at work, prevalent ideas about child sexual abuse, rape and sexual violence and in doing so creating new discourses and resistances and new power relations (see Ramazanoglu and Holland 1993: 250).

At different moments social policy can be seen to be influenced, or not, by these resistances at one and the same time. By example, governments in the USA and UK can be seen as being anti-homosexual, yet funding – albeit limited – is put into AIDS work. At one level social policy presents homosexuality as unnatural, abnormal and dangerous, yet it also puts energy into challenging the idea of AIDS as the gay plague. One reason is clearly to encourage awareness of the dangers of HIV/AIDS to all members of the population, but from another perspective the discourses can be seen as allowing challenges and resistances.

Conclusion

A central aspect of the social policy and sexuality dynamic is the role of social policy as an instrument of disciplinary power, particularly through the process of normalisation, but it is by no means the only process. It is through normalisation, enacted here in social policy, that the ideal of heterosexuality is established as the set of sexual relations and behaviour by which all sexuality will be judged, heterosexual and non-heterosexual, as the 'natural', 'normal' and acceptable form of sexuality. By this measure all forms of sexual behaviours, relations, contexts and activities are judged to be either deviant or acceptable. Through and in social policy the normalising process in relation to sexuality can be said to have a regulatory and social control function.

Regarding the State, we can also see that the application of heterosexual ideology is uneven both in relation to individual and groups of women as well as social policy responses. For example, in 1988 the UK government sought to ban the promotion of teaching about homosexuality and homosexual relations in local authority maintained schools. Initially, control over sex education and teaching around HIV and homosexuality was given to school governors. Education about HIV/AIDS was then included in the National Curriculum in 1992, only to be removed again in June 1993. Now all schools must provide some sex education but parents can exercise the right to withdraw their children. From this example we can see that discourses of sexuality are often uneven and may be intersected by other discourses as, in this case, by discourses of health, parental choice, consumer rights, privacy, health and education.

It is also through social policy that sexuality, or what we know to be sexuality is constituted. This is not, however, a one-way process because what we understand to be the 'truths' of sexuality, or knowledges of sexuality, also constitute social policy in a specific way. This reflects the existing power-knowledge relations centred on sexuality, as well as other discourses, such as 'race', gender, politics and welfarism.

In this chapter I have offered some explanations of how social policy might affect the different ways in which we 'behave' sexually, conceive of, and talk about sexuality, along with the interrelationship of different discourses; and the complex and contradictory nature of power evident in the sexuality/social policy dynamic. In order to illustrate the relationship between sexuality and social policy I have deliberately presented the relationship as more fixed and consistent than it materially is for the purposes of illustrating my argument. Individuals, groups, agencies and organisations are complex, contradictory and conflicting, and operate inconsistently and varyingly depending on the social circumstances and social positioning (Layder 1994: 97). What is interesting, however, is why does social policy tend to adopt a fixed idea of sexuality as heterosexuality, which has normalising effects?

Notes

1 See Carabine and Richardson (1995) for a more detailed discussion of the relationship between sexuality and the discipline of social policy.

2 This approach is one adopted in the 1957 Wolfenden Report on male homosexuality and prostitution. The report distinguished between what should be allowed in public and what would be tolerated in private. However, this view of sexuality as private is tolerated in a number of ways. First, what people do sexually, where and with whom is the focus of implicit and explicit social regulation and control. Foucault has demonstrated that sexuality rather than being secret and repressed in the Victorian era was very much a matter of public concern and discourse (Foucault 1990). Second, challenges to the established 'truths' of sexuality and related analyses of the relationship between sexuality and power from,

amongst others, feminist, lesbian and gay activists, postmodernism and queer theory/activism have brought the issue of sexuality very much into the realm of the public. Finally, despite a strong belief in sexuality as personal, private and beyond the boundaries of State intervention, it is a focus of political and public discourse.

3 Examples include: campaigns against section 28 of the Local Government Act 1988, local authority funding for rape crises centres, the establishment of domestic violence and sexual abuse units by the police, housing and counselling projects for young women experiencing sexual violence, abortion campaigns, well-women clinics, etc.

4 The panopticon was based on Jeremy Bentham's idea for a circular prison/building which had at its centre a watchtower from which a warder or observer could survey all cells and each inmate within them. The observer was unable to be seen so inmates were never sure if they were being observed or not and thus assumed constant surveillance. In believing that they were under constant surveillance the inmates behaved as though they were under continuous gaze: 'individuals begin to oversee themselves, to regulate their own behaviour in the light of this assumed visibility to others' (Layder 1994: 99) (Foucault 1979: 297–8). The idea of the panopticon was employed in a variety of institutions concerned with the control of large numbers of people, for example, prisons, schools and hospitals.

   Through his analysis of the panopticon effect Foucault illustrates how not only is the overseeing 'gaze' internalised by individuals but also that 'the functioning of power becomes automatic rather than the result of the conscious exercise by some external agency (such as a sovereign)' (Layder 1994: 99–100).

5 Vikki Bell (1993: 33–5) provides a clear summary of Foucault's three methods of disciplinary power.

6 Mixed economy of welfare includes all welfare provision, such as that provided by the State, voluntary sector, the family and private sector.

7 Section 28 was introduced as an amendment to the Local Government Act (1988) and sought to ban the promotion of homosexuality and pretended family relationships by local authorities or the teaching of the acceptability of homosexuality in schools. The section came into effect on 24 May 1988.

8 Until February 1994 this had previously been 21 years of age.

9 Norplant is a contraceptive implant consisting of six rods containing the hormone levonorgestral and is effective for up to five years. Implanting the contraceptive involves minor surgery using local anaesthetic.

5

Heterosexuality and the desire for gender

Sheila Jeffreys

The desire for gender, often felt as a visceral excitement, is a crucial component of heterosexuality as a political institution. I shall suggest here that gender is much more than just an annoyingly arbitrary and socially constructed classification system. Feminist theorists have shown how gender dynamically empowers heterosexuality, provides its most powerful pleasures through the sexuality of eroticised dominance and submission, and maintains the cruel power of men over women through turning it into just 'sex' (MacKinnon 1989; Jeffreys 1990). 'Gender' is not an inert filing system but a vital force in constructing and maintaining heterosexuality as the scaffolding of male supremacy. The desire for gender is not just the desire to conform and fit in, though that has a powerful effect, but an excitement felt as sexuality in a male supremacist culture which eroticises male dominance and female submission. In this chapter I shall seek to show how powerful the desire for gender is by looking at some examples of its effects, such as lesbian butch/femme role-playing and transsexualism. In some areas of lesbian and gay theory, influential in the academy, these forms of the desire for gender are being represented as revolutionary, the political way forward for queer activists (Jeffreys 1994). I will suggest that these phenomena, rather than toppling the institution of heterosexuality and the male supremacy it supports, are likely to strengthen the heterosexual regime.

Some lesbian and gay theorists recommend that genders should be played with, as if masculinity and femininity were simply harmless costumes to be exhumed from mother's trunks in the attic and tried on for size (Case 1993). The problem with gender, they say, is that it is arbitrary; men and women are restricted in their access to the delights of gender and forced to choose only one. Feminist philosophers, such as Janice Raymond, have criticised the idea of androgyny which some theorists, explaining that it is unfair that men or women should be restricted to only masculine or feminine characteristics, have seen as a goal (Raymond 1986: 12–13). Such notions see the problem with gender as rationing or restriction rather than its very existence. Masculinity and femininity are seen either as just about performance or as timeless human qualities which in combination could make a whole person. But as the French feminist theorist, Christine Delphy, has pointed out, masculinity and femininity do not represent timeless universal human values (Delphy 1993). They represent, in fact, the values of a male supremacist hierarchy at a particular point in time. Emerging from hierarchy they cannot be expected to survive the creation of a non-hierarchical society.

That which is seen as archetypical 'feminine' behaviour – much of what is reproduced in drag, camp, and transsexualism – is in fact the learnt behaviour of the oppressed, learnt to avoid punishment or gain favours. It is behaviour which shows awareness of low status and suitable respect for the powerful male class. 'Femininity' is learnt behaviour which is recreated every day of a woman's life through her interaction with men. 'Feminine' behaviour shows deference. Girls and women are expected to take up little space, sit with legs crossed and arms by their sides, keep their eyes lowered, speak only when spoken to. Such behaviour is policed, for example, in ticket offices, on public transport, on construction sites, in lecture halls and school classrooms by men and boys who react negatively to girls and women behaving as if they have a right to take up space or time, or who simply wish to show off by putting down a female (Larkin and Popaleni 1994). Masculinity is also learnt behaviour, which demonstrates dominance and maintains a man's place in the ruling class. In a posthierarchical world it is hard to imagine that these certainly non-universal qualities would survive.

Masculinity and femininity, the genders of dominance and submission, are eroticised to create the sexuality of male supremacy which I call heterosexual desire. By the term 'heterosexual desire' I do not mean desire for the opposite sex, but a desire that is organised around eroticised dominance and submission. It emerges from the political system of heterosexuality as the eroticised subordination of women and is seen as natural, as what sex is. The hetero in heterosexual desire means other; in such desire one participant is 'othered', or reduced to subordinate status through dominant/submissive, objectifying sex (Jeffreys 1990). The 'difference' between the sexes which is supposed to give the excitement to heterosexual sex, is, I would argue, not natural but political, a difference of power. Heterosexual desire is formed out of, and requires for its excitement and continuance, the subjection of women. But it is not limited to opposite-sex couplings. Lesbians and gay men can experience heterosexual desire too, through the reproduction of gender through butch/femme role-playing, other stylised forms of gender power difference such as sado-masochism or through eroticising race, class or age differences. The opposite of heterosexual desire is homosexual desire: desire based upon sameness instead of difference of power, desire which is about mutuality and which is more suited to the egalitarian future that feminists wish to create. Heterosexual women and men can experience homosexual desire, but the structural power differences that regulate the relations between women and men can make this particularly difficult to achieve.

Heterosexual desire is crucial to the political system of heterosexuality because it gives it the excitements and satisfactions that can be derived from intensity of sexual feeling. The excitement is the excitement of cruelty, of the exploitation of inequality. But it makes its followers loyal. Elsewhere I have described heterosexual desire as the 'grease that oils the machinery of male supremacy' and that still seems to me a reasonable way to formulate its effect (Jeffreys 1990: 251). It is heterosexual desire that eroticises for men the objectification of women and provides the motivation for sexual violence (Stoltenberg 1989). The sexual violence and harassment that women suffer in childhood, at work, on the street, in the marriage bed provides men with sexual satisfaction from the subordination of women. Heterosexual desire helps to maintain male supremacy by crucially limiting women's opportunities to study, work, travel, feel safe in their homes through all the varieties of sexual violence and the fear of such violence. The construction of 'desire', the construction of what is seen as sexual pleasure both arises from the present political system of male supremacy and reinforces it.

Heterosexual desire requires the construction of gender difference. Catherine MacKinnon argues that gender is constructed to serve the needs of institutionalised heterosexuality:

> Sexuality, then, is a form of power. Gender as socially constructed, embodies it, not the reverse. Women and men are divided by gender, made into the sexes as we know them, by the social requirements of its dominant form, heterosexuality, which institutionalizes male sexual dominance and female sexual submission ... Male and female are created through the eroticization of dominance and submission. The man/woman difference and the dominance/submission dynamic define each other.
>
> (MacKinnon 1989: 118)

Thus gender is not simply the mould in which men and women learn different sexualities, but is a product of sexuality itself. The sexuality of male supremacy, heterosexual desire, requires the constant recreation of masculinity and femininity. Those who are to play the dominant or submissive roles in the sexual drama don the manifestations of inequality that are supposed to mark the appearance of men and women, whether straight or gay, to inform their gestures and signify their place in the sexual hierarchy, the hierarchy of cruel excitement. All of the signs of 'gender' which demonstrate women's powerlessness or men's power are eroticised in the heterosexual system. The symbols of masculinity that are eroticised include boots, leather, uniforms, shoulder pads and belts. These symbols of power and powerlessness are not harmless 'differences' but the uniforms of political class positions which are eroticised in heterosexual desire. Many of the requirements of femininity seem designed specifically to afford to the dominant the excitements of eroticised cruelty on a day-to-day basis, such as high-heeled shoes and constricting clothing. Through these requirements women are to perform their sexual corvée as objects for men's delight. Monique Wittig describes how women are placed into the category of sex in which their duty is to be 'the sex' and also 'sex itself' (Wittig 1992). They are to be available for the sexual pleasures of men.

A sexuality of equality or 'homosexual' desire, should, in theory, be easier to achieve in same-sex relationships where the institutionalised power difference between the sexes does not intrude. If heterosexual desire is to be created, then 'gender' must be imported, or some other form of power difference which can take the place of gender, such as age, race or class, must be eroticised. In the late twentieth century there has been a recrudescence of 'gender' in lesbian and gay culture. Lesbian and gay history has taught us that in the period before gay liberation in the 1970s, gay male effeminacy and lesbian masculinity in the form of butch role-playing were common forms of identity (Jeffreys 1989). With gay liberation and feminism these gender practices became briefly intolerable to politicised lesbians and gay men. Many thought they would never revive, but they have experienced a revival along with new forms of gender practice, the masculine gay man and the feminine or 'lipstick' lesbian. Drag has returned in celebratory form, not just in the pubs and clubs but as a central element of Sydney's Mardi Gras, and has become the popular culture version of male homosexuality once again as in, for example, the 1994 film about drag queens and a transsexual touring the Australian desert, *Priscilla, Queen of the Desert*. Rather than seeing these practices as specific to gay culture or even politically progressive through showing the social construction and flexibility of gender, I suggest that they show the power of the political institution of heterosexuality to pull the potentially dissident practices of homosexuality back into its thrall.

Lesbian role-playing

Butch/femme role-playing in the 1990s is, I would argue, a clear example of the portability of gender for the creation of heterosexual desire. Role-playing in earlier decades served other functions, such as the protection of being able to pass in a rigidly segregated society, and not just erotic excitement. The rehabilitation of role-playing and the promotion of this practice that has occurred over the last decade in lesbian sex magazines and lesbian fiction as well as lesbian theory represents role-playing as serving a specifically sexual function. Lesbian sex therapist JoAnn Loulan, who had a 'conversion experience' and decided that she was a femme, explains that role-playing is about the construction of sexual categories (Loulan 1990). The novelist Lee Lynch, who has played an important part in the rehabilitation of role-playing, says: 'Butch ... is knowing how to stand on a streetcorner and catch a femme's eye' and femme 'Is spotting the butch and knowing how to get her clothes off' (quoted in Garber 1993: 148). Marjorie Garber, commenting on these remarks suggests that 'Here it is *difference* that is erotic; difference within sameness' (Garber 1993: 148). But the difference does not seem benign. It is not difference in the form simply of variety that is in question here, but the difference of power that is enlisted to create the excitement of heterosexual desire.

The femininity reproduced in butch/femme role-playing and much of so-called 'lesbian chic' replicates in rather vivid fashion the most stereotyped requirements of heterosexual femininity, as is clear in the following example from the contemporary role-playing anthology *The Persistent Desire*:

> Being femme for me means wearing a short, tight skirt, garters, and three-inch heels when I'm going out. It means standing in front of the mirror putting on mascara and reddish brown lipstick. It means shopping for a low-cut blouse to reveal a hint of cleavage some nights. It means smiling, or sometimes pouting, when my woman puts her arm around my waist and, with her other hand, turns my face up to kiss hers. It means whispering, 'I'm yours, own me,' when she makes love to me. It means feeling sexy.
>
> (Austin 1992: 362)

This 'Gone with the Wind' type of femininity is surprising in the 1990s after a feminist and lesbian feminist movement offered swingeing critiques of such behaviour, now often labelled 'prescriptive feminism', and it cannot be seen as resulting simply from an absence of alternatives. 1990s role-players choose their roles in opposition to feminism rather than in its absence. Before the 1960s such conscious choice was less possible. A femme from this earlier period, speaking in the research by Kennedy and Davis on role-playing in Buffalo, upper New York state, describes being femme in similar ways but in a rather different historical situation: 'Why a femme? Well because I wore make-up, I wanted to wear make-up and I liked clothes' (Kennedy and Davis 1993: 156).

Kennedy and Davis explain that role-playing prior to the 1960s involved very careful imitation of the heterosexual norms of the period:

> Butch and fem mannerisms were modeled on male–female behaviour as portrayed in the Hollywood movies of the period. They included all the little details of presenting one's self – manner of walking, sitting,

holding a drink, tone of voice. Most butches were expert mimics who had mastered the subtleties of nonverbal communication.

(Kennedy and Davis 1993: 157)

From the practices and writings of role-playing lesbians, past and present, we can learn a good deal about the rules of femininity. Femmes nowadays describe their femininity as being represented in an interest in silky fabrics, in gossip, in lacking a sense of direction, and to Loulan's chagrin it seems that most lesbians she interviewed associated femmeness with doing the housework (Loulan 1990). We can also learn something about the dangers that lie in the adoption of masculinity, since one characteristic of lesbian masculinity that was evident in 1950s butch role-playing in the Buffalo study was violence against femmes:

Most relationships were very violent at that time. And I think that's what happened to most people ... When you loved somebody you owned them, it was an ownership. This is my woman ... She knew that. When a woman got into a relationship with a butch she knew she belonged to them. And that's how it was.

(Kennedy and Davis 1993: 321)

Power in role-playing relationships was expected to follow heterosexual patterns, which included violence. *The Persistent Desire* includes several examples of events in contemporary role-playing which feminists might define as forms of sexual violence, such as initiating sexual activity with a woman who is sleeping (Jeffreys 1994: 73). It is reasonable to assume that the creation of power differences for sexual/emotional excitement might complicate the problem of eliminating lesbian domestic violence in the present.

It is interesting that those lesbian theorists currently who are complacent or enthusiastic about role-playing tend to be contemptuous of the idea that it replicates heterosexuality. For example, Kennedy and Davis remark about role-playing in the past: 'By definition this culture was never simply an imitation of heterosexuality, for butches did not completely adopt a male persona, and fems were aware that they were not with men' (Kennedy and Davis 1993: 190).

Indeed femmes might choose a lover specifically because she was a woman who had adopted masculine characteristics and not a man. However, the ways in which lesbian role-playing is different from the role-playing of heterosexuality are less startling than the similarities. Loulan attributes the feminist idea that role-playing lesbians are 'mimicking male/female roles' to lesbian self-hatred, our fear that lesbians are just an inferior version of heterosexuality. She says that 'somewhere in our deepest homophobic selves, we agree that lesbians are an ersatz version of the heterosexual model,' whereas in fact 'butch and femme have nothing to do with male and female' (Loulan

1990: 48). Role-playing is 'something profoundly female' which instead of deriving from male/female derives from some other root, an archetype or principle which both male/female and lesbian roles stem from, a dualism in nature. According to this essentialist logic both heterosexuals and lesbians and gay men are then able to raid nature's larder and make use of this harmless gift of gender in such ways as they might wish.

Transsexualism

Transsexualism shows even more clearly than role-playing the hold that the desire for gender exerts over people's lives. In the 1970s feminist theorists, and particularly Janice Raymond in her book *The Transsexual Empire* (1994), identified the phenomenon of transsexualism as resulting from the savage limitations of gender roles under male supremacy which forced nonconformists into believing they needed to transsex. Twenty years later transsexualism has no fewer recruits and is exhibiting new forms. The clearest motivation for transsexualism in both sexes has always been a despised homosexuality which caused men and women to believe they could not love their own sex without mutilating their bodies and professing to a new sexual identity which would make them really 'heterosexual' (Lothstein 1983). But men have for some time been deciding that they are 'really' lesbians too in both pre- and postoperative conditions.

A relatively new phenomenon is that of lesbians transsexing to become 'gay men'. Gayle Rubin, an American proponent of sado-masochism, sees this latter phenomenon as emerging from butch role-playing, as simply an enthusiastic extension of the adoption of masculinity by lesbians. She explains, with approbation, that lesbians are reproducing an impressive array of varieties of masculinity (Rubin 1992: 470).[1] These varieties of masculinity are the exaggerated forms adopted by gay men in reaction against the effeminate stereotype of pre-1970s homosexual history. It seems that as a result of the dominant influence of gay men in the lesbian and gay community, male gay forms of masculinity have come to be seen as desirable for lesbians. Where once butch role-playing might have imitated a heterosexual masculinity, the new 'lesbian' transsexualism imitates a gay one. Rubin is angry that the lesbian community in San Francisco is showing so little enthusiasm for the phenomenon of female-to-male transsexualism though 'their numbers are growing and awareness of their presence is increasing' (Rubin 1992: 475).

Judith Halberstam's (1994) contribution to the collection *The Lesbian Postmodern* is a good example of that postmodern lesbian and gay perspective which celebrates transsexualism as socially transformative. She manages to eliminate the seriousness of the phenomenon of transsexual surgery by seeking to establish that there is really no such thing as the transsexual because we are all transsexuals. She suggests that some of us use fabric and some constructed flaps of skin to indicate that we are crossing genders. She gives examples of how the phenomenon is manifesting itself in the lesbian community. Some f-to-ms are seeking to become gay men. One pre-op, Danny, seeks sex with men but only if they will accept that she is a man and therefore has 'gay' sex with them. Danny describes an occasion when a man accepted she was a man but penetrated her vaginally because he had always wanted a man with a vagina (Halberstam 1994: 213). Halberstam describes the video *Linda/Les and Annie* in which a new f-to-m transsexual attempts sexual intercourse with the sex industry personality Annie Sprinkle. Halberstam comments that it is 'remarkable as a kind of post-op, postporn, postmodern artifact of what Sprinkle calls "gender flexibility"' (p. 216). In the video, Les, who was apparently once a radical lesbian feminist, though that is rather hard to believe, 'claims that one of the most pleasurable experiences he has had in his new body is the automatic and immediate respect he receives simply because people perceive him as a man' (p. 218):

> Les's body is scarred and tattooed, a patchwork of stitching and ink . . . Les's imperfect penis is a skin sack formed from skin taken from his forearm and his abdomen. Heavy scars below his navel culminate in the less than intimidating phallus, and below the phallus Les retains his clitoris. Les's breasts have been removed and the testosterone has given him facial and chest hair. In order to make his made-to-order penis erect, Les must insert a rod into the sac – unfortunately, half-way into Annie Sprinkle the rod works its way through the end of the penis, and Les is forced to insert his thumb into the penile skin to give it tumescence
>
> (p. 219)

I suggest that rather than a glorious example of the postmodern tendency to create a socially transformative gender flexibility, there is another way to see these phenomena. Firstly, they demonstrate the lengths to which it is possible to go to reproduce heterosexual desire. In this instance the cruelty of the freak show, the eroticising of mutilation for the pornography video market in a fashion similar to that of disability pornography, is being utilised. A woman endures pain and mutilation for the sexual satisfaction of others. It also demonstrates the oppressive and compulsive force of heterosexuality as an institution which can draw within its thrall even those, lesbians, who might be most clearly seen as the rebels against male power. It shows too the utter inflexibility of gender for Les. If gender is truly flexible then there is no need for surgery; once surgery is accomplished the aim of flexibility is defeated. Playing with 'gender' then would depend on the ability and willingness of surgeons to reconstruct wombs and penises they have removed. Rather than celebrating we should perhaps be thinking of how the self-hatred that oppression as a woman and as a lesbian – especially for those like 'Les'

who has been pursuing her role as sex so literally as to be in the sex industry – still affects many in our community in the supposedly liberated 1990s.

Drag

Another example of the ways in which lesbians are 'reclaiming' the sexual
excitements of gender is that of lesbian drag. Judith Halberstam explains that
genderbending does not require sex-change operations, since in New York,
Annie Sprinkle has been running 'Drag King for a day' workshops with a
preoperative f-to-m transsexual, Jack Armstrong, a 'longtime gender activist'. The workshops show women how to pass and they then have a night
out as 'men'. The American lesbian lifestyle magazine, *Deneuve*, in its
October 1994 edition, includes photographs of the two winners of the San
Francisco Drag King contest. The prizes go to lesbians who can most successfully imitate men, apparently it seems, gay men. Gay men also, to judge
from the blurb, find the winner attractive (*Deneuve*, October 1994: 21). It
is quite hard to recognise the subversive qualities of such a performance considering the energies which lesbian feminists have needed to put into over-
turning the hostile stereotype that lesbians simply want to be men.

But some feminist theorists approach even male drag from a postmodern
perspective which renders it politically progressive (Garber 1993: 151).
Marjorie Garber, for instance, defines drag as 'the theoretical and deconstructive social practice' that puts in question 'the "naturalness" of gender
roles through the discourse of clothing and body parts'.[2] But this questioning does not seem to be necessarily a disruptive one. Transvestism and drag
can be well accepted by malestream culture as she explains:

> the best known of transvestite refuges among the power elite in the U.S.
> today is probably the fabled Bohemian Club of San Francisco, 'the most
> exclusive club in the United States, with 2,300 members drawn from
> the whole of the American establishment and a waiting list 33 years
> long'.
>
> (Garber 1993: 65)

This, she tells us, 'is, after all, the club of Kissinger and Reagan, of political
as well as financial and show-business power'. Transvestism in gay men does
not seem to provoke much disquiet. Currently performers such as the British
artist Julian Clary, whose work could be seen more as camp than drag since
the clothes he wears – such as short shiny chain-mail tunics – are rarely recog-
nisably those attributed to women, can have very popular shows on
respectable TV channels. Wayne Dynes comments that 'Undeniably camp is
subversive, but not too much so, for it depends for its survival on the patron-
age of high society, the entertainment world, advertising and the media'
(Davy 1993: 141).

Transgender activism

A new ingredient in contemporary sexual politics is transgender activism. Transgender activism in the work of exponents such as Kate Bornstein is seen as a politically progressive successor to transsexualism (Bornstein 1994a). Most of those who profess to it are men who have had radical surgery in their obsession with gender. None the less, they are now stating that surgery is not necessarily desirable. Transgender activists, they say, do not need to transsex via surgery. They do not even necessarily see themselves as becoming women as transsexuals traditionally have. They see themselves as a revolutionary third sex or shaman class which can teach the world, including uppity lesbian feminists who fail to be seduced by gender, of its flexibility and artificiality. In fact the very concept of 'transgenderism' relies upon a belief in gender since without the idea of another gender to pass into there would be no point in being 'trans'. The transgender project seeks to 'deconstruct' gender by promoting it. This is a very different project from that of feminism. Whilst lesbian and most heterosexual feminists choose to refuse gender categories, transgender activism represents a religion of gender which worships and celebrates its power.

Presently transgender activists, who represent pre- and postoperative transsexuals born into mainly male but also some female bodies, are demanding a place on gay rights and even 'lesbian feminist' platforms. Their activism includes the demand by male-to-female 'lesbians' for access to women's space through such means as a protest camp at the gates of the Michigan women's music festival, because participation is restricted to 'womyn born of womyn'.[3] There is now a concerted attempt to gain access for transsexuals who decide that they are both women and lesbians to women-only space in all its forms. Male-to-constructed-female transsexuals and their supporters attack the lesbian feminists who deny entry as 'essentialist', as if there were something non-essentialist about transsexualism. Feminist and lesbian separatism has always been based upon the principle of inclusion of members of the sex class of women, those with common experience and concerns, rather than on any notion of female essence. But the belief of transsexuals in a mysterious female essence, which has inconveniently located itself in their bodies, fuels their lives. The male-to-constructed-female 'lesbian' has most frequently been heterosexual in his preoperative state. He related to women from the sex-class position of manhood whereas lesbians, in the subordinate sex class, have chosen to love women like themselves. It would be difficult to imagine how two such different experiences could be confused.

Kate Bornstein recognises, as a result of his relationships with lesbian feminists, that he is not a woman.[4] He does not believe that transgendered people are either men or women, they are a third form. He sees himself as representing the transformative possibilities of the transgender phenomenon. He likens the role of the transsexual to that of the shaman. The shaman, in

Chuckchee culture in Siberia, dressed in the clothing culturally assigned to women and assumed religious functions (Mihalik 1989). The enthusiasm within lesbian and gay culture for the various forms in which men, and more rarely women, might assume the roles and mannerisms assigned to the opposite sex class and even engage in marriage with persons of the same sex class, is vulnerable to some serious political questioning. One concern is of course the appropriation of ill-understood cultural forms by white lesbians and gay men, which could be seen as a form of cultural imperialism. Another difficulty lies in seeing practices such as shamanism as demonstrating gender flexibility rather than rigidity. In many cultures the solution to the problem of people who did not fit into one of two genders was to allow them to swap, and inhabit a specially created category. The creation of such a category might with more justification be seen as a mechanism employed to maintain two dichotomous genders, and the heterosexuality which depends upon them, whilst not causing too much grief to those men inconvenienced by this political arrangement. This is a mechanism aimed at preventing any disturbance to gender rather than dismantling it. Transsexualism in Western culture maintains gender too, by accepting gender and its rules as real and inevitable and demanding only the right to swap rather than evacuate gender. Kate Bornstein, though, believes that the creation of a third category is revolutionary:

> I think it's time for us to use our status as Third to bring some harmony into the world. Like other border outlaws, transgendered people are here to open some doorway that's been closed off for a long long time. We're gatekeepers, nothing more.
>
> (Bornstein 1994a: 98)

Bornstein wants lesbians and gay men to unite under a banner of the transgendered. They should recognise that they too are oppressed for being gender outlaws and they have therefore a common cause with transgender activists. Surprisingly, lesbian feminists who have developed a political critique of transsexualism/transgenderism as a mechanism for maintaining gender categories are attacked by Bornstein for being precisely those who are seeking to maintain such categories (Wittig 1992). According to Bornstein it is mainly men like himself who are really 'deconstructing' gender whereas everyone else, such as 'Judaeo-Christian fundamentalists, radical lesbian separatists, and the more vocal transgender activists' has a 'common need for a fixed gender' (Bornstein 1994a: 132).

Bornstein's determination to move beyond gender is enhanced, he says, by the fact that his lesbian girlfriend has now become 'transgender' too. His 'female lover, Catherine, became my boyfriend, David' (p. 25). But she did not remain his 'boyfriend' long. Bornstein explains in an interview in the British lesbian lifestyle magazine *Diva* that David is 'exploring a gay male identity' and because she does not consider herself bisexual, cannot continue her relationship with him (Bornstein 1994b: 21). Bornstein apparently now wants to 'move out of the area of gender' and says 'What I'm exploring now is S/M' (Bornstein 1994a: 122). Bornstein explains that sado-masochism is 'a consensual way to play with power and gender'. S/M can 'do away with gender', he says, 'when the play reaches the point of almost purely dealing with power' and that is why feminists are critical of the practice:

> This could possibly contribute to the current taboos placed on S/M by leaders of some branches of feminism, as well as by the more vocally conservative patriarchy: they're both too invested in maintaining their genders and the gender system which defines their own boundaries, self-definitions, and ideologies.
>
> (p. 122)

In fact feminists criticise sado-masochism precisely because it eroticises the crude power difference of gender which fuels heterosexual desire, reinforcing rather than ending it.

Intellectual lesbian and gay support for the idea of the revolutionary potential of transgenderism tends to come from postmodern theorists. Some are prepared to take their enthusiasm for 'crossing' so far as to include race as well as gender. Judith Halberstam gives an example of Asian women having cosmetic surgery to make them look more American – eye-widening, the creation of folds in eyelids, nose and chin jobs – to show that race is 'obviously artificial, another fiction of culture' as she believes gender to be. Cosmetic surgery, she explains, can both 'bolster dominant ideologies of beauty and power' and 'undermine completely the fixedness of race, class, and gender by making each one surgically or sartorially reproducible':

> To all intents and purposes, if we are to employ the same rhetoric that pertains to transsexualism, the Japanese woman paying for the face job has had a race change (and here we might also think of the surgical contortions of Michael Jackson). She has altered her appearance until she appears to be white.
>
> (Halberstam 1994: 217)

Indeed, a feminist perspective would see these phenomena as connected but in a different way. Discontent with the body results in both cases from political causes, racism, and an abusive gender-based institution of heterosexuality. But Halberstam is celebratory about the effects of the 'cosmetic surgery' of transsexualism. Like Bornstein she sees lesbians as transsexuals too, since bodies that 'dress up' in gender (presumably her definition of the lesbian) and those that are 'surgically constructed in the image of its gender' are all transsexual. Both the 'transsexual body' and the 'postmodern lesbian body' 'threaten the binarism of homo/hetero sexuality by performing and fictionalizing gender'. The postmodern lesbian body is, she says, 'finding voice finally' in the 'underground culture of zines and sex clubs' (Halberstam 1994: 226). The postmodern lesbian, it seems, is a product of the sex industry.

Judith Halberstam sees learning to 'read' gender as the exciting project for lesbians who must 'become an audience for the multiple performances of gender we witness every day'. This seems to mean the activity of working out whether an over-the-top effeminate woman is mimicking femininity, or an apparently gay man is a drag king, and so on. It sounds a time-consuming project but not revolutionary. Not only are there other things we could be doing to end the oppression of lesbians, gay men and women in general, but the constituency for this new form of fluency is likely to be limited and already converted to its revolutionary possibilities. Lesbian feminists are likely to consider it more revolutionary to be conscientious objectors, refusing the categories of gender. There are many lesbians who resist in the strongest terms dressing up in any gender at all.[5]

The male-to-constructed-female transsexual Sandy Stone in his *Post-transsexual Manifesto, The Empire Strikes Back* also argues that gender is fictional and readable. Stone suggests that we see transsexuals as a 'genre – a set of embodied texts whose potential for productive disruption of structured sexualities and spectra of desire has to be explored' (Halberstam 1994: 226). In fact bodies are not simply texts. The sort of damage done to the bodies we are talking about here is not reversible. Transsexualism and many of the transformations of the body celebrated in postmodern writings have nothing to do with flexibility and fluidity, but the reverse. Organs that have been removed cannot be easily replaced on second thoughts, and second thoughts do happen more frequently than anyone is discussing. Tattooing cannot be removed without great expense and difficulty despite the fact that the images fade and their meanings may fade even more quickly. The silicone used in cosmetic surgery, in noses, chins, penises and testicles, as well as in breast implants is extremely poisonous. Support groups of women and men seeking compensation for the terrible injuries which result from silicone are being set up around the world, such as the Coalition for Silicone Survivors in the US.[6]

The transgender phenomenon in some cultures has a great deal more to do with the demands of the sex industry, in which male clients use transsexuals in order to maintain their heterosexual identities, than with revolutionary transformation. The *travestis* of Brazil, the British newspaper *The Independent on Sunday* reports (reprinted from Calkin 1994), are having silicone injected into cheeks, hips, bottoms and thighs, often several litres at a time, so that they can earn more money in the sex industry. The results are often fatal.

> The silicone could . . . cause allergic reactions; it could fall or slip down the body, accumulating in the testicles or the ankles; it could damage the immune system and cause circulation problems, oedema (swollen

tissue), swollen legs and backache. Some *travestis* had more than six litres of silicone injected.

(Calkin 1994)

The postmodern position of complacency or celebration in relation to these attacks upon the body shows a determination to ignore individual or collective suffering, to exclude any knowledge of the material political reasons which force women and men to wish to cross race or gender. Racial hatred is not just a reflection of the beauty industry. The hatred of homosexuality which has historically produced transsexualism is not just an aesthetic effect. It is cruel to celebrate the effects of these terrible – in its original sense as in to strike terror – forces of oppression, which can cause dangerous and sometimes fatal physical mutilation, as simply interesting performances. In the period of serious medical attack on homosexuality from the 1940s to the 60s lobotomies were performed on lesbians and gay men. Nobody seems to be celebrating this, yet. Surgical attempts to organise deviants into political obedience and correct categories is not a progressive phenomenon. For the lesbians and gay men who are transsexing so that they can love the same biological sex, transsexualism is the lobotomy of the late twentieth century and should cause as much political outrage.

Postmodernism and the desire for gender

The ideas of French gay male postmodern theorists have been adopted to provide a theoretical justification for those practices which have been interpreted as demonstrating gender flexibility, such as camp, drag, role-playing and transsexualism. Postmodern beliefs have allowed their proponents to ignore the cruelty and actual inflexibility of transsexualism. Suzanne Moore has characterised the obsession of male postmodernists with genderbending as 'gender tourism', 'whereby male theorists are able to take package trips into the world of femininity' in her thought-provoking article 'Getting a Bit of the Other – the Pimps of Postmodernism' (Moore 1988: 179). These male theorists, such as Barthes, Deleuze and Guattari, Baudrillard and Lyotard essentialise a notion of the 'feminine' as a place of otherness and transformation. Getting excited about gender, particularly femininity, does seem to be a predilection of postmodern lesbian, gay and particularly queer theory.

Such postmodern writings tend not to be very reader-friendly. Jacqueline N. Zita, in a recent lesbian studies anthology, has proposed an interesting explanation for this. She suggests that the adoption of obscure and elitist postmodern language by most practitioners of the new lesbian and gay studies is a new form of closet. She attributes it to the fear of discrimination quite reasonably felt by gay male academics which causes them to seek respectability for gay studies by burying it in language that fits into a respectable European intellectual tradition to obscure the sexuality involved.

This rapid ascent into the esoteric echelons of academic discourse seems not only related to a quick resolution of male Oedipal tension between disgraced gay sons and forgiving straight fathers, but also a quick cover of the ass – an overreactive if not homophobic attempt to sanitize and intellectualize over the cultural shame and embodied grit that grounds queer studies in the body and its heady sexual desire.

(Zita 1994: 266)

Zita is very critical of the way that gender is conceptualised in this new gay theory. She argues that it loses the material base that gender has always had in feminist theorising, the connection with male dominance and female subjection. In such queer theory, she explains, gender is 'based on performance theory, theatrical aesthetics, and interactionist and liminality models'. From this perspective a concept of gender loses:

... an understanding of gender as materialist and structural and as deeply embedded in nonsexual as well as sexual contexts which are rife with a long history of violent conflict and power struggles between the sexes, races, and classes.

(Zita 1994: 262)

Male gay theorists have 'The luxury of theorizing gender solely as a performance, an aesthetic, or an erotic script' as a result of their privilege, she says. For them gender does not seem to be attached to male supremacist oppression as it is for women and can be 'radically deconstructed as an ontology-free artifice of sexual semiotics by the postmodern constructionists or as a history-free stylistic by whatever-turns-you-on pro-sex liberals' (Zita 1994: 263). But this does not explain why lesbian theorists are making similar arguments. Perhaps both men and women in academic queer studies are too far from the battlelines of heterosexuality to understand how gender is acted out therein.

Quite central to the ideas of the postmodern enthusiasm is the reclamation of practices previously decried as oppressive or resulting from oppression, as potentially revolutionary and transformative. This is a comforting ploy which allows persons who wish to see themselves as progressive to continue to gain excitement from practices of dominance and submission without experiencing any political discomfort. Even heterosexuality itself is being reclaimed as revolutionary, at least as long as 'queers' are doing it. The self-identified 'lesbian' photographer of sado-masochism, Della Grace, who is presently growing a beard, has sex with men and is planning to marry a man whilst still seeking to maintain an identity as a subversive (Orr 1995).

One could argue that the 'gender outlaws' are in fact loyalists rather than rebels. They demonstrate the extraordinary power of heterosexuality as a political system and are involved in the constant reproduction of its basic dynamic, masculinity/femininity. The force which can disrupt this gendered system is feminism. The feminist project has always been the abolition of gender, not the reclaiming of it. Lesbian feminists, in particular, have been the conscientious objectors who have refused to take part in the cruel rituals of gender. In a very conservative time at the end of the twentieth century a great pessimism about the possibility of social change, combined with a renewed belief in biological determinism, have led to men and women taking 'sex' hormones and having surgical reconstruction rather than challenging male supremacy. The potential challenge of homosexuality to the institution of heterosexuality has been undermined by forcing the incorporation of lesbians and gay men into conformity with the rules of gender and heterosexual desire. The transgender activists are not creating a 'third' but merely recreating the two genders of male supremacy, male dominance, in masculinity, and female subordination, in femininity.

Notes

1 Male gay historians who explain this 'butch shift' suggest that these gay masculinities were constructed to replace the 'real men' (i.e. supposedly heterosexual men) who were the romantic objects of male homosexuality before gay liberation. When gay men started to seek sexual partners within a gay community, masculinity had to be created so that a heterosexual desire based upon dominance and submission could still be created.
2 Transvestism is the sexological term applied to heterosexual male crossdressing; drag is the term most commonly used by gay men to describe gay crossdressing. These practices may not be as discrete as both heterosexual and gay practitioners like to assume.
3 This development is described in the American lesbian lifestyle magazine, *Deneuve*, October 1994: 43.
4 I choose to refer to m-to-f transsexuals with masculine pronouns because I place those raised as men in the political class of men.
5 Bornstein sees the very idea of the 'lesbian' as being based upon 'gender', presumably because lesbians choose women to love rather than being polymorphously perverse. But I would argue that lesbians are choosing members of a particular political class, the sex class of women, rather than having any necessary interest in 'gender'. Women do not have to have a gender, they can resist adopting both masculinity (the behaviour of the oppressor) and femininity (the behaviour of the oppressed). But the 'women' of transgenderism and transsexualism do have to have 'gender' because their 'womanhood' is defined by nothing else but some idea of 'femininity'.
6 The Coalition of Silicone Survivors can be contacted c/o Lynda Roth, PO Box 129, Broomfield, CO 80038-0129, USA.

6

Recognition and heterosexual desire

Wendy Hollway

[One could] search for the circumstances in which affection, tenderness and other non-hostile components of love participate in, perhaps even dominate, excitement.

(Stoller 1985: vii)

The secret of love is to be known as oneself.

(Benjamin 1984: 301)

Introduction

My purpose in this chapter is to provide a theoretical sketch of a female sexual desire which eludes and resists patriarchal relations. In everyday usage, I take sexual desire to mean a combination of attraction towards and erotic excitement in a sexual encounter with another person; but this is of little help in understanding desire. Such an attempt requires at least two strands: the development of desire in an individual's history; and the conditions for its expression in adulthood within sexual relations. I concentrate on the former here, since I believe the latter depend on them.

The theorisation of sexual desire in current feminist discourse, as in current psychoanalytic discourse, has been dominated by the proposition that difference or otherness (in terms of power, of gender, of identity) is a condition of sexual desire – in particular, though not exclusively, of heterosexual desire. This proposition has been encapsulated in the idea of women's heterosexual desire as the desire for erotic domination by a man. I believe in the possibility – indeed in the actuality – of sexual desire which expresses other dynamics; dynamics which allow 'self and other to meet as sovereign equals' (Benjamin 1990: 12). Examples are desire for recognition and its fulfilment, and passion in mutuality and shared characteristics. This has led me to be critical of the lack of much space within contemporary feminism for understanding what we might for the moment call (begging a few questions) a feminist sexual desire. Hence my commitment to developing such a discourse.

The political criticism of heterosexuality within feminism, enhanced by the relative silence of heterosexual women, has been one of the recent factors in perpetuating the absence of such a discourse. This absence is amplified by the historical lack of any discourse which offers women positions in which we can recognise ourselves as desiring sexual subjects, without moral opprobrium and sanctions. In this chapter, consistent with the focus of the book, I argue my case in relation to women's *hetero*sexual desire. I do this for three reasons. Firstly because I can draw on my own experience; secondly because it is primarily women's heterosexual desire which has been constructed within feminism as being determined by gender and power difference; and thirdly, this is the most difficult, and therefore most theoretically challenging, case to make – a case which has implications for the understanding of gendered subjectivities. The principles may, however, usefully be applied to sexual desire generally, both homosexual desire and men's desire.

According to both psychoanalytic feminism and radical feminism (which unusually agree on the formulation of heterosexual desire as erotic domination – see Hollway 1995b), gender difference produces otherness, which is a precondition of (hetero-)sexual desire. Reviewing the psychoanalytic literature, Chodorow (1994: 35) refers to this as 'the almost definitional encoding in heterosexuality of intra-psychic and interpersonal male dominance'. Stevi Jackson provides a concise expression of this dominant feminist discourse concerning heterosexuality:

> What is specific to heterosexual desire ... is that it is premised on gender *difference*, on the sexual 'otherness' of the desired object ... Since it is gender hierarchy which renders these anatomical differences socially and erotically significant, it is hardly surprising heterosexual sex has been culturally constructed around an eroticization of power.
>
> (Jackson 1995: 132)

My purpose in this chapter is to argue that this characteristic of heterosexual desire, the eroticisation of gendered power difference, which undoubtedly often renders it problematic, is not inevitable within current social and political conditions as Kitzinger has argued (1994: 207). To the extent that I succeed in arguing for the possibility of a 'feminist' heterosexual desire, the case provides a way of understanding how unconscious dynamics impact upon social change.

In the following section I situate the recent feminist debate about women's heterosexual desire in the context of two currents of feminist psychoanalytic theory – object relations and Lacanian – in an attempt to specify why women's heterosexual desire appears incapable of theorisation outside assumptions of sexual difference and women's passive sexuality or lack. While object relations theory marginalises issues concerning sexual desire in gender development, the Lacanian tradition posits an unfulfillable sexual desire based on the loss of the (m)other due to the Oedipal dynamics which are an inevitable result of sexual difference.

I then critique the universalist Lacanian assumptions of split subjectivity and the unfulfillability of desire, linking his starting point of desire for recognition with Benjamin's work.

In the following section I set up the fundamental precepts of my account of the development of subjectivity. Subjectivity is seen as more or less integrated (and by the same token more or less split). Carried through life and varying according to how anxiety-provoking circumstances and relations are, this will profoundly affect relational dynamics, especially sexual relationships, in which issues of intimacy and its absence figure so crucially. I argue that the basic processes by which subjectivity is achieved are not initially gendered; that is they precede and can survive gender difference. The fact that individuals plot different, and more or less integrated paths through primary object relations and anxiety mean that different people, men and women, will experience the 'imperatives' of gender difference more or less strenuously, with more or less damage. I introduce a Kleinian model of the Oedipus complex which does not put sexual difference at the centre of child development as do the Freudian and Lacanian models.

In the penultimate section I focus on identifications as the raw material of subjectivity, using Benjamin's work to argue for the possibility of multiple and crossgender identifications which survive in the child's successive encounters with gender difference.

In the final section I attempt to link these relational dynamics that can elude and resist patriarchal relations specifically to sexual desire.

Heterosexual desire and erotic domination

Radical feminism gave us the crucial insight that sex and power are interwoven in ways that manifest in men's sexual violence towards women through rape, pornography, child sexual abuse and sexual harassment, as well as in the more mundane arena of the asymmetries in women's and men's relation to active sexuality. Radical feminism also gave us the slogan 'sleeping with the enemy' and too often treats all men as sexual villains and the power that they manifest through their sexuality as monolithic in contrast to women's powerlessness and victim status. The contours of this debate are now well known. A series of phrases has come to characterise the dominant critique of heterosexuality: 'compulsory heterosexuality' (Rich 1980), 'heteropatriarchy' (Jeffreys 1990) and 'the heterosexual matrix' (Butler 1990a), emphasising the entrapment of women, especially heterosexual women. I broadly agree with the radical feminist assertion that within patriarchal structures heterosexuality functions as one of the primary institutions reproducing gender difference.

Whilst these critiques have articulated and elaborated an important political truth, they have been characterised by the tendency to see the structural and material features of women's subordination within heterosexuality reflected at the level of heterosexual women's desire, with deterministic effects; hence 'the eroticisation of inequality' (Dworkin 1981) and the 'eroticisation of power difference' (Jeffreys 1990; Kitzinger 1994; see also Hollway 1993, 1995a and 1995b for elements of a critique). I am therefore going to address primarily the psychic dynamics which can construct heterosexual desires which have the capacity to resist patriarchal heterosexuality and the reproduction of gender difference.

It is still unfortunately contentious to claim that forces exist at the level of the psyche which interrupt the way that the material and social world would otherwise determine subjectivity.[1] Yet without such an analysis it is difficult to theorise the forces of change. Psychoanalysis, which 'claims human desires as its area of special study' (Person 1989: 21), has been profoundly influential (in negative as well as positive ways) in providing and limiting the available frameworks within which to analyse sexual desire, both heterosexual and homosexual. It is thus impossible to circumvent an encounter with psychoanalysis in what follows; I have been faced with the problem of how to make it accessible to a social science audience which is often unfamiliar with, and sometimes hostile to, its perspectives. For all its limitations, it has the merit of addressing the consequences for adult sexuality of the origins of desire in early life. Recent uses of psychoanalytic theory emphasise the imagination: 'the imaginary nature of the unconscious . . . is at once a constitutive source of human practice and agency, as well as the force locating human subjects within unacknowledged conditions of action through the barrier of repression' (Elliott 1992: 10). In its widest sense, this force deriving from the unconscious is desire.

In psychoanalytic theory, it is impossible to talk about sexual desire and sexual object choice without talking about gendered subjectivity (see Chodorow 1994 for a useful critical account). Feminist psychoanalytic work has tended to divide into two approaches: those for whom Oedipal dynamics are central in accounting for gender difference, often as interpreted by Lacan,[2] and those who draw on some version of object relations theory, which emphasises the development of self in relation to others, in particular the mother-infant dyad,[3] therefore focusing on pre-Oedipal relations.

In the first tradition, following Freud, the sexual drive is seen as the driving force in the formation of human subjectivity. The Oedipal dynamic refers to the point when the child is forced to concede the father's power through his priority over the child in terms of possessing the mother.[4] What the child, boy or girl, wants of the mother gets understood as sexual possession, which through its prohibition instates desire and gendered identity. In this sexual drive paradigm, difference is understood in terms of genital difference and gender difference comes to revolve around the phallus/penis, the castration complex and women's 'lack'. In Lacan's rereading of Freud:[5]

> this linguistically constructed and structured unconscious *is* our sexuality: subjectivity emerges out of unconscious sexual drives. This sexualization and subjectivity are by definition constituted in terms of difference, or opposition, between the sexes.
>
> (Chodorow 1992: 188)

In the second tradition, sexual desire virtually disappears from the picture, while concern with separation from the mother provides the problematic within which girls' and boys' gendered development is understood. The boy is more threatened by his desire to merge with the mother, and defensively uses his difference and his identification with the father to separate. The girl may never fully separate, but continue in a series of unconscious mutual identifications with her mother. Coupled with her overvaluation and idealisation of the father (see especially Contratto 1987), this supposedly ensures her femininity and, in the process, instates a passive sexuality.[6]

These different emphases reflect divergent traditions in psychoanalysis revolving around whether Oedipal dynamics or pre-Oedipal relations are privileged in the account of how gendered subjectivity is achieved in children's development.[7] According to Benjamin,

> this shift from oedipal to preoedipal – that is from father to mother – can actually be said to have changed the entire frame of psychoanalytic thinking . . . The last twenty-five years have seen a flowering of psychoanalytic theories about the early growth of the self in the relationship with the other.
>
> (Benjamin 1990: 11–12)

This split in feminist psychoanalytic traditions means that pre-Oedipal, mother-based accounts do not talk in terms of desire, while accounts which have kept sexual desire in the frame – notably Lacan-inspired – have been fixated on Oedipal dynamics. The Oedipal story, revolving as it does around the castration complex and penis envy, hinges on the idea of sexual difference, which simultaneously produces gender-differentiated subjectivities and sexual (supposedly heterosexual)[8] desire differentiated into active and passive. Nevertheless, because it is the body of theory that focuses on sexual desire, it is usually this Lacanian tradition which is drawn on in feminist attempts to use psychoanalytic theory seriously to understand the impact of the unconscious in producing heterosexual desire. For example:

> Both the boy and the girl have to submit to castration to allow the emergence of desire, that investment of the object with erotic value which makes the object relation possible . . . The whole economy of desire is rooted in the phallus *and* this phallus is attributed to the father . . . So

if desire is the investing of the object with erotic value, this investment is not made in relation to difference as such, but in relation to a gendered difference . . . Desire is *engendered* by difference.

(Adams 1989: 248)

In this account, the object (or person) relation is only made possible by its investment with erotic value (sexual desire). In pre-Oedipal accounts this argument would be reversed, since the infant is seen as inherently object-relating, attaching to later erotic investments a pre-established connection with the other. Benjamin takes this connection as primary and theorises it as recognition, which is arguably consistent with Lacan's principle of desire for the other, even though it draws primarily from the object relations tradition. In other words, there is potential for some productive theoretical cooperation in this area.

Desire and recognition

For Lacan, desire is 'desire for the desire of the other' (Macey 1995: 78). There are two steps in this formulation. The first is that the object of desire is another being – desire for the other – rather than a drive, state or a material object for consumption. The second is that what is desired of the other is also not something that can be exchanged or consumed, not material or grounded in reality, but remains at the level of that elusive, imponderable category, 'desire', made more elusive by its echo-like quality: desire for the desire of the other. According to Lacan, while desire for the other is originally desire for the mother, this desire is inevitably alienated in successive developments (for a detailed account, see Frosh 1987). The child thereby enters the social and symbolic world as a subject whose integration is illusory, who is condemned to be split, and whose desire is therefore based on lack 'resulting from the unattainability of the wholeness which is desire's constant objective' (Jefferson 1994: 17).

In this view subjects are seen as inevitably split (and therefore inevitably unfulfilled), leaving no room for theorising specific intersubjective and psychic conditions which lead to the possibility of wholeness, the fulfilment of desires and the attainment of anything but illusory integration. For my purposes, the strength of Lacan's theorisation of desire is that it is within a tradition of Hegelian philosophy which links desire to recognition (Macey 1995), and therefore to the social conditions of intersubjectivity. However, it is in overgeneralising the account of the failure of recognition and thus rendering splitting a universal principle that Lacan becomes so didactic: it is 'the very generality of [Lacan's] theory that is so problematic, the very abstraction of a subject which never exists "in situation" . . . that becomes an opaque obstacle to the understanding of concrete subjectivity' (Macey

1995: 81). Macey adds that this leads to 'a curiously asexual (and affectless) psychoanalysis' (p. 81).

It is Lacanian psychoanalysis that has been appropriated in most post-modern theorisations of self in which, according to Elliott, 'the self is little more than image, simulacrum, blank fiction' (Elliott 1992: 9). As Benhabib points out, psycho-historical accounts of how children actually develop have been notable by their absence:

> The historical and cultural study of diverse codes of the constitution of subjectivity, or the historical study of the formation of the individual, does not answer the question: what mechanisms and dynamics are involved in the developmental process through which the human infant, a vulnerable and dependent body, becomes a distinct self with the ability to speak its language and the ability to participate in the complex social processes which define its world.
>
> (Benhabib 1992: 217)

In my view these failures have affected feminist theorists in the postmodern tradition such as Judith Butler (1990a) who, even while they seek to incorporate the idea of an unconscious desiring psyche into their accounts of gendered subjectivity, are derailed by the grand narrative of the phallus, the lack of specificity and the inattention to the developmental histories of desire. These developmental histories, while being gendered through language and social structures in a shared way, are also those of unique subjects who make sense of the significance of sexual difference and gendered power relations through their inner world. The coordinates of this inner world are already developed prior to language, harnessed by phantasy, within object relations.

I am going to preserve Lacan's proposition that desire is for recognition but argue that, while it is elusive and easily derailed (by Oedipal dynamics), desire is possible to fulfil in intimate relations if the conditions of external and internal world permit. The external conditions refer to the actual relationship with an adult partner (including the structural influences upon it), while the internal refer to the products of the psychic and intersubjective history which constitute subjectivity.

Jessica Benjamin's analysis of erotic domination (1984, 1990) also follows in the Hegelian tradition, putting the concept of recognition at the centre of her understanding of the intersubjective relations within which gendered subjectivity is formed, and using the paradigm of the 'master-slave' relationship to provide a power dimension to this analysis. However, unlike Lacan, she draws from the insights of the pre-Oedipal tradition, thereby taking seriously relational dynamics in theorising subjectivity. These dynamics are based on recognition:

> In order to become human beings, we have to receive recognition from the first people who care for us. In our society it is usually the mother

who bestows recognition. She responds to our communications, our acts, and our gestures so that we feel they are meaningful. Her recognition makes us feel that vital connection to another being as necessary to human survival as food.

(Benjamin 1984: 293)

The need for recognition, which Benjamin argues is constitutive of subjectivity, involves a paradox: namely that 'at the very moment of realizing our own independence, we are dependent upon another to recognize it' (Benjamin 1990: 33). The most obvious way to defend against the anxiety of dependency is to control the one on whom we depend. This is where Benjamin's analysis of erotic domination begins. Rather than being an inevitable outcome of desire for the complementary other's difference to compensate for the lack in oneself, for Benjamin, erotic domination is the result of an attempt to control dependency transferred into the sexual relation.[9] However, control is an inherently unstable solution because 'if I completely control the other, then the other ceases to exist' (Benjamin 1984: 295) and then there will be no one there to recognise me. Thus control of the other as a way of resolving dependency is an instance of false differentiation: 'psychological domination is ultimately a failure to recognize the other person as like, although separate from oneself' (p. 294). Rather, 'true differentiation means maintaining the essential tension of the contradictory impulses to assert the self and respect the other' (p. 295). This ability depends on the early object relations usually played out between infant and mother and these, therefore, are central in determining whether adult sexual desire follows the pattern of erotic domination, the pattern of mutual recognition or, of course, a mixture.

Subjectivity and differentiation in early object relations

The new-born infant is not only dependent for its survival on adult care, but it is 'undifferentiated'; that is, it can achieve no organised distinction between itself and the objects on which it depends. (In relation to early infancy, the term 'objects' is used because it is only later, and then not fully, that babies can relate to an integrated other; that is, a person.) In this view, identity[10] is, in the words of one psychoanalytic dictionary, 'the sense of one's continuous being as an entity distinguishable from all others' (Rycroft 1972: 68). This is a crucial, but not automatic, developmental achievement and relies fundamentally on the infant's unconscious relations with primary objects, notably the mother. It affects the subsequent history of desire in a person's life.

The infant does, however, experience itself through bodily sensations, being at the mercy of its physiological needs and functions: notably the sensations of hunger and satisfaction of hunger, discomfort and comfort. It has recently emerged from a life where there could be no distinction between it (the 'foetus') and the body carrying it. Moreover, it has no sense of time: that is, of the predictability of sensations and events. For now, it is bathed in satisfaction or gripped by some unpleasant physical sensation, like hunger or pain, which it cannot relieve by itself. Frustration is therefore experienced as acute hostility: 'separate worlds of timeless bliss in one ideal universe of experience, and terror and persecution in another alternative universe' (Britton 1993: 38).

These two basic states – satisfaction and frustration – have been characterised by Melanie Klein as 'good breast' and 'bad breast' in an attempt to represent the radically split nature of the objects characterising the infant's presymbolic world. The infant's reality is also split in the sense that it cannot make the distinction between phantasies and reality, between internal mental life[11] and external reality (what actual people are doing to it), and therefore between itself and the maternal object. Note that for Klein, unlike for Lacan, a measure of integration succeeds splitting, although its achievement is sometimes tenuous and never entirely free of the splitting defences of early infancy.

Integration in the self of the separate part objects which have constituted early experience is part of the same achievement as the ability to recognise another person as an integrated whole, continuous in time and space. This ability is also tied up with the achievement of differentiation, the baby from the maternal object (now experienced more as 'mother', that is, person), and thus the achievement of a sense of self. The self is made up of the parts which are introjected from others, in particular from the parents or other primary carers: 'In the earliest phases the good object which is felt to be singular at any one moment is of particular importance, since its secure introjection forms the basis of the ego's stability' (Hinshelwood 1991: 312). This achievement, which Klein refers to as the depressive position, depends considerably on the capacity of significant others to be differentiated from the baby, in the sense of knowing whose feelings belong to whom. Without this capacity in the other, one cannot be recognised for oneself, rather than as a projection of the other's unresolved parts: 'the real mother is not simply an object for her child's demands; she is, in fact, another subject whose independent center must be outside her child if she is to grant him the recognition he seeks' (Benjamin 1990: 24).

These developmental processes are triggered by infants becoming 'acquainted with reality through the deprivations it imposes on them' (Klein, quoted in Britton 1993: 82). The first and most important deprivation that reality imposes is the deprivation of the maternal object which, for the young infant, exists only in relation to the infant itself. Gradually, the baby's experience of the mother's independent centre outside the child will come through the reality of her other relationships.[12] For Klein,

> the oedipus situation exemplifies this knowledge ... just as in the
> depressive position the idea of the permanent possession has to be given

up, so in confronting the parental relationship the ideal of one's sole possession of the desired parent has to be relinquished.

(Britton 1992: 39–40)

If recognition is not working, desire for the other (the other's recognition) will indeed dictate relationships. If, however, integration, differentiation and recognition are successfully established, the threat can be worked through; the threat precipitated by the loss of the phantasy that the mother is there only for the child. In this case the actual relationship, with what it crucially provides in terms of continual reaffirmation of the self as knowable and lovable, will not be lost through competition:

it is through mourning for this lost exclusive relationship that it can be realized that the Oedipal triangle does not spell the death of relationship, only the death of an idea of a relationship.

(Britton 1993: 94)

Recognition is unfulfillable to the extent that subjectivity is dynamic, always needing reaffirmation through others who can be trusted to recognise. It is fulfillable to the extent that recognition can continue to be experienced, significant others permitting.

The move from experiencing the world in terms of two-person relationships to three-person relationships provides a 'triangular space . . . [which] includes the possibility of being a participant in a relationship and observed by a third person as well as being an observer of a relationship between people' (Britton 1993: 84). Kristeva has similarly pointed to the importance of a third party (the 'imaginary father of individual prehistory') in the baby's development, not just as a way of coming to terms with loss, but 'the creation of a space outside into which the subject can look – making it possible both to be with the mother and to develop' (Frosh 1994: 138).

In this account of the Oedipal situation, importance is given to the child's recognition of the fact that the relationship between the parents (or parental figures) differs from that between parent and child. While conventionally this aspect of Oedipus has been read through *sexual* difference (the father has the right of possession over the mother by virtue of the penis/phallus), it is, in my view, significant that the Oedipal encounter is to do with generation, and maybe more superficially to do with gender. That is, it can be read as about the privileges and potency of adulthood, not inherently about those of adult males. True, deprivation of the mother is important, but under the conditions I have outlined above, sexual difference would not trigger the chain of dynamics normally theorised in Oedipal terms. If the baby can come to terms with the fact that the mother has an existence beyond itself, and if it continues to feel recognised, as separate, both by its mother and a widening circle of others, it will be in a good position to hold to a secure self in relation to the gender differences experienced through the reality of triangular relationships.

Identifications and identity

Benjamin (1995) argues for the need to replace the idea of a singular identity with the notion of identifications. Gender difference (in the singular)
relies on an idea of unitary, and therefore oppositional, gendered identity in
the parents (and significant others) with whom the child will identify and
from whom it will derive the parts making up its own identity.

Pre-Oedipal infants experience themselves as omnipotent – before, that is,
they have to come to terms with the realities of their physical limitations,
dependency and competition. During this phase, they want everything. For
Benjamin, the significance of the pre-Oedipal period is therefore 'not signifying two-not-three, or separation from the mother, so much as believing you
can have or be everything' (Benjamin 1995: 108). This is when a more or
less integrated self is being formed through identification. Identification, or
more particularly introjection,[13] is the process through which external
objects are relocated within the self and potentially identified with, to become
part of the self. While in early infancy these introjected objects remain separated off from each other, the process of integration to form a secure sense
of self relies crucially on the integration of the good objects experienced in
primary relationships. Importantly, these identifications are not exclusive to
the same-sexed parent:

> In my view, toddlers are struggling equally to maintain identification
> with both sexes, to keep both parents available as objects of attach-
> ment and recognition. Optimally the identification with both parents
> allows the child to assimilate much of what belongs to the other –
> identification is not yet limited by identity. In this phase, gender identifi-
> cation is much less rigid than the oedipal organization that comes after
> it: cross-sex identification can coexist with same-sex identification;
> sexual identifications have not yet hardened into polarities.
> (Benjamin 1990: 113)

The burden of the Oedipal story for girls is that they must transfer their
desire from mother to father, give up the phantasy of being the phallus for
the mother and reconcile themselves to having babies; that is to being the
object of a man's desire. In other words, they must give up masculine identifications. However, most girls (at least in the West) continue to identify with
so-called masculine characteristics of the father and others[14] at least until
adolescence, well beyond the Oedipal stage. There is a considerable measure
of agreement among psychoanalytic feminists that boys have a much harder
passage through the Oedipal period. Girls, like boys, have the task of differentiating as a separate person, and while it is not complicated by the task
of constructing themselves in opposition to the mother's gender, this also
leaves her with 'no obvious way of disidentifying from her mother, no hall-
mark of separateness' (Benjamin 1990: 78).

The usual Oedipal emphasis is on the desirability of the boy's separation from the mother by whatever psychic means possible. This is typically achieved through repudiation of the mother and exclusive identification with the father: 'to the extent that identification [with the mother] is blocked, the boy has no choice but to overcome his infancy by repudiation of dependency' (Benjamin 1990: 162). When this happens, 'the whole experience of the mother–infant dyad is retrospectively identified with femininity and vice versa' (Benjamin 1990: 162) (witness the tendency in little boys to assume that all babies are 'she'). Given the importance of identification with the good object/mother, the boy loses something crucial to his self. His desire (for the m/other) is thus constructed out of loss and is experienced as unfulfillable. Maybe this was Lacan's own trajectory, but we cannot assume it of women, nor indeed of all men.[15] Consistent with my arguments in the previous section, Benjamin uses Fast's distinction between repudiation and renunciation to make the point that a longer period 'of allowing both feminine and masculine identifications to coexist, would aid boys in becoming more differentiated from mother and obviate the need for such defenses as repudiation, distance and control' (Benjamin 1990: 169).

Here I would like to offer an example of an alternative trajectory for a man, which also demonstrates the variability of gendered characteristics across the sexes. The usual story of the acquisition of singular gender identity hinges on the parents having singular gender identities themselves, identities which therefore contrast with each other: masculine and feminine. Desire for the (gendered) difference only to be found in the other hinges on this assumption. Discussing this question with a man I know well, I asked 'why do you identify with your mother so strongly?' (I asked this since I suspected that it had a great deal to do with his capacity to relate to women through likeness as well as difference, therefore to recognise them and treat them 'as sovereign equals' in sexual relationships too.) The reply was multifaceted, but one thing that struck me was that, as a young boy, he was not only uncomfortable with some of his father's traditionally patriarchal attributes (which he therefore consciously sought to reject), but also with his father's 'feminine' ones. For example, as a young boy, he was ashamed by the fact that his father could be very emotional, to the point of crying. His mother, in contrast, was calm and steady, never showing emotions outside a familiar and predictable range (she sounded 'containing'). He is like his mother, not his father, in this respect.[16]

Analytically I would argue that he successfully introjected a good object deriving from a mother who was herself integrated and containing. He evidently did not repudiate the mother (in Benjamin's and Fast's terms), but, for whatever complex of reasons, was able to retain those positive identifications in his gradual achievement of a core 'masculine' identity. He may have been helped in this by the lack of gender polarity between his parents.

Benjamin sees this in terms of being able to renounce, rather than repudiate the mother (and therefore femininity). Repudiation involves 'a defence against envy, not an acceptance of difference' (Benjamin 1990: 116), since it involves giving up something that is desired above all else, resulting in 'loss' and unfulfillable desire. Renunciation, in contrast, is based on the realistic acknowledgement of sexual difference (in the sense that one cannot be both a woman and a man). Renunciation, unlike repudiation, preserves the capacity for recognition:

> As we give greater value to the preoedipal world, to a more flexible acceptance of difference, we can see that difference is only truly established when it exists in tension with likeness, when we are able to recognize the other in ourselves.
>
> (Benjamin 1990: 169)

In this account, in place of the Oedipal logic of either/or (mother or father, girl or boy, penis or breast, having or being), the principle of recognition can reinstate both/and, which is the 'overinclusive' principle of pre-Oedipal identifications (see Benjamin 1995). To the extent that this is achieved in both boys and girls, it overturns the principle of desire for the other of gendered difference.

I would agree that 'loss of mutual recognition is the most common consequence of gender polarity' (Benjamin 1990: 171). If, however, it is possible to conceptualise a path through the intersubjective development of children which does not involve giving up identifications of likeness with both parents – that is, multiple cross-sex identifications – then it follows that mutual recognition is possible in heterosexual relationships. If the child learns that mutual recognition characterises the parental relationship, it can be experienced as inclusive rather than exclusive. To the extent that the possibility of recognition is lost in the exclusionary principle of Oedipal dynamics, through repudiation, adult desire for the other will be dependent, defensive and driven, a combination recognisable in many adult relationships, with men especially exhibiting the last two characteristics.

It takes two . . .

Let me first summarise these dynamics that can elude and resist patriarchal relations (I will then attempt to link them specifically to sexual desire). First, their origins are in early object relations, when internal and external forces begin to maintain that tension between self-assertion and dependency which is the key to non-defensive differentiation. When the people who are an infant's primary objects are able to recognise the infant as separate and dependent (and be separate enough themselves to be able to provide true recognition) the conditions are in place for mutual recognition; which can be reproduced in adult sexual partnerships where these conditions obtain on both sides. (I think that this is a good definition of love.)

Second, these conditions of integration need to be reasonably secure by the time the baby or child faces the realities of gender difference, especially as experienced in the parents' relationship. If children continue to have access to multiple, cross-sex and crossgender identifications,[17] they will not feel depleted of part of their potential selves and will not seek in an idealised or denigrated other what they have lost.

The question remains, what is it about the mutual exchange of recognition which renders a relationship sexually exciting, rather than platonic? For me it revolves around the way that the pleasure of mutual recognition can be exquisitely signified in the intimacy of sex. Under such circumstances, sex reproduces the physical intimacies which I characterised as the 'state of bliss' side of infantile experience, which depended entirely on the communications of physical bodies: warmth, heartbeat, smell, the movement of skin against skin, the pressure of hands and lips acting as a constant reminder of being in relation to another. If the dynamics I have described work out well enough, later these will be retrospectively experienced as security, trust and predictability. Experience of oneself as loved is not a once-and-for-all achievement and so will be sought and desired repeatedly as affirmation. This is the sense in which I see desire as both fulfillable and unfulfillable at the same time.

While we unconsciously seek this in all relationships, it is in the sexual relationship – if it is based on mutual recognition – where it will feel most trustworthy, because of the repetition of early intimacy through the inevitability of physical contact in sex. If a sexual partner is relatively unknown, the desire would be to be known through physical contact and still wanted, still (sexually) desired.

It is commonplace for women (and men) to experience false recognition in heterosexual relationships, which may well trap them into being the objects of men's sexual desire. In this case, however, any aspects which remain hidden (as they surely will) will undermine true recognition, that is, to be recognised for the entirety of who one is. If one is recognised in this way, and one is still desired, then one is not (or no longer) a sexual object (or a maternal, or paternal object). Such desire invites engagement of one's full potential, one's active subjecthood. It is more like Cixous' desire than Lacan's based on lack: 'full desire, a desire rooted in abundance rather than loss, creativity rather than absence' (quoted in Frosh 1994: 27).

Sexual abundance requires a discussion about fear of loss of control, given the widespread ambivalence towards it. For men during heterosex, loss of control at orgasm can either be experienced as safe (in the context of mutual recognition), or as the feeling of losing a differentiated self, which would lead to defensive control, even over orgasm, maybe through maintaining a dominant position over the woman or rejecting her afterwards (Person 1989). It may also make him fear and disapprove of a desirous woman (for anything more than a few disconnected encounters) (Heyn 1992). In such circumstances a woman cannot feel recognised and will likely lose pleasure in sex, except through erotic domination. If she (if they both) can lose control and still feel safe, this parallels the containment that infants need from parents, that they will remain unharmed by the infant's negative projections – thoughts, feelings and phantasies – but rather transform them into safe objects whereupon they may be reintrojected by the baby or child: 'The parent-figures need to be actual containers, in emotional experience, for the angry, greedy and frightened feelings of their child' (Rustin 1991: 190). We are likely to feel greedy and frightened (if not angry too) at orgasmic moments, given the dominant discourses on women's sexuality, given also our appetites and the threat of loss of control. To feel safe, to trust that we shall feel safe again next time (and in between times), is surely a central condition for the free and active sexual desire that I am talking about.[18]

In this chapter, I start from a personal conviction that mutual recognition within contemporary heterosexual relationships is possible and that it does not only create the condition for love, but also for an active and fulfillable sexual desire. Because of the discrepancy between this personal knowledge and the knowledge offered by feminist theory, I have tried to theorise how this 'feminist' heterosexuality is possible, given the manifold and powerful forces working against it. The emphasis of my account is on the achievement of recognition, integration and differentiation in early childhood relations and its implications for the preservation of crossgender identifications and therefore recognition of likeness across the sexes. I try to theorise a passage through Oedipal dynamics, for girls and boys, where the polarities and prohibitions of gender difference do not inevitably produce defensive heterosexual relationships based on false recognition. If two people both bring to a sexual relationship these capacities, produced by 'good enough' intersubjective circumstances in their histories (circumstances which are not directly related to material conditions and are in principle available to all, irrespective of social difference), then a desire may be forged which is based on likeness as well as difference, on recognition as well as idealisation or denigration; a desire which is both fulfillable and insatiable.

I feel that the weakest part of this argument is the move from desire for recognition to sexual desire. I have done little more than point to the importance of physical contact in early object relations. The significance of these early experiences of body contact for the later sexualised body, and for the expression and fulfilment of sexual desire, requires a good deal more exploration. Touch, caresses, holding, warmth, smell, heartbeat: these form the prelinguistic bedrock of the experiences of both safety and bliss. All being well, and despite the powerful discursive factors militating against such safety for women (and differently for men), the safety will later translate into the experience of trusting specific others with an uncensored sexual self. Within this safety, the infantile experience of bliss may be translated into the adult experience of *jouissance* and experienced time and again – and therefore desired time and again – in sexual relating.

The arguments sketched here have implications for a theory of change which hinges on the creative role of unconscious fantasy in ensuring that people are never ciphers of their social conditions; in this case, ciphers of the patriarchal structures and relations which are still so influential in the reproduction of gender difference and oppressive heterosexuality. For those sociologically minded feminists who see the prefiguring of egalitarian social relations as either impossible or irrelevant,[19] I believe this sketch for a theory of feminist heterosexual desire shows how powerful patriarchal forces need not be determining at the level of the psyche, and therefore in gender relations. Defences against anxiety are not just at the root of damaged and damaging human (and sexual) relations, but provide the conditions also for creative imagination which, in human (and sexual) relations, can transcend the real.[20] The desire for recognition is a powerful moral and political force.[21] In my account, it suggests not only that women's heterosexual desire is not inevitably for erotic domination by a man, but that gender-differentiated subjectivities are not determined by patriarchal discourses.

Notes

1 This remains the case despite the influence of psychoanalytic theory within feminism and cultural studies.
2 For example, Mitchell (1974); Mitchell and Rose (1982); Adams (1989); Brennan (1989, 1993).
3 For example, Eichenbaum and Orbach (1982) and Chodorow (1978, 1992, 1994). Object relations theory is 'a set of accounts about the constitution of self in the context of primary emotional relationships'(Chodorow 1992: 7). However, there are differences between what is now called object relations (and interpersonal) psychoanalysis on the one hand and Kleinian and post-Kleinian psychoanalysis (H. Segal 1979; Rustin 1991; Anderson 1992; Parker 1995), where the concept originated, on the other. Where object relations traditions stress the real conditions of emotional relating that the infant experiences, Kleinian and post-Kleinian traditions take the infant's imagination and capacity for phantasy to mean that these 'real' relations are never determining of the child's development. In my view, the Kleinian approach provides for creative and imaginative forces in the human psyche which disrupt any notion that the psyche is a reflection of external forces. In this chapter, I use the concept of object relations in the Kleinian sense; that is, incorporating the principle that a person's object relations are not just reflections of real interpersonal relations.
4 This psychoanalytic literature is permeated with references to the mother, which have irked feminists wishing to move from 'mothering' to 'parenting'. However the dynamics described in terms of the maternal relation can refer to any primary love object, woman or man. The assumptions of continuity with foetal experience and suckling experience would, however, need reworking. In this chapter I take the 'father' to mean any man who becomes a sexual partner to the mother, thereby occupying the social, and potentially the emotional, position referred to

in psychoanalysis as the father. I use the term 'parents' in the same spirit (see Holloway, forthcoming).

5 See Lynne Segal (1994: 130–40) and Chodorow (1992: Chapter 9) for two accessible feminist discussions of Lacan's relevance for feminism, and Gallop (1982) for a lot more detail.

6 For example, Ernst (1987); Benjamin (1990); Flax (1993); Mens Verhulst et al. (1993).

7 It has been remarked that these traditions are themselves gendered, in their relative privileging of the breast and the phallus (Frosh 1994).

8 See O'Connor and Ryan (1994) for a critique of this orthodoxy in the context of clinical psychoanalysis and the pathologisation of lesbians and homosexual men. Chodorow (1994) provides a detailed theoretical critique of the tendencies within psychoanalysis which normalise heterosexuality.

9 For an account of how also 'domination is anchored in the hearts of those who submit' (Benjamin 1990: 52) – usually presumed to be women – see Benjamin (1984, 1990).

10 The terms 'person', 'subjectivity', 'self' and 'identity' are not entirely interchangeable. 'Person' is used here in the everyday sense to distinguish between that and the objects and part-objects of the infant's early experience. 'Subjectivity' comes from poststructuralist theory, carrying with it a critique of the 'individual' as the rational unitary subject of psychology (Hollway 1989: Chapter 2). 'Self' implies reflexivity (not another but oneself) and 'identity' suggests the self-conscious understanding of that self as it is experienced by others.

11 One of the earliest ways the infant has of coping with the paranoia of its separate worlds is by phantasising the breast in its absence. This is an example of 'the imaginary nature of the unconscious'(Elliott 1992: 10). From theorising this capacity, Klein emphasised that the infant is never a passive object on to which experience is written.

12 Whereas orthodox Oedipal theory has a strong tendency to universalise the child's acquisition of gender and sexuality by relying on the idea (symbolically and actually) of two parents of 'opposite' sex, this Kleinian version of Oedipal theory has greater potential for recognising the variability of different family configurations and the effects these will have on the developing psyche of the infant. Apart from Chodorow's influential, but early (1978), arguments in *The Reproduction of Mothering* this is an almost untouched theoretical area. I return to it in a collection of essays (coedited with B. Featherstone) to be published by Routledge.

13 The technicalities of the different meanings of identification and introjection in Freud and Klein are discussed in the relevant entries in Hinshelwood (1991).

14 Benjamin's discussion of the role of the father in the daughter's development of subjectivity explores the pre-Oedipal as well as the Oedipal father:

> When, in rapprochement, the father first begins to represent freedom, separation and desire, this is not simply an earlier version of the oedipus complex. The father here is not a restrictive authority, not a limit to the child's desire, but rather a model for it, whereas the Oedipal father is both.
>
> (Benjamin 1990: 101)

15 However, the dynamics associated with Oedipus will affect the way that the defences of introjection and projection are deployed. Craib (1987: 732), for

example, claims that 'for women, the central defense mechanism is introjection ... for men, projection or denial'.

16 While this example is removed from the Oedipal stage in age terms, it none the less demonstrates the perseverance of identifications from what Benjamin (1995) calls the 'overinclusive' stage into post-Oedipal identity.

17 The utility of preserving a distinction between sex and gender is evident here. 'Cross-sex' refers to identifications which go, for example, between son and mother, or daughter and father. 'Cross-gender' identifications might proceed with a parent of the same sex, but refer to characteristics which are socially marked as characterising the other sex: for example, if a girl gets into home improvement because she identifies with her mother's competencies in that area, when these do not characterise her father (or other significant adult male in her life), or if a boy, through identification with his father, is capable of expressing painful emotions through crying.

18 I was recently picked up on this point, that is not acknowledging that women can have desirous sex with strangers. Since this cannot, by definition, involve recognition, desire must here be driven by a different dynamic. Maybe it has something to do with the safety of not being recognised for expressing a sexuality which opposes moral conventions.

19 I have disagreed with Denise Thompson on the issue of how to understand political change in heterosexual relations in a wider debate on heterosexuality in the pages of *Feminism and Psychology* (Thompson 1994; Hollway 1995a).

20 At a recent conference where I gave parts of this chapter as a paper, I was asked 'What's wrong with erotic domination?' My answer was along the following lines: within what I regard as necessary boundaries of safety and trust, erotically playing out themes of domination and submission (as well as other themes) may explore an imaginary world which escapes the confines of the real and may help us approach occluded aspects of past relationships, not just gendered power relations, and mitigate the anxiety associated with previous vulnerability or ambivalent control.

21 See Rustin 1991 for a full exploration of the relevance of Kleinian theory for a socialist politics.

7

Heterosexuality and masculinity: theorising male power or the male wounded psyche?

Victoria Robinson

The theoretical gaze has recently turned towards that previously thought unfathomable construction and identity we call masculinity. Given the (socially constructed) emphasis we place on the sexual – our sexual desires, practices and relationships – it is inevitable that the new male writers on masculinity, with whom I am concerned, should place an examination of the male sexual self at the centre of their analysis.

The men exploring and analysing their sexuality range from the male academic who uses postmodernist theories, to anti-sexist men involved in the men's movement, to Robert Bly's men's therapy movement which 'seeks to liberate the Wild Man (the fierce, instinctive, irrational, intuitive, emotional, sexual, hairy essence of man) from its centuries of imprisonment inside each living male, to re-unite the sons with the fathers' (Segal 1994: 270). Men's popular magazines ask men whether they are new men, new lads, wild men or simply unreconstructed macho men. This academic and popular interest, which is generally concerned with a heterosexual sexuality, is intimately connected to feminist theories and ideas, whether that connection is made explicit or not.

In this chapter, I want to look particularly at recent theoretical attempts by male academics to explore heterosexuality. This raises questions about the relationship of the writing by men on masculinity to feminism as a theoretical body of work, and about men's (sexual or otherwise) relationships with women. A central concern is whether this new and evolving interest by some men in the construction of masculinity challenges male power and privilege, as well as allowing men to redefine male sexuality in new and diverse ways. The chapter also reveals the diversity of opinion and approach to masculinity/masculinities and sexuality which characterises this writing.

Before discussing in detail the ideas and theories expounded by men writing on masculinity, it is worth examining briefly the contemporary debate around the institutionalisation and practice of women's studies, gender studies and men's studies/masculinity writing, and their relationship to each other. The writings by men on sexuality – and heterosexuality in particular – can, at one level, be critiqued within this context (see Canaan and Griffin 1990; Cornwall and Lindisfarne 1994; Robinson and Richardson 1994). Some feminists have been critical of the new developments of gender studies and men's studies, arguing that their appearance within the academy is at the expense of women's studies, which is still situated somewhat precariously (if less so now) in the institutions. In the United States, there are now courses and journals entitled 'men's studies' within universities, whilst in Britain this new interest in men and masculinities has, so far, been mainly apparent in research publications and conferences, with courses on masculinity just beginning to emerge. Gender studies too has found some support in terms of how it accommodates a problematising of masculinity:

> For men have not previously confronted themselves as 'masculine'; masculinity, and male sexuality, remained largely unproblematized, while it was women who were the 'dark continent'. The move towards gender studies hence seems in general to be a progressive and fruitful one.
>
> (Polity Press 1994: 3)

Male theorists have varied both in terms of their relationship to feminism and to women's studies itself. For example, the US academic Michael Kimmel (1988: 20) has asserted that 'Men's Studies doesn't seek to supplant women's studies. It seeks to buttress, to augment women's studies, to complete the radically redrawn portrait of gender that women's studies has begun.' Some feminist writers are more sceptical of claims that men's studies is the natural complementary field of study to women's studies (see Canaan and Griffin 1990; Hanmer 1990; Cornwall and Lindisfarne 1994), whilst other male writers have been suspicious of naming this area of study 'men's studies' (see Hearn 1987; Hearn and Morgan 1990).

It is also argued that gender studies, as opposed to women's studies, allows men to feel more comfortable, exploring masculinity in the context of the premiss that men, like women, are oppressed by their gender (see Robinson 1993b).

There are valid feminist concerns about the writing on masculinity, its institutional location and relation to women's studies. For example, there are fears that the theoretical spotlight will now return to men again, and that in the competition for scarce resources women's studies will lose out. Writings on male sexuality, specifically on heterosexuality, need placing within the framework of these specific feminist concerns. Elsewhere I have argued that the themes and issues prioritised under men's studies and writings on masculinity have primarily been concerned with masculine subjectivity, for example, men's relationships with feminism, parenting, male bonding and feelings about their own sexuality (Richardson and Robinson 1994). The focus in men's studies and writing on masculinity in the UK has also tended to be on research publications, rather than on the use of such research for political and social change.

The work of Andrea Cornwall and Nancy Lindisfarne (1994) also serves to illustrate the various facets of this critique by feminists of masculinity theory and its institutionalisation as men's studies. They place their study of hegemonic and subordinate masculinities in terms of a reconsideration of anthropological approaches to gender, and consider a scrutiny of men's studies and writings on masculinity central to their project. Concerned to 'disrupt the premises which underlie much recent writing on and by men' (p. 2), they conclude that a writer such as Harry Brod (1987) emphasises the personal at the expense of the political. His writings reproduce dualisms such as passive/active, body/mind and reason/emotion which, they assert, are deeply implicated in gendered inequalities in the West.

Drawing on postmodernist conceptual critiques, Cornwall and Lindisfarne also accuse male writers on masculinity – such as, for example, Michael Kimmel (1987) – of using terms such as 'masculinity' and 'femininity' in an unreflexive and unproblematic way, so as to ignore the ambiguities and contradictions (as well as a variety of perspectives) when examining gendered relationships.

It is historically inaccurate and theoretically simplistic to assert that women's studies and feminist theory have only been concerned with women's experience, femininity and female sexuality, and that the new men's studies and writings on masculinity will complete the portrait of gender, only half drawn, by scrutinising masculinity (see, for example, Kimmel (1987) for this latter viewpoint).

In 1978, in *About Men*, Phyllis Chesler wrote about men and patriarchy, men's relationships with other men and relationships with women. She considered men and sex, pornography, sexual fantasies and male violence:

> I wrote this book in order to understand men. First, I turned to books already written by men, about men. I found them of limited usefulness. Only some men, mainly poets and novelists, spoke about themselves in a personally authentic voice; only some men wrote about the male condition with an awareness that it is different from the female condition.
>
> (Chesler 1978: xv)

To their credit, some male theorists, such as Hearn and Morgan (1990) and Morgan (1992), have acknowledged that women theorists have indeed analysed the problematic nature of masculinity, citing feminist writers Delphy (1977), Chesler (1978) and Friedman and Sarah (1982). Canaan and Griffin (1990) argue that one of the great contemporary myths is that the women's liberation movement and feminist research is only of benefit for (and is interested only in) women. They quote the work of Brah (1988) and Davis (1982) for work on 'race', class and masculinity; Hanmer and Maynard (1987) for work on male violence; Driver and Droisen (1989) for research on sexual abuse; Dworkin (1981) for analysing men's use of pornography; and Russell (1989) for work on the links between military institutions and hegemonic masculinity.

With regard to recent writings by men on masculinity, the titles of the books by men give some theoretical clues to their methodologies and chief concerns: *Male Order: Unwrapping Masculinity* (Chapman and Rutherford 1988), *The Making of Masculinities* (Brod 1987), *Men in Feminism* (Jardine and Smith 1987), *Rediscovering Masculinity* (Seidler 1989), *Refusing to Be a Man* (Stoltenberg 1989), *Men's Silences* (Rutherford 1992). What exactly is being 'unwrapped' and to reveal what? The title *Refusing to Be a Man* is perhaps indicative of early attempts to disown or disclaim masculinity, as opposed to more recent attempts not to reject but to transform masculinity or even masculinities. What are the gaps and silences around masculinity and sexuality which men are to reveal? Will attempting to articulate the silences result in more myths? For instance, is the 'new man' and his arguable appropriation of feminist theory another manifestation of 'macho man' with his overt pride in his masculine attributes and power over women? Will male power and privilege be unwrapped along with a subjective account of male sexualities, or is it the male, wounded, narcissistic psyche which receives theoretical scrutiny? Some heterosexual men make no pretence – authentic or otherwise – at either responding to the challenges of feminism or at deconstructing/constructing different sexual masculine identities and behaviours. This is illustrated by writers such as Desmond Morris (1994) who, with works like *The Naked Ape*, captured the popular imagination with his extreme biologically essentialist views on 'human mating' patterns. These writers still have a purchase on common-sense views of heterosexual practices and relationships, accepting gender polarities in the context of a behaviourist biological and psychological framework.

The male theorist Adam Jukes (1993) argues that men are

> dominated by the urge to conquer and penetrate women . . . heterosexual desires [are] to penetrate the female and impregnate her . . . the erect penis is a rock of stability to which most men turn in times of stress . . . the bottom line is that male abusiveness and violence, our power and control, are not negotiable currency.
>
> (quoted in Segal 1994: 291)

This is hardly an analysis informed by feminist criticisms, nor by the concerns of the male new masculinity writers who problematise masculinity and recognise the social constructed nature of male heterosexuality (or the so-called 'crisis in masculinity'). In our desire to explore the writings of male masculinity theorists, we should not forget that some men still write as unreconstructed misogynists who sanction the biological inevitability of gender roles and violence against women.

But it is the work since the 1980s with which I am chiefly concerned in this chapter, when writing by men on sexuality and masculinity either began to have a new perceived legitimacy within men's studies as a separate field of enquiry, or as a new and much publicised area within academia generally. (See Robinson and Richardson (1994) for a full discussion of publishing trends and research on masculinity by men.) As Lynne Segal writes:

> Throughout the 1980s the shifting nature of men's lives, their behaviour, experiences, anxieties, fears and cravings, have been debated with new passion and concern. Books researching fatherhood, men's violence against women and children, male identities and male mythologies now interrogate man, as a sex, in a way until recently reserved for women – as a problem.
>
> (Segal 1990: x)

What areas, issues and questions have men writing on heterosexuality, and as heterosexuals, been particularly engaged with? Certainly pornography, sexual harassment and child sexual abuse have received attention, for example, but it is pertinent to ask certain general questions about these analyses. Has heterosexuality as both institution and experience been explored, or has heterosexuality itself remained an uncharted given, even when specific issues such as pornography and violence have been addressed? Another relevant concern is that heterosexuality, when discussed generally, often tends to be theorised in relation to sexual identities, relationships and practices and not seen in dynamic relation to the world of politics or work, for instance. (These questions can also be addressed to writings by heterosexual feminists in recent publications: see, for example, Wilkinson and Kitzinger 1993, and in this collection.)

An anthology of articles taken from the British men's sexual politics magazine *Achilles Heel* (1978–92) voices the personal and theoretical endeavours of some anti-sexist men to re-examine masculinity. The editor, Victor Seidler, states that the magazine was sympathetic to feminism and gay liberation, and feels that it was important for heterosexual men to relate to both movements:

> Even though heterosexuality functioned as an oppressive norm within a patriarchal society, we did not feel that heterosexuality in itself could be renounced. In this sense our sexuality could not be presented merely

as political choice but we had to learn to accept and in some sense to celebrate our own sexualities. We had to face how little we understood about ourselves sexually and how estranged we often were from our bodies that we had learned to use in instrumental ways. As men we had to face our own fear of intimacy and learn to question the ways in which a whole range of needs were somehow compressed into our social desire.

(Seidler 1992: xii)

These sentiments are a mixture of both the political language used by and desires of women in the early 1960s women's liberation movement, many of whom put their energies into understanding their sexuality and recognising their estrangement from their own bodies. An example of this was the concerns of women's groups and their emphasis on self-examination, for instance, as well as more recent concerns expressed by heterosexual feminists to 'accept and celebrate' their heterosexuality (Wilkinson and Kitzinger 1993).

The essays cover heterosexual relationships (for instance, sex in long-term relationships), childhood sexuality, pornography, sexism, sexuality and male violence, homophobia, sex, health and therapy. The accounts are often experiential with some theoretical framework. At times, the essays are almost confessional – with titles such as 'How I gave up pornography' by John Rowan – but many of the essays display an authenticity of good faith by revealing both masculine desires and practices and the contradictions of masculinity which are involved. Some of the writers do consider male power and privilege, as well as being interested in the personal implications of heterosexuality for themselves. For example, when talking about men's violence Tony Eardley accepts that it is precisely men's silence and an apparent lack of disquiet among men on male violence which justifies women's suspicions that even those men who are least personally violent secretly enjoy the benefits to be had from the violent actions of others. Whilst Victor Seidler, talking about heterosexual and homosexual relationships, argues the need for men to take more responsibility for their emotional lives in relation to partners and with their children. (See also Giddens (1992) for an analysis of men's emotional dependence on women.) Seidler also recognises men's role in challenging patriarchal institutions, founded on images of traditional masculinity – as well as effecting personal change.

Dorte Marie Søndergaard, in her analysis of the book (1993), argues that despite the defensiveness on the part of some of the contributors, she was generally impressed by the balance shown, avoiding the weak capitulation and aggressive self-insistence stereotypical of male responses to the feminist challenge around sexuality and other issues. What she did feel was apparent was a somewhat ambiguous treatment of masculinity: presented as negative in terms of a shaping masculine identity, yet also as valuable, 'something one must take care of' and develop, not allowing the feminist challenge to wash 'it overboard' (p. 396).

If we are to see masculinity as contested, contradictory and open to change, then I feel that this ambiguity around male sexuality – simultaneously both vulnerable and powerful – is necessary. Certainly the most recent discourses on masculine sexuality by men would not seek to reject their gender because the renunciation of masculinity was a way of coping with their guilty feelings or their power (see Seidler 1989, 1994). John Stoltenberg's book (1989) entitled *Refusing to Be a Man*, may reflect this tradition of rejection. The emphasis by some writers is more on a reworking of masculinity in an attempt to open up new ways of thinking about men and male identities, of opening up a dialogue on masculinity between men. (Though this begs the question, which men?) For instance, Victor Seidler (1994) asks whether it is possible to conceive of heterosexuality as a relationship of power in society, and as a legitimate sexual orientation.

Some of the articles in the *Achilles Heel* collection are concerned with men's relationship to intimacy and emotion. Indeed, this reflects a tendency for some of the writing by men on masculinity to write about issues of emotional conflict and suppression. Victor Seidler (1989), for instance, argues that traditional male sexuality is often not seen to be connected to vulnerability, intimacy and contact. Further, men's sexuality is seen to be related to performance, with men often being 'control freaks' in sexual relations.

In his book, *The Inward Gaze: Masculinity and Subjectivity in Modern Culture* (1992), Peter Middleton argues that much recent writing on masculinity by men tends to engage uncritically with these concepts of intimacy and emotion.

He cites writers such as Tim Beneke (1989), who suggests emotional suppression may be one cause of rape, and the members of the anti-sexist men's movement magazine *Achilles Heel*, with their concerns about men's alleged difficulties with emotion and their involvement with the promulgation of the more humanistic psychotherapies. A number of the essays in the book *The Sexuality of Men* (Metcalf and Humphries 1985), which was compiled by *Achilles Heel* contributors and has served as a case-study for a number of writers critical of some men's writing on sexuality, are also scrutinised by Middleton. Middleton, like others, argues that these essays reflect this uncritical emphasis on emotion and, even, in the process, somewhat disown issues of sexuality.

Middleton concludes that this has a number of unfortunate implications. For instance, emotion, subjectivity and identity are not universal concepts, which the collection tends to assume, and that in relying on object relations psychoanalytic theorists there is a tendency to mother blame. Jonathan Rutherford (1992) also finds that this emphasis on feelings in *The Sexuality of Men* can mean that men may turn their back on rationality and reason, and see feeling as leading to the 'truth'.

Earlier criticism from Kobena Mercer and Isaac Julien (1988) on *The Sexuality of Men* can serve as a framework to critique men's writings on sexuality generally. They argue that specific essays ignore the socio-economic context of men's violence by locating the root of the problem at a solely psychological level. Furthermore, by emphasising inner feelings and the 'person-centred' stress on identity at the expense of the environment, issues are only addressed in a limited way. A 'self-centredness' of white sexual politics generally is seen to be individualistic and 'excludes questions of race and ethnicity because it is so preoccupied with the "self", at the expense of the "social" ' (Mercer and Julien 1988: 119). Lynne Segal (1990) also gives a critique of accounts of masculinity which reduce a consideration of male power (with its social, economic and political dimensions) solely to the intricate workings of the psyche. Her discussion on Lacanian theory, which she argues is indifferent to particular historical processes (and utilised by some male writers on masculinity), is seen to be characteristic of all psychoanalytic thinking.

Middleton, in his very thorough and detailed chapter on theories of modern masculinities, asserts that a general feminist acceptance of the aims of the men's movement has been counteracted by a belief that the emphasis on emotional expression and development has sidestepped important issues; furthermore, it was possibly both self-indulgent and self-exonerating. He concludes: 'Men's deafening silence about their own sexuality as opposed to the objects of their desire continues' (Middleton 1992: 126).

An example of how analysis of men's heterosexuality can be sidetracked into the personal (at the expense of political action or wider connections to structural inequalities between women and men) is to be found in how theoretical ideas are frequently discussed and utilised in popular magazines for both sexes. Books on men and the media/popular culture such as Chapman and Rutherford (1988), Easthope (1990) and Craig (1992) do, to varying extents and from different perspectives, provide theoretical explanations which link analysis on masculinity to social relationships. They also consider how the media serve to construct masculinities, examine how men read the media, and show how popular representations of masculinity can reinforce male dominance and power.

Antony Easthope (1990), from a psychoanalytic viewpoint, considers masculinity in the specific Western tradition, arguing for its non-universality and reflecting on masculinity, homosexuality and homophobia in the context of the mass media, whilst the essays in Craig's edited collection (1992) are concerned, amongst other topics, with media theory, the representation of men's relationships, advertising images of men in sport, and men and the news. Clay Steinman, in his essay 'Gaze out of Bounds: Men Watching Men on Television' re-examines the idea of the gaze and asserts: 'Viewing affirms a subjectivity that validates desire for a certified star, but has no truck with acknowledging homoeroticism on screen. For heterosexuals, viewing denies its own eroticism' (Steinman 1992: 213).

But are these particular theoretical arguments and insights translated into the popular? How are the recognised concerns of homophobia and the construction of masculine heterosexuality discussed and presented for wider consumption? An article in the British edition of *Cosmopolitan,* entitled 'Under Pressure: What the Media is doing to Men' (Baker 1994), stresses issues such as the male body on display in the media and the increasing number of men opting for cosmetic surgery – for example, the insertion of silicone pectorals, removal of 'tummy fat' and penis extensions. Heterosexual men's lack of confidence about their own sexuality and image is highlighted by a discussion of men's feelings of inadequacy about being the nine-stone weakling. The article emphasises the increased pressure and constraints on men. Even if heterosexuality can be seen to be tacitly acknowledged (though always implicitly, not explicitly), this covert, even unrecognised critique of heterosexuality focuses on the crises in masculinity for men, rarely on the implications for women. Even if within this particular article it is acknowledged that women too face media pressure, it is only mentioned to illustrate how heterosexual men face similar pressures to look attractive. Indeed, feminists themselves are quoted in an effort to show how changes in masculinity mirror equally those which have affected women:

> Using images from male homosexual subculture, advertising has begun to portray the male body in a beauty myth of its own . . . As this imagery focuses more closely on male sexuality, it will undermine the sexual self-esteem of men in general.
>
> (Naomi Wolf, quoted in Baker 1994: 132)

An emphasis on men's personal sexual identities informs both popular representations of masculinity and academic theorising by men on sexuality. Jalna Hanmer (1990), concerned with the latter discourse, asks if work by men on masculinity is going to tackle issues of violence against women or whether they are willing to take on questions and theoretical perspectives developed in women's studies in the area of human reproduction. She writes: 'The study of men conceptualised solely as the study of personal identity, of masculinities, is too narrow to do so' (p. 34). How far, then, have men writing on heterosexuality been willing to look beyond purely the personal, at the structural manifestation of both the contradictions around masculinity for men and how the attendant male power and privilege is connected to women's oppression?

Harry Brod (1990), in an examination of pornography and its effect on the alienation of male heterosexuality, is forthright about popular conceptions of 'normal' male sexuality being seen as consensual, non-violent heterosexuality. He argues that this definition is problematic, to say the least; its other side emphasises both compulsory heterosexuality and the implicit or explicit coercion or violence so associated. His analysis here is concerned with male subjectivity, but he is also aware of competing definitions of heterosexuality and the implications of this for women.

Elsewhere, Brod's earlier work (1987) on male violence has come under feminist scrutiny. Andrea Cornwall and Nancy Lindisfarne (1994) examine his work on violence as part of his implication that the 'new men's studies' is a necessary corrective to feminist work. They conclude that his account of male violence emphasises militarism, not rape or battery. Furthermore, they argue that his discussion of pornography is virtually devoid of comment on the multiple forms of violence this can entail. His account is concerned generally about the effects of pornography on men. It is necessary to explore contradictions of masculinity and male subjectivities in relation to sexual processes and identities, but feminists would argue that this focus is in danger of again making women's diverse experiences invisible. So when Brod recognises women's studies and feminist ideas (Brod 1987), how much of this is lip service being paid to feminism, before he can get on with the 'real job' of exploring masculinity?

Some individual men have attempted to extend their analysis of sexuality beyond the realms of the personal. Jeff Hearn (1992) is concerned to explore male domination in the public worlds of work, politics, sexuality and culture. He analyses the diverse connections between public patriarchal organisations and male heterosexuality and homosexuality, and states that, whilst problematising his terms, 'the powers of men and of public men applies especially to the power of able-bodied, heterosexual, "middle-aged"/older, middle/upper-class, white men' (Hearn 1992: 3–4).

The specific issues around sexuality and heterosexuality which the new masculinity theorists address are informed and underpinned by the more general theoretical assumptions around masculinity implicit in their discussions.

R. W. Connell's work on a 'critique of hegemonic masculinity' has been particularly influential in shaping the terms of the debate on masculinity. His definition and analysis of this concept (Connell 1987) sees heterosexual men as entrenched in the defence of patriarchy, but also finds reasons for men to want to change this system, even though they are the beneficiaries of such an oppressive structure. He argues that not all men are the same, and some groups such as 'effeminate or unassertive heterosexuals' may not be part of the dominant masculinity.

Generally, there has been an acceptance of masculinity as a social construction which, as such, sees masculinity as fluid and open to both contestation and change:

This has led to a recognition that the dominant forms of men and masculinities are themselves not merely 'natural' and unchangeable ...

Thus men and masculinities are not seen as unproblematic, but as social constructions which need to be explored, analysed and indeed in certain respects, such as the use of violence, changed.

(Morgan 1992: vii)

A way in which this change is seen to occur is through alliances between feminists, gay men and progressive heterosexual men (Brod 1987), though such alliances are neither automatic or easy.

There has also been a move to recognising hegemonic masculinities, making explicit to enquiry how 'particular groups of men inhabit positions of power and wealth and how they legitimate and reproduce the social relationships that generate their dominance' (Brod 1987: 92). It is then argued that most men do not correspond to the hegemonic model, but that many men are complicit in sustaining it. The hegemonic model of masculinity is also heterosexual (see also Carrigan et al. 1985).

The idea of hegemonic masculinity (Connell 1987) also allows for the deconstruction of the term: there are not just a plurality of masculinities, hegemonic masculinity is one which is 'white, heterosexist, middle class, Anglophone, and so on' (Hearn and Morgan 1990: 11). This model allows us, they claim, to look at the various subordinations, stigmatisations and marginalisations men may experience because of their sexuality, ethnicity, class, religion or marital status, within a patriarchy.

Feminists too have contributed to this conceptualisation. For instance, Lynne Segal's study of masculinities (1990) has been influential in its attempt to shed light on the category of masculinity which, she claims, still remains deeply obscure. Segal argues that we need to look at the specific nature and significance of masculinity, not merely emphasise its complexity and contradiction. She therefore emphasises specific masculinities, for instance macho, black, gay and anti-sexist, to illustrate how an understanding of the differences between men is fundamental to the struggle for change.

Other feminists (Cornwall and Lindisfarne 1994) have explored the concept of a hegemonic masculinity. As well as arguing that masculinity varies over time and setting, they also argue that

Hegemonic versions of masculinity frame relations of inequality. However, hegemonic forms are never totally comprehensive, nor do they ever completely control subordinates. That is, there is always some space for subordinate versions of masculinity – as alternative gendered identities which validate self-worth and encourage resistance.

(p. 5)

This idea of change is a prevalent concept in recent literature on masculinity. R. W. Connell (1995) further examines the concept of hegemonic masculinity by stressing multiple masculinities and by exploring groups of men undergoing different experiences of change. Some are seen to be wanting to transform gender relations, and some are resisting these transformations. His general thesis is to combine, in his analysis, both personal life and social structure. So a notion of 'compulsory heterosexuality for men', for example, is seen to reveal both the complexity of change in masculinity and also the diverse possibilities of change.

A feminist response to this emphasis might be a concern that the current notion of emphasising changing masculinities should not ignore or minimise men's continuing power at both a structural and personal level. For example, compulsory heterosexuality may be a reality for women and men but their experiences of it, and the power and privilege that accompany it, are different.

Other men, for example Harry Christian (1994), are also concerned to dislocate the idea of hegemonic masculinity. Christian argues that, though a common conception of heterosexual men's experiences of sex is one of domination and control, his personal experience has been that sex is about shared physical enjoyment. Thus, he argues against general statements about heterosexual men, based on limited empirical evidence, which ignore variations amongst straight men and concludes: 'The non-macho non-gay identity needs to be distinguished' (p. 188).

What has been the relationship of these male writers to feminism, both in terms of the women's movement and feminist theory? Some men, as I have already indicated, have either not acknowledged feminism's contribution to the analysis of heterosexuality and masculinity or, arguably, have made only a token gesture to feminist theories. Even when some men attempt to engage genuinely with feminist discourse, they can, sometimes unconsciously, reproduce patriarchal ways of thinking (see Jardine and Smith 1987). Others have more openly acknowledged the debt to feminism:

> Most of the radical theorising of gender has been done by women or by gay men. I am a heterosexual man, married, middle-aged, with a tenured academic job in an affluent country ... I owe an account of what I am doing here.
>
> (Connell 1987: xi)

This situating of oneself in relation to feminism, gay men and individual location reflects the feminist tenet that the personal is indeed political. Connell is also scathing about the notion, put forward by the 'men's movement' in the United States in the 1970s, that men too are equally oppressed as women, which he sees as 'demonstrably false'. Heterosexual men – more so than others, he claims – are advantaged by the current social structure. He also maintains that there are few heterosexual men working on sexual politics issues in the institutions.

Other writers, for example Victor Seidler (1994), also mention the debt that theoretical enquiry on masculinity owes to feminism. In his recent study of masculinity, modernity and social theory, for instance, Seidler argues that feminism has made a challenge of a fundamental nature to modernity. Yet the same writer's views on heterosexuality – in their relation to feminist ideas and the women's movement – are more debatable, for example his understanding of the complexities of feminism as a political project and a diverse body of theory: 'But it is one thing to understand the institutional power of heterosexuality and another to think that sexual orientation is a matter of "political choice"' (Seidler 1994: 100).

On the other hand, Seidler accepts the institutionalised position of heterosexuality, and rightly wonders if heterosexuality can be simply abandoned. Yet he is also dismissive of those who have constructed their sexuality as political choice, for example political lesbians. Many women who have 'chosen' to be lesbians for political reasons do not automatically expect heterosexual women to follow suit, realising women to be straight because they either have to, say for economic reasons, or because they want to, and see that as a political choice too.

As well as having a specific relation to feminism, the new writings on masculinity also have a historical and contemporary connection to the gay men's movement and theory. Gay men's studies has been chiefly concerned with documenting sexuality's importance. As Tim Edwards (1994: 1) writes: 'In addition, men's study of masculinity added some insights into masculinity and male experience though frequently excluded full consideration of sexual orientation and heterosexuality as a component of masculine identity.'

Edwards also states he is tired of some gay men's sexism and that many gay male theorists themselves have not accepted connections between masculinity and gay sexuality. But in some ways heterosexual men have more power than gay men within the academy, and Edwards is also critical of tendencies in men's studies which he feels has been 'profoundly uncritical of the role of sexuality in masculine identity, particularly the component of heterosexuality, and excluded consideration of gay studies' significant critique of the naturalness of [any] sexuality' (p. 10). Generally, this can be seen as an indictment of what has been perceived as the fundamental concerns of the new masculinity theorists.

It is interesting to note that in Britain and elsewhere, most of the work on masculinity, and that which has gained prominence, has been written by heterosexual men. In contrast, the writing on heterosexuality by feminists, has, until relatively recently, been largely by lesbian theorists.

If a concept of hegemonic masculinities assists the analysis of the diversity of men's experiences, then a related question for this evolving body of theory is whether or not there has been a real engagement with issues of difference between men. Feminists have had to address theoretical and political charges of ethnocentrism, and have taken on an explanation of differences between women in terms of 'race', class and sexuality to an extent, whilst age and disability have yet to be adequately theorised.

Joyce E. Canaan and Christine Griffin (1990) have stated the possibility of 'the new men's studies' marginalising radical analyses of 'race', class, age, disability and sexuality as merely another set of variables which draw us back to a narrow political agenda. But, as with other issues, there are differences between the new masculinity writers on how they theoretically address difference. Certainly, masculinity writers writing before the mid-1980's, as Edwards (1994) has noted, did not deconstruct masculinity. Heterosexual writers have also noted these accusations, that masculinity theory has not written about the multiplicity of male roles (Brod 1987). Brod also asserts that steps are being taken now to address this issue (see also Hearn and Morgan 1990). Other writers are not convinced that the steps taken are meaningful ones. John Goetz (1987), discussing the oppressive experience of lesbians and gay men, writes that 'A men's movement which neglects this history and this continuing oppression is deeply homophobic' (p. 5). This homophobia, he concludes, is something that men from the men's movement, and outside it, have to address.

Gary Kinsman (1995) also puts forward an analysis of how heterosexual men, even those influenced by feminism and in the process of questioning some aspects of male privilege, have not questioned the institution of hetero-sexuality. He further argues that the literature of the men's movement has produced an image of men that is white, heterosexual and middle class.

Around 'race' and ethnicity issues also, white straight men in the late 1980s had yet to make such insights fundamental to their analysis. Mercer and Julien (1988) specifically use *The Sexuality of Men* (Metcalf and Humphries 1985), to argue that generally white sexual politics has been impoverished in an obsession with 'self'. Thus a consideration of 'race' has been absent, not only from the essays in that collection, but also from white men's politi-cal agenda overall. (Though rightly, they also assert that white feminists, as well as anti-sexist men, need to take up 'race', ethnic and cultural differences in their analyses.)

Robert Staples (1995), writing about stereotypes of black male hetero-sexuality, attempts to 'penetrate the superficial images of black men as macho, hypersexual, violent and exploitative' (p. 375). Despite the unre-flective use of the word 'penetrate', this is an important theoretical task. He concludes, however, that for black men, rape is often an act of aggression against women because they do not receive status through work due to their unemployment and underemployment. He thus reveals a different stance on rape to feminists, who have stressed the power relation in acts of sexual vio-lence towards women.

Feminists and men writing on masculinity and sexuality may well have different agendas and therefore different questions to ask. Only if male writers incorporate a full consideration of men's power, whatever their class position, can their analyses be empathic to feminist concerns.

Another theoretical framework, that of queer theory, has also been employed by some masculinity writers. Some support these moves, like the 'white, middle-class, heterosexual man' writing in *Body Politic*, a magazine which he asserts, 'has recognised that the time is right for new conversations between feminine/masculine, black/white and gay/straight to be stirred up, at the same time as acknowledging diversity and difference' (D. Jackson 1993: 7). Others have been more sceptical of such developments generally, in terms of whether the study of masculinity benefits from such 'queering'. (See for instance Diane Richardson's article in this book.)

The different perspectives and approaches used by masculinity writers to explore heterosexuality are of relevance in themselves: they reveal not only the writers' particular 'biases', but, to an extent, also what issues are selected, which concepts are utilised, as well as what questions are asked.

Jalna Hanmer (1990) asserts that there are aspects of the approaches to the study of men which worry her, particularly the US use of role theory and socialisation theory. She sees this as limiting the study to the individual, or else attempting to explain social formation and processes purely at the level of the individual. Some masculinity writers themselves have criticised this approach (see Pleck 1987).

Victor Seidler (1994), when discussing 'men's studies' as it has developed in the United States, posits the argument that its development has left behind 'difficult personal terrain' for theoretical engagement. (See Morgan (1992) for a discussion on experience and methodologies in the context of men engaged with an exploration of masculinities). This suspicion is connected to the strength of a positivist social science methodology in men's studies, which Seidler feels is related to the disciplinary strength of psychology, and leads to his criticism of a behaviourist approach. This is seen to be a simplistic explanation for the connection between empirical research and feminist theory: for example in the relationship of pornography's effects on men and on their behaviour and relationships with partners.

Some have argued that the writings on masculinity and sexuality have overused or relied upon particular perspectives and theorists. Peter Middleton (1992) argues that work on male sexuality, such as Metcalf and Humphries (1985), relies on object relations psychoanalysis, particularly Nancy Chodorow's *The Reproduction of Mothering* (1978). Men in the men's movement have accepted this perspective, he says, because it accepts the premiss that men grow up emotionally suppressed. Indeed, Chodorow has the 'honour' of being one of the major feminist sources used by men's studies in the United States (Cornwall and Lindisfarne 1994).

Though it is fair to agree with David Morgan (1992) that there has been no automatic response on men's part to the ideas and practices of feminism, Jalna Hanmer's (1990) view that men working on the study of masculinity need to appreciate the diversity of feminist views is important. She argues that only some feminist work is recognised, and consequently 'Some women are apparently elevated into the male scholarly world by being identified as asking questions and providing theory judged relevant to the study of men' (p. 26).

Another response by some men writing on masculinities has been to caricature and stereotype particular feminist positions. Victor Seidler (1994), when discussing aspects of sexuality such as rape, stereotypes radical feminism by asserting: 'On the other hand, what about the radical feminist assumption that "all men are potentially rapists"?' (p. 99). Given that this assumption would generally be attributed to radical feminists, he thus colludes with the myth that all radical feminists are biological essentialists. Similarly, his reasonable assertion that it is important to hold on to a recognition of the sources of power men have in heterosexual relationships, as well as accepting the ways men and women collude in such relationships, is unfortunately supported by his blanket statement that radical feminism would only stress men's power and its connection to women's oppression. Further, radical feminists, he asserts, argue that women should separate from heterosexual relationships with men to discover their own autonomy and independence. Such an unacknowledgement of the richness and complexity of feminist thought is particularly characteristic of this stereotyping of radical feminism (see Douglas 1990; Richardson 1996) and is representative of some masculinity writers' seemingly genuine but unsubtle and theoretically simplistic use of feminist ideas in their explanation of masculinity. Another example of this tendency is given by Cornwall and Lindisfarne (1994) who quote Brod (1987) as conflating the different stances within socialist feminist theories in his analysis. Others, such as Stoltenberg (1989), are more generous and theoretically authentic when he writes about his relationship to radical feminism which, he says, energised him with its emphasis on social construction theories and which helped him see within the present male-supremacist structure of gender, a possibility of men as not being brutish and loutish.

As with the subtleties and richness of feminist thought as a body of theory, the new male masculinity writers are diverse in terms of approaches, politics and their general empathy to key feminist concerns. If, however, their ideas are to inform popular opinion and affect the lived experience of both sexes, then this evolving theoretical endeavour must, as some male writers acknowledge, engage with the multiplicity of men's experiences in a systematic way. They must also attempt not to stereotype feminist thought, even if feminist concepts and ideas on male power are uncomfortable for men involved in examining men's position, the male psyche and subjective experience. As with feminist theory and practice, the truism of the personal being political needs to inform both the theory and the actions of men who are striving to alter and transform men's power and their own experiences.

8

Which one's the man?
The heterosexualisation
of lesbian sex

Tamsin Wilton

The foundational assumption of feminism is that women are subordinate to men, and that this is neither biologically determined nor morally defensible. Rather, this relation is social and political (albeit determinedly naturalised within patriarchal discourse) and is in the interests of men who, as a class, profit from it materially and socially. Moreover, many radical feminists argue that the categories whereby this subordination is organised and implemented – the categories 'women' and 'men' – are themselves both the product of and instrumental in maintaining the regime of male power (Wittig 1981). In brief, the binary system we call gender is intrinsically political.

Integral to the political organisation of gender, indeed to the very idea of gender itself, is the notion of sex. It is clear from the semantic slipperiness of 'sex' that its relationship to 'gender' is one of radical inseparability. 'Sex' means both the state of being male or female and the sexual (i.e. erotic) field of human behaviours. We speak of people 'having' a biological sex – on to which some (simplistically and inadequately) suggest the social structure of gender is mapped (Gatens 1991) – and of 'having' a sexual orientation, preference or identity, by which is meant a *gendered* direction of erotic desire and/or practice. Indeed, as I have suggested elsewhere (Wilton forthcoming), the generally accepted meanings for biologically 'sexed' bodies depend upon the heterosexual imperative, such that a vagina is understood to be 'for' penetration by a penis.

The radical inseparability of sex (as in 'gender') and sex (as in 'the erotic') has important implications for lesbians, and for lesbian feminists in particular. Because feminism is a politics of gender, and because discourses of gender and sexuality are inextricably interwoven (Butler 1990a, 1993a), the meanings of 'lesbian' and 'heterosexual' are strategically significant to feminists. Sexual behaviour is policed by the deployment of stigmatised/anathematised gender identities – 'calling gay men "feminine" or calling lesbians "masculine"' (Butler 1993a: 27) – a strategy which shames by attacking *gender* identity on the basis of erotic desires/behaviours. It is equally the case that gender behaviour has been policed by the deployment of stigmatised *sexual* identities. Boys and men are kept to the masculine straight and narrow by the threat of being called queer,[1] and successful or strong women – especially in traditional male occupations – are likely to be labelled lesbian. Since the nineteenth century those trying to discredit feminist political movements have used 'lesbian' as an accusation to force fearful women back into line (Abbott and Love 1972): a strategy which depends on constructing 'lesbian' as an alien monstrosity prowling outside the fold of gender conformity.

These disciplinary manoeuvres in the fields of gender and the erotic depend for their intelligibility on their mutuality. It is by reason of our position outside our proper *gender* that queers[2] are monstrous aliens: to be a faggot or fairy is to be tainted with femininity and to be excluded from the masculine (and hence, to be the proper target of male violence as a 'female' creature outwith male protection); to be a dyke is to be guilty of pretensions to masculinity and to be excluded from the protected sphere of femininity (and hence, to be the proper target of male violence as a 'male' creature outwith male protection). The sociopolitical infrastructure of gender, in other words, coalesces around and is enforced by the threat of violence (itself seen as 'properly' male). Thus the disciplinary regimes of gender and the erotic are intrinsically codependent and foundational of the superordination of men to women.

Telling the difference

It is crucial to identify the instrumentality of the heterosexual master narrative in this. Heterosexuality means 'other-sexuality', homosexuality means 'same-sexuality'. To be homosexual means to desire people the same as oneself, to be heterosexual means to desire people who are other than oneself, in a relation of complementarity. Moreover, this 'otherness' has become identified with *oppositeness*, with polarity, and has therefore (illogically) been naturalised by association with a wide range of scientific/philosophical discourses including alchemy, Taoism, Tantric Bhuddism, mediaeval Christianity, physics and chemistry. As Janice Raymond memorably put it, 'Hetero-relational complementarity becomes the "stuff of the cosmos"' (Raymond 1986: 12). We speak unthinkingly of the opposite sex, yet there is no biological or somatic sense in which the bodies of women can be understood as opposite to the bodies of men. Even at the most fundamental biological level, male and female bodies occupy a complex and shifting field within which musculature, bone structure, endocrine function, genital structure, etc. demonstrate a wider range *within* 'one sex' than they do *between* the 'two sexes' (Kaplan and Rogers 1990; Birke 1992). This profoundly ideological notion of complementary gendered polarity – heteropolarity – has become the mystified and naturalised organising principle which saturates Western culture, structuring thought and social organisation around notions of binarism, complementarity, unidirectionality and polarity.

This polarity is not natural, but socially constructed. Thus, in order for heterosexuality to be maintained, it is imperative that *otherness* or *difference* be maintained. To erase or conceal the identifiable differences between women and men is to shortcircuit this heteropolar model (for more on the idea of heteropolarity, see below), so disobedience to gender becomes intolerable. To demonstrate that desire exists between individuals located at one or other pole – that two positives or two negatives may attract rather than repel – is to demonstrate the artificiality of the heteropolar model, so homosexuality is inconceivable to the straight mind without the insertion of 'difference'. Hence the homophobe's anxiety to have an answer to the intolerable puzzle posed by lesbian existence: which one's the man!

This heteropolarity is necessary to patriarchy, for it must be possible to distinguish men from women in order to institute and reproduce a power differential that is (precisely) predicated upon that difference. Thus the hegemonic construct of heterosexuality must either deny the existence of lesbian desire altogether (as in 'you're only a lesbian because the right man hasn't come along yet'), or must cast lesbian desire and behaviour within the heterobinary – as masculine or feminine and an always already inadequate simulacrum of masculinity or femininity at that (Butler 1991). By this insistence on reading 'lesbian' in a heterosexual paradigm, the phallocracy[3] is reproduced rather than challenged by the supposed existence of women whose desire for other women must otherwise be recognised as disobedient to the doctrine of heteropolarity. Thus the challenge posed to phallocentrism by lesbian existence is efficiently denied. If one partner in a lesbian dyad is 'the man' and the other 'the woman', the heterosexual imaginary thereby insists that *all* lesbians desire the penis: the one-who-is-the-man wishes s/he had her own penis, the one-who-is-the-woman wishes (as heterosexual women are presumed to wish) to be penetrated by the penis of the other. Hence the enduring belief among (supposedly empiricist) scientists in absurdities such as the over-developed lesbian clitoris capable of penetrating a vagina (Hemmings 1986; Ruse 1988).

'Heterosexuality' is a patriarchal narrative told about bodies and desires which polices women's and men's adherence to proper gender and erotic behaviours and makes women's liberation unimaginable. The givenness of gender and of sexuality and their necessary coterminosity have been challenged by (some) radical feminists, by gay liberationists and sexual libertarians and, most recently, by Queer theorists and activists (notably Judith

Butler, Eve Kosofsky Sedgwick, Sue-Ellen Case, Teresa de Lauretis, etc.) in the interests of gender/erotic[4] liberation struggles. It is therefore both ironic and politically troubling that a particular construct of heterosexuality has been deployed by some feminists (see, for example, Leeds Revolutionary Feminist Group 1981; Bev Jo 1984; Jeffreys 1990) in order to police lesbian sexual practice. Judith Butler (in an earlier avatar as 'Judy Butler') writes of 'the lesbian feminist tendency in recent years to legislate politically correct and incorrect behaviour' and suggests that 'The trend has become alienating for many women within the lesbian-feminist movement because it appeared that sexuality was being made radically *public*, opened to communal scrutiny, verbalised out of existence' (Butler 1982: 171).

More troubling than this laying bare of sexuality to public scrutiny is, I suggest, the heterosexualisation of lesbian sex that has taken place as part of the particular strand of lesbian feminism which Butler critiques. I want to start by considering the current general disengagement of the labels 'heterosexual' and 'homosexual' from both sexual practice and gender.

No longer necessary fictions? Queering as power struggle

The expression and maintenance of power has much to do with naming. Indeed sociologist Anthony Giddens asserts that power *is* the power to name (Giddens 1992), for power over groups, individuals and behaviours depends on the act of naming them. Social scientists have long recognised that gender and sexual identity are what Jeffrey Weeks (1985) calls 'necessary fictions' rather than straightforwardly descriptive of presocial biological or psychological 'realities', and that the naming of such identities is always political.

The last decade has seen an overt struggle over the assigning of individuals and groups to particular gender and/or erotic categories, a struggle both intensified and complicated by the HIV/AIDS epidemic. The imperative to fix and reify these fictions has been confronted by an extraordinarily broad-based impulse to destabilise and undo them. From the early days of the epidemic of HIV disease in the West (and elsewhere), the attempt to reaffirm discrete categories of gender/erotic identity has been framed in a discourse of contamination, seepage and quarantine. That this should be so is unsurprising: once HIV was (misleadingly) perceived as a disease *of* homosexuality then it became imperative (for misinformed, paranoid non-homosexuals) to maintain distance not only from homosexuals, but from homosexuality. A cordon sanitaire was hastily drawn around 'heterosexual safety' by naming/claiming *as heterosexual* institutions and groups – the family, the public, society, the nation, the human race – from which homosexuals were excluded by virtue of their queerness (Wilton 1992) and which became the paranoid insignia of heterosexuality. This tendency was deeply rooted in the familial ideology of the New Right and the 'moral majority' and in the hate politics of religious fundamentalism:

Dear Family Member,

Since AIDS is transmitted primarily by perverse homosexuals, your name on my national petition to quarantine all homosexual establish-ments is crucial to your family's health and security ... Only your contribution can help us protect Americans from the 'Gay Plague' and its perverted carriers.
(American Family Association c.1983, quoted in Patton 1985a: 85)

From this discursive association of AIDS with homosexuality comes a new meaning for heterosexuality: 'not at risk from AIDS'. Thus, as further groups became visible among those with clinical manifestations of the syndrome, they joined the ever-widening ranks of the 'not-properly-heterosexual', in what Cindy Patton has aptly termed 'the queer paradigm' (Patton 1985b). Within this informal paradigm, ideas about normality and deviance, although still including specific sexual behaviours, take on a new set of mean-ings proliferating around this highly specific AIDS infection binary: 'at-risk' and 'not-at-risk'. Thus 'heterosexual' becomes somewhat detached from its usual moorings in 'properly' gendered erotic behaviours and a range of deviant behaviours – such as the use of injected street drugs – becomes 'queered'.

This unmooring of heterosexuality is paralleled in oppositional AIDS dis-course by Patton's alternative binary. By summarising safe-sex advice as 'Don't get semen in your anus or vagina', Patton proposes a subdivision of sexually active people into those who take semen into their bodies and those who don't. Whatever your gender or sexual 'identity', you belong either to the 'safes' or the 'unsafes'. Patton's model, ignoring/negating as it does pre-existing categories of male/female, queer/straight, effectively queers the entire field of the erotic.[5]

It is not only within AIDS discourse that heterobinarism has been dis-rupted. Luce Irigary's influential notion of 'hom(m)osexuality' indicates that sexuality, whether gay, lesbian or hetero-, may be organised (and generally is organised) in the interests of men (Irigary 1974). Eve Kosofky Sedgwick (1985) introduces the notion of male homosociality as the shaping force of Anglo culture and co-opts the idea of the closet (Sedgwick 1990) to refer to wider notions of hiddenness and revelation, turning it into 'the primary struc-tural relation of knowledge/ignorance' (Crimp 1991) and asserting that 'modern cognition itself hinges on the hetero/homo impasse' (Koestenbaum 1991). From a different angle some lesbian writers (for example, Rich 1980; Faderman 1981; Onlywomen Press 1981) have, by replacing women's desire for women with 'woman-identification' in their definition of 'lesbian', sought to claim as lesbian women whose sexual orientation is heterosexual. This strategy neatly queers all feminists, and constructs an oppositional polarity: lesbian = feminist, heterosexual = non-feminist. The radical implication of this is, of course, that biological males may claim that they are women-identified feminists and therefore lesbians. This is just what some genetic males are choosing to do, sometimes – though not always – through surgical castration (Stone 1991; Zita 1992; Bornstein 1994a). To object to their doing so is to take strategic refuge in essentialism (whether biological, sociological or psychological), a logically untenable position within the political lesbianism paradigm. This supposedly radical detachment of 'lesbian' from bodily desires and acts has clearly not succeeded in disentangling itself from the determinism which so saturates heteropatriarchal discourse.

Buying into heterobinarism: revolutionary feminist 'heterosexuality'

Radical/revolutionary feminists such as Charlotte Bunch, Catharine MacKinnon and Sheila Jeffreys have developed a peculiar form of determinism whereby gender is seen as originating in and intrinsically reproductive of *sexual* (here meaning erotic) regimes of subordination. Judith Butler sums up this erotic-determinist position thus: 'In theories such as Catharine MacKinnon's, sexual relations of subordination are understood to establish differential gender categories, such that "men" are those defined in a sexually dominating social position, and "women" are those defined in subordination' (Butler 1993a: 27).

The implications of this construct are that gender – as a product of relations of erotic subordination – floats free of biological sex, signifying not genital difference but rather a polarity of sexual/social dominance and subordination. Furthermore heterosexuality itself has been constituted within this strand of radical feminist discourse as a free-floating sign, signifying not relations characterised by gender disparity but relations characterised by 'eroticised inequality' (see Jeffreys 1990 and this volume). Heterosexuality is *embedded in the erotic* in contrast to 'lesbian', which purportedly transcends it. In other words, women may call themselves lesbian if they have (a) the right kind of sex with women or (b) no sex at all with women or men, but the correct politics. If they (a) consent willingly to any kind of sex with men,[6] (b) have no sex at all but the wrong kind of politics, (c) have the right kind of sex with women but the wrong kind of politics or (d) have the wrong kind of sex with women, they are heterosexual.

From this position lesbian (and gay) sexual relationships and behaviours may be 'heterosexual' (Jeffreys 1990) or may reproduce heterosexual masculinity and femininity (Jeffreys, this volume), not only through the putatively 'transparent' heterosexualisation (seemingly) intrinsic to transsexual/transgender surgery, but through behaviours and rituals characteristic of (urban, first world) queer communities such as drag, camp and S/M or butch/femme role play. Detaching heterosexuality from its embeddedness in the presumptive polarity between sexed/gendered bodies enables it to be re-situated as a property of queer couplings: 'Heterosexual desire is eroticised power difference. Heterosexual desire originates in the power relationship between men and women, but it can also be experienced in same sex relationships' (Jeffreys 1990: 301). If heterosexual desire is understood in its common-sense meaning as the erotic desire of men for women and of women for men, clearly it is nonsense to assert that it may be 'experienced in same-sex relationships' (unless as a desire for different-sex individuals outside the relationship). Nor does Jeffreys's own definition of heterosexual desire as 'eroticised power difference' necessarily enable her to claim that it may be present in same-sex relationships. To claim that heterosexual desire is eroti-cised power difference is not at all the same thing as claiming that eroticised power difference is, therefore, heterosexual desire. Boxing may be ritualised male violence, that does not mean that any and all kinds of ritualised male violence are boxing.

It will be objected by some that I am engaging in pointless semantic game-playing here, but this elision is important, for it is what enables Jeffreys to make use of the 'charge' of heterosexuality against women who identify as lesbians. It also enables a whole range of sexual behaviours to be collapsed together under the sign of the heterosexual,[7] a device that gives rise to a mis-chievous and tendentious intervention in the project of lesbian feminism.

> Once the eroticising of otherness and power difference is learned, then in a same-sex relationship, where another gender is absent, otherness can be reintroduced through differences in age, race, class, the practice of sadomasochism or role playing. So it is possible to construct hetero-sexual desire within lesbianism and heterosexual desire is plentifully evident in the practice of gay men. The opposite of heterosexual desire is the eroticising of sameness, a sameness of power, equality and mutu-ality. It is homosexual desire.
>
> (Jeffreys 1990: 301)

Jeffreys does in some sense have etymology on her side. While the generally accepted meaning of the words 'heterosexual' and 'homosexual' – and the reason they were coined in the first place – takes 'same' and 'different' to refer to biological sex, choosing alternative markers of difference does not necessarily do overmuch violence to semantic intelligibility. Yet there are major problems with her analysis. The first is highlighted by her cynical exploitation of 'age, race, class' as simple and, by implication, comparable, markers of difference. Age, 'race' and class are not comparable either in their effects on individuals or in their social effects within lesbian communities. By reducing her critique to the narrow arena of what people with certain genitals do to get sexual pleasure, Jeffreys reduces racism, ageism and class oppression to the status of sex toys. And this, of course, is what she is doing with gender. A penis penetrating a vagina has, *per se*, no political or symbolic significance. It is the material, cultural, social and ideological apparatus of heteropatriarchy which gives it its meaning. Men's power over women is both expressed in and maintained by their sexual access to women's bodies (Wilton 1992; Frye 1993). It does not *consist in* that access.

Similarly, white supremacy is maintained by and expressed in white men's assumption of sexual access to the bodies of black women *and* the use of the racist construct of the hypersexualised black woman to support the racist construct of the sexually pure and cold white woman. Both constructs are at the same time racist, sexist and heterosexist (there are class issues too). It is both intellectually/politically naïve and offensive to reduce this complexity to a simple question of eroticised difference.

The second set of problems with this disengagement of 'heterosexual' from gendered or sexual bodies is strategic. The choice of an alternative/oppositional set of markers of difference makes of the words themselves strategic political instruments. If 'heterosexual' is assigned a primarily *political* meaning in this way (i.e. if it is used to mean 'involving relations of dominance and submission') rather than the generally accepted meaning, this introduces a level of opacity which may hinder rather than help the struggle to expose the already strategic/political nature of the word. It may also reinforce the very heteropatriarchal construct of gender which lesbian feminism critiques, and, moreover, may collude with the lesbian oppression spawned by that construct. It is this point that I wish to discuss next.

Shooting feminism in the foot?

If feminists believe it is important to expose the instrumentality of the heterosexual imperative in women's material and ideological oppression (and I for one most certainly do), heterosexuality must be stripped of the invisibility attendant on its status as hegemonic norm (Wilton 1993, 1994). To do this, we need to write the 'heterosexual' into statements such as: 'Women are an integral part of man's leisure' (Griffin, quoted in Wilton 1993a: 172), or 'At a time when women are heavily dependent, both emotionally and economically, on their partners, they can place a relatively low premium on *his* active involvement in childcare and housework' (Graham 1993: 100; added emphasis) or 'Black women see their unpaid domestic work more as a form of resistance to oppression than as a form of exploitation by men' (Collins 1990: 44). By writing in 'heterosexual' to such texts (and these are all feminist examples), it becomes possible to assess the significant role that relating intimately/sexually to men plays in women's oppression. It also makes visible the erased alternatives: spinsterhood, celibacy, lesbianism. Lesbians are not an 'integral part of men's leisure' in the way that non-lesbian women[8] are, so something else *is* possible. It is likely that the division of domestic labour/childcare in lesbian couples is unlike that of heterosexual couples, so something else *is* possible (Blumstein and Schwartz 1983; Caldwell and Peplan 1984). And what light does it throw on the interaction between racism and heterosexism when we ask what black lesbians feel about their unpaid labour?

It is for reasons such as these that the visibility of heterosexuality and of a lesbian alternative are crucially important to feminist struggle. However, in order to make the workings of heterosexuality visible, we have to be able to name it. Naming it tends to denaturalise it (the power of the heterosexual imperative largely rests on its self-ascribed 'natural' status) and, in the words of Gill Dunne, exposes 'the arbitrary nature of gender-specific experiences and patterns of living' (Dunne 1992: 86), which the naturalisation of heterosexuality conceals.

Clearly, if it is to remain strategically useful in such contexts, 'heterosexual' must retain its gendered meaning. It would be almost impossible to identify the centrality of heterosexuality – meaning precisely the imperative to relate sexually to men – in women's oppression if 'heterosexual' were a sign that floated free of its historical attachment to gender/sex. To speak of 'a heterosexual imperative' or of 'compulsory heterosexuality' in the sense of an eroticised relation of dominance *unattached* to gender is not to eradicate gendered inequality, but rather to collude in the invisibility that protects it. As such, detaching heterosexuality from gender difference is counterproductive, a self-imposed hindrance to feminist theory and activism.

The revolutionary feminist prick – being a good 'bad' girl

There has been a 'four legs good, two legs bad' tendency within certain strands of radical feminism insisting that to be a good feminist one must be a good lesbian.[9] Ever since Charlotte Bunch declared that 'Lesbianism threatens male supremacy at its core' (Bunch, quoted in d'Emilio and Freedman 1988: 317), heterosexuality has been seen by some to disqualify women as feminists. Thus, in a now famous paper, the Leeds Revolutionary Feminists stated that 'serious feminists have no choice but to abandon heterosexuality' and that 'Men are the enemy. Heterosexual women are collaborators with the enemy' (Onlywomen Press 1981: 5 and 7). In the US, the CLIT Collective excluded heterosexuals from the category 'women' altogether:

> Dykes don't know any humans. They know men and they know women. Straight women are not what dykes call women and therefore [we] do not lust after them as straight women like to think. Straight women think, talk, act, cross their legs, dress and come-on like male transvestite female drag queens.

> (CLIT Collective 1974: 362)

To be a heterosexual woman in this discourse is to be cast out of feminism as a traitor and to be cast out of womanhood as a man (albeit one masquerading as a woman). Additionally, even to experience heterosexual desire is to be implicated in something which feminism is dedicated to destroying, and hence to be at risk from feminism itself, for 'The demolition of heterosexual desire is a necessary step on the route to women's liberation' (Jeffreys 1990: 312).

Within this strand of revolutionary feminist discourse, 'heterosexual' operates as a stigmatising label carrying the threat of punishment – exclusion from the political struggle and comradeship of women, eventual destruction by feminism – much as 'lesbian' does within heteropatriarchal discourse (Rich 1980). Such stigmatising labels are far from being simple descriptive terms, rather they represent efforts to control the behaviour of both labelled and not-labelled alike, and to do this through fear and/or guilt. As such, they affect lesbian women far more powerfully than non-lesbian women. There can be no doubting the damage caused to some non-lesbian feminists by this opportunistic labelling. Defensiveness, hurt and a deep suspicion of radical feminism continue to characterise the approach of many non-lesbian women to the subject of sexuality (for example, see essays in Wilkinson and Kitzinger 1993). But non-lesbian women are located (willy-nilly) within a structure that gives them access to male protection and heterosexual privilege.[10] Despite what the recent vogue for lesbian chic might suggest to the naïve, lesbian women are in a far more beleaguered and vulnerable position. Survival, in the teeth of widespread and entrenched hostility against lesbians, is difficult without access to what June Arnold evocatively calls 'the safe sea of women' (quoted in Zimmerman 1992). Inclusion in a feminist peer group is therefore likely to be more important to lesbian than to non-lesbian feminists, simply in terms of social support, and hence the threat of being labelled 'heterosexual' is concomittantly greater.

Additionally, the accusation of lesbian heterosexuality is most generally predicated upon specific sexual desires and practices (see Jeffreys, this volume), and it is precisely by our sexual desires and practices that we gain access to the name 'lesbian' in the first place. The performative ritualisation of some sexual practices (butch/femme, S/M, piercing, gender-fuck, etc.) is also an important social glue in certain lesbian, queer or lesbian-and-gay communities, as has long been the case (Nestle 1987, 1992). Such practices may be experienced by many lesbians as foundational of their lesbian status, identity or desire; to stigmatise them as heterosexual is profoundly disrespectful. This fundamental lack of respect for specific lesbian desires, acts or identities can make feminism appear hostile to many lesbians, while the relative openness of the lesbian and gay movement and the new queer activism appears far more inclusive of lesbian diversity. This can mean that, for some lesbians, there is an apparent need to chose between gender (privileged by feminism) and sexuality (privileged by queer) as the organising principle of their subjectivity and their resistance.

It is also the case, and this has been politically disastrous, that this attempt to eradicate the taint of heterosexuality from lesbian sexuality has been done in the name of feminism. This has foregrounded a particular kind of radical feminism saturated with readings of the erotic that insist on discipline and restraint rather than empowerment and autonomy as the necessary components of women's sexual pleasure. It has been a gift to commentators (and they include people of all genders and sexual preferences) seeking to discredit radical feminism.

Being a nice dyke for daddy

The political lesbian ideal of eroticised mutuality resonates problematically with the dismissive heteropatriarchal construct of lesbian sex as non-phallic and hence not 'real' sex. New Right romantic (presumably heterosexual) philosopher Roger Scruton imagines lesbian sex thus: 'there is an extremely poignant, often helpless, sense of being at another's mercy . . . she can only wait, and wish, and pray to the gods, with . . . troubled fervour' (Scruton 1986: 308). This paranoid Disneyesque fantasy is uncomfortably echoed in the words of left-wing gay AIDS commentator Simon Watney, who dismissively characterises lesbian feminist sex as a 'technicolour feminist Shangri-La, all tender, feeling, oceanic, tranquil – and deathlike' (Watney 1987: 74).

Once more there seems to be a disturbing parallel between revolutionary feminist ideal and what the boys want lesbians to be. With revolutionary feminists seeming to advocate precisely the kind of lesbian sex least disruptive of patriarchal erotic/gender regulation[11] and most pleasing to straight men like Scruton, and insisting moreover that it is not necessary to desire or have sex with women to call yourself a lesbian (Leeds Revolutionary Feminist Group 1979) nor to desire or have sex with men to be labelled heterosexual (Jeffreys 1990), it is unsurprising that many lesbians wrote feminism off as yet another factor in lesbian oppression:

> The attraction of queer for some lesbians is flavoured by a rebellion against a prescriptive feminism that had led them to feel disenfranchised by the lesbian feminist movement. There was a feeling that the importance of identifying politically as a lesbian had obscured lesbianism as a sexual identity. 'Acceptable' ideas of lesbian sexuality and desire were constructed around notions of sameness and a desexed androgyny, and anyone who disagreed with the 'right on' line, regardless of her sexual practice, would be dismissed at best as an SM dyke, and at worst as a fascist.[12]
>
> (Smyth 1992: 26)

Confronted with the heteropolar interpenetration of gender and the erotic, the revolutionary feminist strategy has been to detach heterosexuality from gendered/sexed bodies, and to detach lesbianism from desire and sexual activity and to associate it with a political position. This has some theoretical usefulness, in that it denaturalises both, and offers a position eccentric to heteropatriarchal discourse from which to read and speak about gender and sexuality. However, the elision of 'lesbian' with 'feminist' which developed historically from this theoretical position is flawed by a classic catch-22. Although becoming a lesbian is seen as a feminist act, there is no guarantee that becoming a lesbian will mean that you are no longer heterosexual, since certain relationships are instrinsically heterosexual regardless of the gender of the people concerned. This means, logically, that it must be possible for a relationship between a man and a woman to be a homosexual relationship, or at least, be founded on homosexual desire – although Jeffreys deals with this point somewhat inadequately in *Anticlimax* by saying that such a relationship is 'difficult to imagine' (Jeffreys 1990: 316).

Ironically, this revolutionary feminist tactic may itself be read as heterosexual, according to its own logic. Control, mastery, dominance, the imperative (and the power) to name and exclude the 'other', are the definitional prerogatives of male power. To take upon oneself the right to name 'proper' behaviour – perhaps especially behaviour proper to sex role or gender role – is, in Lacanian terms, to seize control of the symbolic order, to claim the phallus (Lacan and L'Ecole Freudienne 1982). Within the terms of feminism – a movement whose resistance to patriarchal structures and norms has traditionally been indicated by its commitment to giving women a voice and taking seriously what they have to say – presuming to judge another woman to be not a proper feminist, not a proper woman or not a proper lesbian smacks of patriarchal behaviour. This point has been made by several critics of the Leeds Revolutionary Feminist paper (Onlywomen Press 1981). As Christine Delphy insists, 'one needs to be a nominalist in political matters. Feminists are those who call themselves feminists. It is not up to me, or anyone else, to award or withold the term as if it were a title' (Delphy 1994: 18).[13]

To make use of an ungendered set of meanings for heterosexuality in an attempt to establish lesbian sexuality as a bridgehead of radical feminism has been, I believe, counterproductive. The result has probably been to make both lesbian and non-lesbian women less likely, rather than more likely, to call themselves feminists. I am also deeply uncomfortable with the disciplinary imperative manifest in this strategy, which seems to me more akin to classic fascism than radical feminism. But revolutionary lesbian feminists have not been alone in the deconstructive project.

Straight straits and queer straights

The interlocutions between discourses of gender and the erotic manifest a complexity which I suggest indicates that they may not usefully be distinguished one from the other. At the most straightforward, as Butler points out;

> Sexual practices . . . will invariably be experienced differently depending on the relations of gender in which they occur. And there may be forms of 'gender' within homosexuality which call for a theorization that moves beyond categories of 'masculine' and 'feminine'. If we seek to privilege sexual practice as a way of transcending gender, we might ask, at what cost is the *analytic* separability of the two domains taken to be distinction in fact?
>
> (Butler 1993b: 27)

Since both queer activists and some revolutionary and radical feminists (Jeffreys 1990; Penelope 1992) seek precisely to 'privilege sexual practice as a way of transcending gender' – the one by performative erotic strategies such as gender-fuck, packing dildos and doing drag, the other by eroticising mutuality – Butler's caveat is apposite. She suggests that 'it seems crucial to retain a theoretical apparatus that will account for how sexuality is regulated through the policing and shaming of gender' (Butler 1993a: 27), to which queer project must be added the feminist reminder that such an apparatus needs to account as much for how *gender* is regulated through the policing and shaming of sexuality.

Heterosexuality: theories and queeries

I remain convinced that the doctrine and institutions of heteropolarity are oppressive to women. Indeed, women's liberation consists in liberation from heteropolarity as it permeates, structures and is expressed in the material and ideological arenas:

> our survival demands that we contribute all our strength to the destruction of the class of women within which men appropriate women. This can be accomplished only by the destruction of heterosexuality as a social system which is based on the oppression of women by men and which produces the doctrine of the difference between the sexes to justify this oppression.
>
> (Wittig 1992: 108)

Wittig is quite clear that heterosexuality is a *social* system; she is not here restricting her analysis to what people do in bed. However, the word 'heterosexuality', by reason both of semantics and of usage, inevitably tends to reference the erotic, and hence risks a reading which (perhaps in some cases wilfully) reduces oppression to the level of the erotic and identifies sexual activity between men and women as the cornerstone of women's oppression. I suggest that we speak instead of heteropolarity. Although it resists being reduced to the erotic, heteropolarity saturates and structures the social fields of gender and the erotic, and renders them indivisible. Heteropolarity is intrinsic to women's oppression and eradicating it must be a central part of the feminist project.

It is in Queer Theory that the signs, practices and instititions of gender and the erotic have been most vigorously/rigorously shaken and stirred, and it is under the sign 'lesbian' that the most vociferous and richly productive chaos is to be found. Eve Kosofsky Sedgwick aptly summarises the general assumption among Queer theorists that Queer is taking the insights of feminism a stage further by privileging the erotic rather than gender, and suggests that the intrinsic gendercentricity of feminist thought renders it in the end obsolete: 'It is unrealistic to expect a close, textured analysis of same-sex relations through an optic calibrated in the first place to the coarser stigmata of gender difference' (Sedgwick 1990: 32). For Sedgwick gendercentricity is, by definition, heterocentricity, and hence, she suggests, 'It may be . . . that a damaging bias towards heterosocial or heterosexist assumptions adheres unavoidably in the very concept of gender' (p. 31). Butler goes further, suggesting that feminist discourse by definition (in both senses of the phrase) ends by undermining its own emancipatory project: 'Foucault points out that juridical systems of power *produce* the subjects they subsequently come to represent . . . And the feminist subject turns out to be discursively constituted by the very political system that is supposed to facilitate its emancipation' (Butler 1990a: 2).

The very foundation of feminism as a political and theoretical intervention has its roots in this troubling paradox. Indeed, unless we can instigate a transformational paradigm shift, feminism appears already anachronistic. I would (tentatively!) suggest that Queer Theory offers at least the possibility of such a transformation. As one of the originators of Queer Theory – a paradigm privileging the homo/hetero divide rather than the male/female divide as its organising principle – Sedgwick's work proposes that 'many of the major nodes of thought and knowledge in twentieth-century Western culture as a whole are structured – indeed, fractured – by a chronic, now endemic crisis of homo/heterosexual definition, indicatively male, dating from the end of the nineteenth century' (Sedgwick 1990: 1).

Sedgwick calls herself a feminist, and has produced what one commentator refers to as 'feminist gay male theory' (Plummer 1992). She explicitly acknowledges feminist thinking as her starting point, specifically its detachment of gender from chromosomal/biological sex. She writes of the 'great heuristic leap of feminism . . . the recognition that categories of gender and, hence, oppressions of gender can have a structuring force for nodes of thought, for axes of cultural discrimination, whose thematic subject isn't explicitly gendered at all' (Sedgwick 1990: 34). Her conclusion – that gender and the erotic are distinct – is not one I agree with, but in her hands it offers a powerful theoretical tool for dismantling the institutional practices which legitimate and implement lesbian oppression:

> An essentialism of sexual object-choice is far less easy to maintain, far more visibly incoherent, more visibly stressed and challenged at every point in the culture than any essentialism of gender. This is not an argument for any epistemological or ontological privileging of an axis of sexuality over an axis of gender; but it is a powerful argument for their potential distinctness one from the other.
>
> (p. 34)

Feminists and Queer Theorists (although they are not, of course, discrete sets of people) tend to approach what Rubin (1984) calls the 'sex-gender system' and what I think of as the gender/erotic field[14] from different directions. Feminists tend to privilege gender, and concern themselves with the erotic in so far as it impacts upon relations of gender, while Queer Theorists tend to privilege the erotic and concern themselves with gender in so far as it structures the erotic. One important difference – which may simply be due to the historical fact that feminism pre-dates Queer Theory – is that Queer critics and writers tend to be explicit about their reasons for foregrounding the erotic and to acknowledge the importance of gender, whereas most feminists leave implicit or take for granted their reasons for foregrounding gender and seldom consider the erotic as a possible alternative paradigm. What happens to heterosexuality within this Queer paradigm?

To speak from a lesbian or queer position is to speak from a location eccentric to (cast out from) the heterosexual centre of gravity. 'Being' lesbian or queer makes heterosexuality immediately and directly questionable in a way that being feminist doesn't (necessarily), and it is lesbians, not straight feminists, who have initiated feminist critiques of institutional heterosexuality (Frye 1977; Rich 1980; Wittig 1981; Rubin 1984; Kitzinger & Wilkinson 1993a, 1993b; Wilton 1993a). This makes 'lesbian' a uniquely powerful position from which to speak. Yet a queer position is profoundly limited: 'Queer is and always has been a gay male phenomenon, essentially white and middle class, with sex ("whatever and whoever you want") as the main focus' (Hayes 1994: 15). Lesbians need much more than that.[15] Additionally, it has been suggested (I think rightly) that 'feminist' represents another such powerful position. Both Sue-Ellen Case and Teresa de Lauretis argue that 'feminist' can offer an escape route from the female subject position, constructed by and bound to patriarchal ideology (Case 1993: 295).[16] The position 'lesbian feminist' is unique in that it offers what is currently the only available position from which to critique and resist both the gendered and the erotic imperatives of heteropolarity.

Yet lesbian feminism has historically been perceived as dominated by the question of political lesbianism which, as I have shown, reinforces and strengthens both the institution of gender and male supremacy.[17] Case on the other hand offers a way forward which is positively blasphemous in the context of the kind of revolutionary feminism I have been criticising here:

> Focusing on the feminist subject, endowed with the agency for political change, located among women, outside the ideology of sexual difference, and thus the social institution of heterosexuality, it would appear that the lesbian roles of butch and femme, as a dynamic duo, offers precisely the strong subject position the [feminist] movement requires.
>
> (Case 1993: 195)

Given that the doctrine of heteropolarity proscribes the very idea of female sexual agency, that sexual drive is located in and defined by masculinity, and that heteropolar femininity consists in the 'dissimulation of a fundamental masculinity' (Butler 1990a: 53), butch and femme lesbians do, indeed, offer a most potent challenge to its coherence.

It is essential to deconstruct the gender and erotic fictions of heteropolarity, to disengage notions of strength, weakness, submissiveness and agency from gendered bodies. In order to do that, we must dispense with the essentialism which sees penetration, role play, etc. as inherently heterosexual, i.e. gendered. Although Jeffreys dispenses with one kind of essentialism – that which links sexual identity as homosexual or heterosexual to bodies possessing specific genitals – she replaces it with another kind of essentialism: one which links (specifically erotic) dominance with masculinity and (again, specifically erotic) submission with femininity in a rewrite of heterosexuality. This merely reinscribes, with a docility which is ironic, the hegemonic heteropolar paradigm on to the field of the erotic, and on to the bodies, desires and practices of lesbians who may be said to be engaged in resisting the dominance of that paradigm.

Because of this reinscription of heteropolarity on to resistant sexualities (and because of the confusion it introduces into the political critique of the heterosexual imperative), it is unhelpful to detach the meaning of 'heterosexuality' from its roots in the heteropolar regime of gendered power. The diversity of lesbian sexual desires, practices and identities – rather than representing a backlash or heresy against feminism – may in the long run be instrumental in transforming the paradox at the root of feminist theory.[18] The heterosexualising of lesbian sex is, I suggest, not only profoundly disrespectful and patronising towards lesbians at a personal level, but is both intellectually moribund and politically counterrevolutionary.

Notes

1 In this chapter I use 'queer' to refer to individuals and groups of people who call themselves queer, and to activists in the queer movement. When capitalised, 'Queer', it refers to the elite academic praxis of Queer Theory, exemplified by writers such as Judith Butler and Liz Grosz.

2 'Queer' has been publicly reclaimed by some lesbians and gay men since the late 1980s – although there have always been lesbians and gay men who have been assertive enough to identify themselves as such, as a quick glance at the literature will demonstrate. At the time of writing, its use denotes a non-assimilationist stance which asserts and celebrates queer people's difference from non-queer people, seeing that difference as transgressive of the regulatory norms which restrict not only sexual expression but also *gender* behaviour. Although I reject the 'broad church' approach of queer activism – which holds that any 'deviant' sexual behaviour, from bisexuality to transvestism, is enough to make you queer – I find the unapologetic intransigence implied in calling myself queer a powerful tool for unsettling heterosexual liberalism.

3 I use 'phallocracy' here to refer to the heterosexual world-view organised around the reign of the mythic phallus, that all-powerful imaginary organ of 'masculine' dominance whose potency (and please note the 'masculine' nature of that word!) drives the conceptual machinery of heteropolar culture.

4 That is, the struggle for women's liberation *and* for the liberation of men and transgenderals from the constraits of gender, and the struggle for sexual liberation, that is, freedom of sexual expression.

5 Although, by ignoring the power differential which distinguishes heterosexual women's capacity to prevent semen entering their bodies from gay men's, Patton's queer intervention disempowers women who have sex with men.

6 Clearly rape and other coercive sex acts – such as some forms of prostitution – must be excluded from this analysis.

7 A device, as many readers will no doubt be quick to point out, that parallels the tendency for queer to collapse many varied behaviours under its own sign. See the *Queer Power Now* leaflet cited by Cherry Smyth: 'There are straight queers, bi queers, tranny queers, lez queers, fag queers, S/M queers, fisting queers' (Smyth 1992: 17).

8 I use 'non-lesbian women' to refer to heterosexual and bisexual women, women whose sexual 'identity' incorporates a significant continuing erotic role for men.

9 Not just any old lesbian, of course. Butch/femme lesbians, S/M dykes, lipstick lesbians, lesbian boys and queer dykes are just a few of the 'bad' lesbians excluded from the ranks of 'good feminists'.

10 Although it remains imperative to recognise and acknowledge that this access is differentially structured by power relations of 'race', class, age, etc.

11 Though revolutionary feminists would, of course, claim the opposite: that inequality is necessary to heteropatriarchal sex and that sex from which all inequality has been purged is therefore revolutionary.

12 It is, of course, not only one side which has had the monopoly on put-downs. For example, some 'sex-radical' lesbians or S/M dykes clearly regard 'vanilla' (ie, non-S/M sex) as a put-down, and use it as such.

13 Of course I lay myself open here to the charge that I am appropriating the phallus

in exposing revolutionary feminism as 'not proper feminism'. It is not my intention to do any such thing, but rather to caution, with Audre Lorde, against expecting the master's tools to dismantle the master's house. By naming certain lesbian desires and practices as 'heterosexual', Jeffreys is insisting that they are 'the master's tools'. I think this argument comes from a false premiss and, further, that it is dangerous to lesbians and to feminism. This does not make Jeffreys either 'not-a-proper-feminist' or 'not-a-proper-lesbian', but it does, I suggest, make 'master's tools' out of her argument.

14 'Field' seems to me to be useful because it carries connotations both of electrical charge and discharge (and hence of relations of power and of sexual 'charge') and of a field of war or contest (and hence of struggle, dominance and subordination). I choose 'erotic' over 'sex' because sex carries meanings associated with biology – being of the male or female sex – whereas the erotic is unequivocally to do with desires, pleasures and sexual activities.

15 This is one reason, I suspect, why the majority of 'serious' Queer Theory is produced by women.

16 Both Case and de Lauretis are lesbians as well as feminists.

17 This is why, although I 'am' a lesbian I chose to call myself politically a 'queer feminist'. The baggage of assumptions made about 'lesbian feminists' is something I no longer have the energy to refute, and has led to my work being misrepresented by people who have not even read it (e.g. Gorna 1992: 177).

18 Or it may not. I am not utterly convinced by queer – just certain that transformation is never achieved where dogma has replaced questioning.

9

In the same boat? The gendered (in)experience of first heterosex[1]

Janet Holland, Caroline Ramazanoglu, Rachel Thomson

Q: How was it [with] both of you being virgins? Was it all right the first time? I mean sometimes it's a bit problematic.

A: No, it was funny. I mean you've got to get rid of your embarrassment and you're both in the same boat. You both know, and it's just a laugh isn't it? It's not a . . . I didn't find it like a nerve-racking experience like a lot of people do. I just sort of took it as it comes. If it doesn't work the first time you have another go. You laugh about it.

> (young man, aged 18 at the time of first heterosexual intercourse, white/Asian ethnicity, middle class)

Feminism and heterosexuality

Young people on the brink of heterosexual intercourse are in the same boat in that they have to take the same step from inexperience of intercourse to experience (although not necessarily with an inexperienced partner). In contrast to previous generations, where gendered notions of virginity were institutionally linked to marriage, paternity and the transfer of property over generations, young people are now very generally exposed to pressures to become sexually active, and the age of first intercourse appears to be decreasing.[2] While the acquisition of sexual identities is increasingly detached from moral discourses of purity and sin, responses to the meanings of virginity and its 'loss', and the acquisition of heterosexual identities, continue to be socially gendered and differently embodied for men and for women.[3]

We do not have space here to enter fully into current debates on the nature of heterosexuality, but in this chapter we draw on interview accounts of their sexuality from young women and young men in the Women, Risk and AIDS Project and the Men, Risk and AIDS Project as a contribution to these debates. In analysing the interview accounts, we have taken first hetero-sexual intercourse to be a critically gendered moment in the development of heterosexuality. The young people in our studies told differing stories of becoming sexually experienced and of what rocks the boat, but in this chapter we consider their accounts of their first heterosexual experiences of sexual intercourse as one way of making institutionalised heterosexuality visible.[4]

The moment of 'first sex' is not the only constitutive moment of hetero-sexuality. Becoming heterosexual occurs at differing levels of social activity, from the most grounded meeting of bodies to the most abstracted level of institutionalisation. Sexuality is simultaneously both variable bodily states, desires and physical practices, and also culturally variable understandings of this embodiment and associated identities and social practices. Sexuality is embodied in the sense that it entails bodily activity; there is a physical aspect to sexual desire, gender and reproduction.[5] Heterosexuality is grounded in this bodily sexuality, but it cannot be understood independently of the vari-able beliefs, values, ideologies, discourses, identities and social relationships through which people become socially heterosexual and practice hetero-sexuality. Heterosexuality is lived in distinctive lifestyles (especially those tied to marriage/household arrangements) and in discourses of masculinity/ femininity, normality/abnormality.

Discussions of heterosexuality have generally been absent or constrained within feminism, yet lesbian theorists (for example Butler 1990a, 1993a; Fuss 1990; Stanley 1992, Wilton 1993a) in different ways have made consider-able progress in rendering heterosexuality and its effects visible. These decon-structions of heterosexuality show how far heterosexual women give up their social power to determine their own sexuality, and the extent to which women as well as men actively support and reproduce heterosexual identi-ties, practices and values. When a young woman becomes aware of what it is to be a woman, she is, in Foucault's terms, in the grip of power; the deploy-ment of sexuality requires her to discipline her unruly body, to guard her own reputation, and to police other women (for example by naming 'slags') (Smart 1992; Lees 1993). Adrienne Rich argued that 'compulsory hetero-sexuality' leaves 'numberless women' trapped in the normal (Rich 1983: 165), although 'everywhere women have resisted it' (p. 161). The invisibility of heterosexuality as an institution allows women's absence of choice over their sexuality to go unrecognised so they can be denied the collective power to experience their own needs or determine the meaning and place of sexu-ality in their lives (p. 167).

In this chapter, we make the case that heterosexual 'first sex' is an induc-tion into adult masculinity for young men, within which the woman, whether sexually experienced herself or not, plays an ambiguous role. We are arguing that heterosexuality is not a balanced (or even unbalanced) institutionalis- ation of masculinity-and-femininity, it is masculinity. We take young people's accounts to support our claim that first heterosex is a double construction: the young woman is under pressure first to consent to the constitution of adult heterosexuality as the construction of masculinity, and then to fit herself to this construction. Within this construction of masculinity, young women must find ways of existing and making sense of themselves and their 'otherness'. Sexual intercourse with men becomes something for them to manage as best they can. This construction of adult heterosexuality as mas- culinity offers within it limiting identities of both masculinity and feminin- ity. Femininity is constructed from within heterosexuality and on male territory, yet this territory can only exist with female consent and collusion.

It is not difficult to document the gendering of 'normal sexuality' from young people's accounts of their first sexual experiences. First intercourse is generally a consciously critical moment for young people whether they are actively seeking sexual intercourse, allowing the intercourse to happen, or having it thrust upon them.[6] But, we argue here, it is also part of a much more general, and less visible, process of induction into the dominance of masculine norms and meanings as 'natural'. Significantly, most young women arrive at their first experience of heterosexual intercourse already constituted as 'woman'. From the moment that puberty is marked by first menstruation, they are conscious of what it means to be a woman and the attendant requirements to discipline their bodily unruliness (Prendergast 1995; see also Martin 1987). Yet for young men in most Western cultures, puberty has no such exact marker, and 'first sex' is the key act by which they become a man. As a result, their sexual agency is expressed through 'doing' rather than 'being'.

The question of sexual agency has important implications for the possi- bilities of female sexual pleasure and the gendering of its expression. Decon- structing heterosexuality to show its masculine face exposes not only the exclusion and silencing of lesbians, but also the absence of a positive hetero- sexual femininity. Lucy Bland (1994), in discussing the journal *The Free- woman*, shows the tensions raised by nineteenth-century and early twentieth- century feminists in their attempts to talk about sexuality and to claim the right to *be sexual*. 'I would suggest that the exploration of sex as something other than simply physical and reproductive was easier before the *fixing* in popular speech of "sex" as "sexual intercourse" (and "sexual intercourse" as "penetration"' (p. 4). The terms 'homosexuality' and 'heterosexuality' only entered the English language in 1869, and Bland documents a 'brief moment in which a space was opened up for feminists to discuss sex, or rather heterosexuality' (p. 8).

Young people in our studies recognised a range of activities as sexual, but also showed how tightly the space for discussion of sexuality has been closed.

'Proper sex' was widely defined as a specific version of heterosexual intercourse in which the man's penis penetrates the woman's vagina; it starts with his arousal and finishes with his climax. 'First sex' in this embodied but fragmented guise is the young man's moment. There is no equivalent definition of the 'sex act' in terms of female agency, action or desire; her orgasm is his production. This is shown by the absence in public discourses of sexuality of positive conceptions of active female sexuality, positive female desire or performance; an absence that clearly characterised most of our interviews with young women (Holland *et al.* 1992b). The female heterosexual subject is absent – except as the feminine object of men's desire, the sexual deviant or the sexless mother (see also Bland 1994; Jackson 1994; Jackson 1996; Smart 1996). This lack of female heterosexual identity, and the often stressful contradictions between feminist and heterosexual identities, is explored in Wilkinson and Kitzinger (1993, 1994).

Our findings, together with those from other studies, suggest that the cultural values and social practices of heterosexuality today still divert much of young women's agency, energy and identity towards meeting men's 'needs'.[7] Feminism challenges institutionalised and internalised heterosexuality by making it visible as a social production that rules out the possibility of female power/autonomy and so women's right to be sexual. Gillian Rose has commented that feminism has then focused on women's disempowerment: 'A woman needs to be a Lover and by that I mean something creative, very strong ... feminism never offered me any help, for it fails to address the power of women as well as their powerlessness' (Williams and Rose 1995: 15). We have argued elsewhere (Holland *et al.* 1992a, 1992b, 1996b) that heterosexuality cannot be understood without identifying both female power/empowerment and the social processes which work against it. There is no public language of independent femininity (nor of the imagination and erotic and spiritual ingenuity that Gillian Rose (Williams and Rose 1995: 15) calls for) outside the insubordinate discourses of feminism.

In this chapter, we suggest that the subordination of female sexual agency can be identified at the moment of first heterosexual intercourse. Yet the salvaging of such agency is not merely a question of resistance. Young women are not simply victims of heterosexuality, but the moment of 'first sex' is currently constructed in such a way that much resistance can safely be accommodated. Young people arrive at the moment of 'first sex' in ways that mean the subsequent division of sexual labour into her 'being' and his 'doing' appears inevitable.

How was it for him?

In the Men, Risk and AIDS Project, young men's interview accounts of 'first sex' were predominantly positive. Although a number of them reported anxiety, apprehension or nervousness, these feelings were related to concerns about the adequacy of their own performance. First intercourse for young men was a challenge that could threaten their successful achievement of manhood. Their potency was at stake, they did not necessarily know what to do with their bodies, and there was a good deal of concern about doing it right. But in these positive accounts, the main point was to *do* it – a masculine performance in which they were the star player. This element of performance was clearly recognised by young women:

A: And I suppose he must have been on a right high, you know, just, you know, broke someone's virginity – a sixteen year old girl.
> (young woman, aged 19, ESW,[8] working class)

The issue of 'how was it for her?' is largely irrelevant to the young men's accounts, unless they are actively subverting 'normal' masculinity. Their inexperience as adult males was rectified by the act of intercourse, and this in itself constituted pleasure:

A: Yeah, it was quite a good experience. I thought I'd done alright, like – never doing it before. I was quite pleased really.
> (young man, aged 18, ESW, working class)

A: I mean it's the old saying, 'you enter the bed a boy and you leave it a man' or words to that effect. I felt the same, I didn't alter physically, but I felt different after that first time. I did definitely feel different.
> (young man, aged 19, ESW, working class)

We discuss in the next section the lack of any comparable meanings in the young women's accounts of their first experiences of intercourse. The absence of female pleasure, of Gillian Rose's strong and creative Lover, is marked in the following excerpt:

A: We had both had a bit too much to drink and we ended up in bed. As far as I know she never regretted it. I definitely didn't regret it . . . I didn't have a clue, just did not have a clue, and just sort of went in and hoped for the best.
Q: How was it?
A: Oh I enjoyed it, I thought it was great.
Q: What about her, do you think she enjoyed it?
A: Yes, she seemed to enjoy it, from what I can remember of it. I had a bit too much to drink. So as far as I know, she enjoyed it. She never complained afterwards, and she never complained subsequent times afterwards. But whether she was thinking of my feelings, or whether she genuinely enjoyed it, I don't know. I never really asked.
> (young man, aged 19, ESW, working class)

In this young man's account, what is much more significant than his girl-friend's experience is his own transition to manhood that can be told to others. 'First sex' experiences are not only happening in private, they are also performances in a peer group – events that are made meaningful by talking about them. It is in this talk, and its constitution of gendered sexual reputations, that heterosexuality is reproduced and social meanings attributed in ways that are difficult to escape (Holland *et al.* 1996b). This is particularly marked in the case of young men who became sexually active as young teenagers:

> A: At the time I was thinking, if only my mates could see me now, and stuff like that, and I must admit I didn't really think of the girl at the time.
>> (young man, aged 16, African Caribbean, working class, first intercourse at 16)

> A: It hasn't been pleasurable all the time, but like it was more like if I worked my heart out – oh, my God. Like the first time I was like saying, 'Oh, God, yes! Now I've got something to chat about. Yes! Yes!' sort of thing like that. 'Yes,' I was saying to myself, 'now I am a man, I'm a man', sort of thing.
>> (young man, aged 16, African Caribbean, working class, first intercourse when just 15)

If a young man can produce apparent pleasure in his partner, this is the icing on the cake, and confirms his own performance as a positive one:

> A: I didn't really know what to expect – but it went quite well. And sort of what made it really nice was afterwards she –
> Q: Yeah? [laughs]
> A: My ego just went WHOOMPH, you know.
>> (young man, aged 18, ESW, middle class)

Some young men were more reluctant to define their first experiences in terms of achievement of manhood, especially if they later regretted not having their first experience with someone they loved, but they still framed the experience in a conception of performance:

> A: It was in the back of a friend's car, it was so tacky. We went to a club to meet some girls, and we met them and that was that really. [later in the interview] It was big deal, I remember feeling 'Wow!' afterwards, but it wasn't really a good deal – it wasn't 'I'm in love!' or whatever.
>> (young man, aged 17, 'other' ethnicity, middle class)

A few men explicitly denied that for them first intercourse was an induction into manhood, but they still showed awareness of a rite of passage, and felt they had missed it, or avoided it. The following young man described being unexpectedly 'dragged off into the bedroom' by an unhappy, sexually experienced girl, because he resembled her ex-boyfriend:

> *A:* It wasn't something I really thought was a sort of major crossroads in my life or anything. 'Now I have lost my virginity. Now I am a man', sort of thing.
>
> (young man, aged 20, ESW, middle class)

But he commented that he 'thought it a good idea at the time'.

These accounts are characterised by an awareness of intercourse as performance that is completely missing from the young women's interviews. There is a marked sense of agency in the young men's reflections on their performance, and their accounts are also more embodied than those of the young women. Embodiment was explicit in anxieties about getting and maintaining an erection and reaching orgasm during penetration, when nervous and unsure of themselves. The young men obliquely defined the power of the female partner as a threat to their performance of masculinity in three main ways: she could refuse his advances, 'I thought God, she's going to say, "forget it!"'; she could be more knowing than the man, through prior experience or, most threateningly, she could ridicule and publicise his failure to perform as expected:

> *Q:* Did you feel confident?
> *A:* No, I felt bloody nervous. I thought, what if I don't get a hard-on? It all goes to pot.
>
> (young man, aged 19, ESW, working class)

> *Q:* Is there a sort of feeling do you think amongst men to think they have to be good at sex?
> *A:* I think so, yes, especially if you have seen the girl about and stuff like that, and like you know she is going to open her mouth to everyone else if you are not good, so yes, you have to perform quite well, if you know the girl like, and you have seen her about.
>
> (young man, aged 16, African Caribbean, working class)

Yet this threat is not sourced in the female sexual partner, nor in a critical femininity, but in the male peer group, the men's world that he is entering through this initiation. This sense of threat made young men very reluctant to explore women's pleasure. They did not usually know how to access it, except through their own bravura performance, and any expression of lack of pleasure on the woman's part could undermine the man's achievement. The important thing for a young man was to do it right, and hope the woman, or other women, would come back for more.

There are some similarities between the accounts of young men and young women in terms of a mismatch between expectations and reality, particularly if men's first experience of intercourse was with an older, or a more experienced woman; but there are also some significant differences. Sex is still something that they do to women, and so their sense of agency is strong, and success is judged by how well they think they have performed. A young man who reported being seduced at the age of fourteen by an older woman commented:

> A: I mean, it was a bit disappointing actually. Because I mean there are a lot of boys who spend so much time thinking about sex that they build it up to be this incredible thing, and the first time you're so inexperienced that it's not very good, or at least not as good as you expected it to be.
>
> (young man, aged 19, 'other' ethnicity, middle class)

Young men, like young women, talk of losing their virginity. What they lose is not the intact, material hymen, but their own inexperience, in their achievement of an appropriately situated climax. Sex, in this sense, is what a woman gives to, or allows a man. Significantly, this moment of dominance is achieved by the man losing his bodily control, something which the woman is not allowed, which she has been trained to discipline.

The constitution of the moment of first heterosex as a moment of agency and achievement for the young man can be partly explained by what leads to it. There were some differences here in how first intercourse came about. In some of their accounts of relationships with women, young men reported first intercourse being achieved through a war of attrition in which he progressively worked towards sexual access, leaving the young woman with little space other than to say yes or no:

> A: So anyway, we sat up until about two o'clock, we were in the launderette, I managed to persuade her to have sex.
> Q: I mean how did you persuade her? How did that work?
> A: It was very grinding. I had to grind her down, 'Come on now, you know you want it, go on.' Eventually I pissed her off so much she said yes.
> Q: What to shut you up?
> A: Yes. But anyways she said, 'Right, condoms.' I runs over to the toilets, she says, 'God, you're eager.' She said, 'When was the last time you had it?' I said I hadn't. She went 'Oh, no!' like this. I thought, God, she's going to say 'forget it!'. We got back to the launderette, did it in the launderette.
>
> (young man, aged 19, ESW, working class)

In this approach to male achievement, women are explicitly targeted to meet a male 'need', and female resistance is not only expected but may be a prerequisite of his agency. One young man described how he had felt himself under pressure to put pressure on a girl in order to initiate himself into manhood. When he was 16 he asked a girl he had known for a while if she would have sex with him, and to his surprise she accepted. He felt nervous and guilty:

Q: You said you were guilty. Why do you think you shouldn't have done it?

A: I mean seeing as we were such good friends, right, I don't think I should have gone on doing that. So, when I had finished doing it, I was kind of – I think I did plead to her, you know, it was wrong and so on, and I think she did admit. But I think she didn't really need to have it, you know, and she kind of forced me to do that. She didn't force me, but she said, 'yes, right', you know, 'go ahead', but if she had said, 'no', I would have left it at that, forget about that.

(young man, aged 19, African, working class)

This young man's reflections on his experience entangle his sense of the dangers of sexuality, the impropriety of the woman not putting up any resistance to his proposition, and yet the lack of her own 'need to have it'. 'It' was what he did to her that has changed his own status. The woman figures here as someone who has failed to exercise control over him.

Another man discounted a young woman's claims to virginity on the basis of her unseemly lack of resistance:

Q: Was it her first time?

A: She said it was but I – I don't know whether it was or not. Because like it was too quick like for her like, for a girl to say it was, like in a couple of hours. It would have been more if like she was a virgin, so I reckon she wasn't.

(young man, aged 18, ESW, working class)

In young men's accounts of first experiences of intercourse, there were examples where the construction of male and female as respectively active and passive was absent. Significantly, these examples arose where, whether through circumstance or endeavour, the definition of what constituted 'first sex' was broad enough to dissipate anxieties about male performance. Usually these were couples in an established relationship who felt able to communicate with each other about the timing of sexual intercourse, to negotiate the experience openly and so to offer some resistance to conventions of masculinity and femininity.

A young man who did not have intercourse until he was 18 commented that this had left an unresolved tension in his relationships, but that it was useful in terms of what he was able to learn about sex before embarking on intercourse:

A: When you do go out with someone you are not having sex with you happen to learn a great deal about the workings of the female body which I think has helped me a great deal. I think other than just blindly closing your eyes and having sex, I just couldn't do that, so I actually learned a great deal about what a woman enjoys and wants to get out of sexual things in general.

(young man, aged 19, ESW, working class)

Another commented on his first experience being both good and bad – he succeeded in achieving manhood, but the quality of the experience was limited. He had learned the difference by getting to know a subsequent sexual partner well:

Q: Are you sort of worried about your performance and things like that, getting it right?

A: Yes, it's all the time it's on your mind, because it's also like with someone you don't know, you don't know whether they are appreciating what you are doing or not, so it's sort of hard as well to know what to do. Whereas with my girlfriend Sara, it was different because we knew each other well enough to say, 'Do you like this? Do you like that?' It was easy. But the first time it was good, but it was bad.

(young man, aged 16, ESW, middle class)

Although first intercourse was generally viewed as the establishment of male performance, there was also some resistance to the constraints imposed by conventions of masculinity. Accounts of first intercourse showed considerable variation in the kinds of relationship established between the sexual partners. Where there is a more negotiated relationship, or the influence of feminism (particularly from mothers), then there could be more awareness of the possibility of differences between male and female experience.

The dominance of masculine meaning, and the surveillance of the male peer group, in the construction of heterosexual identity is most acute where sexual encounters are impersonal and transitory. Intimacy, friendship and an equality of inexperience make space within which individual subjectivities can be expressly 'in the same boat'. However, the excerpt at the beginning of this chapter is not typical of the young men's accounts. Being able to laugh together at inexperience, rather than her having the power to laugh at him; exploring desires together, rather than her being expected to service him, requires some initial deconstruction of heterosexual pressures. The extent and problems of effective resistance to heterosexuality seemed clearer in the responses from young women.

How was it for her?

When we compare men's and women's accounts of their first experiences of intercourse, the claim that they are all in the same boat becomes more confused. While young men's accounts are varied, the very general acceptance of first intercourse as a positive step to manhood have no equivalent in the young women's accounts. Conceptions of first intercourse as about women's pleasure, performance or achievement of adult status are strikingly absent, and the women's accounts are generally much more disembodied and distanced from the experience than those of the young men. For young women, sexual intercourse within a masculine construction of heterosexuality presents specific risks. As she takes him into her body for his pleasure, she confronts problems of how to manage this experience in terms of successful femininity, protect both her body and her reputation, and make sense of the experience for herself. It is not then surprising that young women's accounts of first intercourse seemed more varied and contradictory than those of young men.

In contrast to the young men, young women do not seem to embark on their first experiences of sexual intercourse with the idea of becoming women. In the heterosexual/masculine boat, young women do not gain womanhood through sexual intercourse, so much as offer their virginity to men. Drawing on the work of Shirley Prendergast on menstruation (Prendergast 1995), we argue that young women's conceptions of 'now I am a woman' are formed at puberty (and confirmed by pregnancy). It is in the management of first menstruation that a young woman begins to become aware of what it is to be a woman, with its attendant requirements to discipline and conceal her bodily unruliness. Through this discipline she develops a sense of negative power, built upon ideas and experiences of bodily constraint and control (Holland *et al.* 1994a).

For women, first intercourse is socially part of a much longer process than the incident itself. Young women's sense of negative power, the power of control and restraint, is confirmed and compounded by the war of attrition that characterises much early heterosexual interaction. Young women are positioned to resist, to slowly cede bodily territory and finally to consent to intercourse. Unless they were directly influenced by feminism, these young women were not generally aware of heterosexuality as anything other than the natural order of things. This put them under considerable pressure to accept the male domination of the entire process of 'first sex' as natural, and not to rock the boat.

Offering their bodies to men gives young women a range of problems which it is often difficult for them to articulate. Since 'first sex' is not primarily initiation into womanhood, it can be a moment of considerable ambivalence for young women. In most of their accounts, there is a sense of awareness that 'sex' is what is happening for their male partner. 'First sex' can then be the price of keeping a social relationship with a boyfriend:

A: I didn't really want it. He provoked me into it, you know . . . it was like a one-off. You know, I didn't want it really, I just wanted someone to love at that time. He just wanted a bit of – you know.
(young woman, aged 19, ESW, middle class)

Many young women faced a good deal of uncertainty in knowing how to develop the loving relationships they desired, while also having to manage young men's expectations. Young women are positioned within masculinity in such a way that there is always the possibility of force, or other pressure beneath the surface. These pressures may be generally avoided, but young women were still aware of them and the dangers they posed:

A: Normally when you just know a boy's going to try it on or something, you know, like – and, you know, that's when you say 'No' or something, but I didn't. I wanted – I did want to do it. It wasn't like I was – like I say – I wasn't forced or anything. I knew what was going to happen and, you know, I wasn't worried.

(young woman, aged 19, ESW, working class)

A more general problem for young women came from the construction of first intercourse as the man's moment, leaving women to cope with first experiences that did not match their expectations of love, romance, or the earth moving:

A: I was 14. It was complete infatuation, you know, like amazement – these people *like* us, or whatever, and I slept with this boy then. I just didn't feel anything. I didn't think, 'Oh, it's really – or whatever, I just sort of thought, 'Oh, great', and I sort of felt – I wasn't very happy about it afterwards. I mean he didn't force me or anything, you know. He said, and I agreed, but afterwards I sort of felt dirty. I think partly because I was so young, and I was infatuated with this person, and he turned out to be so ordinary.

(young woman, aged 17, ESW, middle class)

The range of young women's responses reflects different approaches to the problems of managing their lack of agency. His achievement of manhood is her loss of autonomy. One way of claiming agency was through defining first intercourse as the young woman giving the man something valuable:

A: Well, just – losing your virginity for them – it's just, I don't know it just seems important to me personally.

(young woman, aged 17, ESW, working class)

An extreme version of this strategy was to treat first intercourse as knowingly bestowing a gift. In the following example, this is offered almost with pity at the point at which she has decided to end the relationship with her boyfriend:

A: I know it sounds stupid now. All right, we was going to split up, but I wanted to be – it was right –
Q: The right time for you to split up?
A: No, it was right to have sex, even though we were splitting up. I

mean he was older than me, but like we'd been together for like
seven months, and we hadn't done anything in seven months, and I
just thought, this is what I want . . . he was totally besotted with me
. . . he'd jump through hoops for me, and I think that's what –

Q: And it was that that finished it?

A: Yeah, I split up with him, but I think it was my way of trying to
apologise.

Q: Was it a big thing for you losing your virginity? Did it mean lots of
things to you?

A: No. It just meant that – um – I'd give him anything – oh, it sounds
sick this – I'd give him something I could never give anything else,
something special, and that's why I did it.

(young woman, aged 18, ESW, working class)

Further variation in women's management of first intercourse occurs
because young women reported a number of possible ways of accepting
sexual experience while offering some resistance to male domination of its
meaning. These strategies, which are echoed in the young men's accounts of
'pushy partners', tend to be associated with the disruption of the chronology
of diminishing resistance to sex over time, for example, by rushing into it:

Q: Do you think you made the right decision the first time?

A: No. I suppose I wanted to just get it over and done with – I didn't
want to rush into it, just because he was there, and I'd been going
out with him anyway. I didn't like him. I just finished with him. I
hated it. It's not great the first time. Never.

(young woman, aged 18, ESW, working class)

In other accounts, attempts to usurp the chronology and to position themselves as actor rather than object seemed to be ineffective in escaping the
power of masculinity masquerading as heterosexuality, and may be met with
regret:

Q: Why did you do it?

A: I don't know. I liked him, but I don't know why – I wish I didn't do
it.

(young woman, aged 16, ESW, middle class)

Although women did not usually present first intercourse as a positive
experience, some of their accounts echoed men's conception of virginity as a
constraint on their own life and freedom to love. In this case the choice of
partner did not matter, as the point was to get first intercourse over and done
with. The following young woman was 16 at the time; her boyfriend was 22
or 23. She says he loved her and wanted to marry her:

A: He was just gross. And – and I did it with him. I just wanted – do
you know what I mean? I just wanted to get it over and done with

> – it was like, you know, I've done it now, I can go and do it with someone I like or something, you know. But in actual fact I didn't actually do it again for ages.
>
> (young woman, aged 19, ESW, working class)

This young woman seems to lack an appropriate language to talk about what she means, so this example remains opaque and contradictory, but it does seem to suggest that by losing her virginity she could open up her body so that she could use it for her own desires, or with someone she loved.

Young women's varied approaches to first intercourse signal the absence of female agency, power and pleasure within masculinity/heterosexuality. Women had varying strategies of acceptance of, or resistance to, intercourse as his performance, but the main way in which these absences could be accommodated was by situating first intercourse within a social relationship with a boyfriend. They made sense of this accommodation through the acceptance of a careful chronology. There is a clear sense, which is not found so clearly in the young men's responses, that there is a right moment, a point at which the woman is ready for what comes next, so that intercourse is part of a 'natural progression' in a relationship:

> A: That was like my first sexual relationship, and I could have done it beforehand, but I chose not to. I don't know – I don't know. To a certain extent you feel that you ought to wait till you feel ready and I felt I could do that, I was just lucky I suppose . . . it was just the right thing to do at that time. That explains it really. There's a sort of natural progression.
>
> (young woman, aged 20, ESW, middle class)

> A: I don't know if either of us was that keen really. I don't know if he – I think – I don't think he was eager to have it, but it was – it was something there that we was going to do together and then it was time. The time came and we did it. It wasn't 'Oh quick! Let's have it now!' It was just – it just came naturally really.
>
> (young woman, aged 18, African Caribbean, middle class)

This chronology could also relieve young men from the pressure to prove their manhood. Where young women expect men to demand intercourse, which they can then either accept or resist, it could be up to the man to respect this sense of timing, and to allow space for a relationship to develop before he made his move:

> A: We was going out for nine months. He waited for about five months. I really got to like him.
>
> Q: Was it your decision to do it or was he hassling you?
>
> A: No, he's so shy you see, he's nice looking and – so, he made the first

move. I was shocked because lads sometimes wait about a week and then jump in your knickers.

> (young woman, aged 17, African Caribbean, working class)

Ros Coward (1984) has argued that female heterosexuality is constructed so that women are positioned in ways that only enable them to choose between 'yes' and 'no'. Perhaps, through their acceptance of a careful chronology, young women are also attempting agency, learning from their established experience in resisting young men's sexual advances. By accepting that men will be making advances, and that these advances do not have to be accepted, they can manage their sexuality by refusing intercourse:

> A: If I – I – if I wasn't up to that, if I didn't think it was that close, I'd just say no – I wouldn't sort of stand by and say all right, I don't mind.
>
> > (young woman, aged 17, Asian, working class)

> A: There was one boy that just pushed me a bit too far, and I got rid of him as well, because I thought, 'Well, I don't need this. What right have you to push yourself on me?' And that was on the first night.
>
> > (young woman, aged 18, ESW, middle class)

Yet if the time somehow is right, then they can find that their agency is simply ceded to the male partner to define the sexual situation, and they lose the right to say no:

> Q: Do you feel in relationships in the past you've been able to make decisions?
> A: Yeah, but not sexually, because he's the first one I've slept with – but we really do make equal decisions apart from that one.
>
> > (young woman, aged 16, African Caribbean, middle class)

By adopting different strategies of acceptance and resistance, young women can position themselves within first heterosex encounters with differing degrees of power, thereby challenging the symbolic meaning of the moment. However with little or no previous experience to draw on as to the nature of female sexual pleasure, it is difficult for them to be constituted as agents rather than objects; they have no boat of their own. The young woman quoted above who had found her first sexual partner gross commented:

> A: If I could go back then and change my mind I would, not because I lost my virginity, but because he was so horrible [laughs]. But I can't. And it wasn't very nice, like it was –
> Q: You didn't enjoy it?
> A: Oh. Well, not like – you know, like you were saying do I like my job. But – because I've got nothing to compare it against, then you don't know . . . in one sense I think you might enjoy it because, you

know, like you're having sex and, you know, you don't really know what to enjoy it is like.

(young woman, aged 19, ESW, working class)

Positive, empowered experiences of first heterosex were, in contrast to the accounts of young men, rare among our female respondents. The constraints of first sexual experience for women were widely recognised. Making the experience a positive one depended on transforming conventional male behaviour into practices in which he was detached from his peer group, and communication about female desires was possible. One young woman illustrates this: with the benefit of age and experience she was able to revisit 'first sex' by having a relationship with a male virgin, inducting him into her own tailor-made version of heterosexuality:

A: The bloke I am actually going out with is about three years younger than I am and we can talk for hours and we get on really well. And he hadn't actually had a sexual experience before that . . . and it was like such a reversal of positions. He had got all these ideals about having sex before marriage and it was only going to be with someone he really cared about or had been married or whatever. And it just sort of developed because we became very close and he changed his ideas about it. So I was like the experienced one although I had only done it about four or five times. So the way I used to ask questions, I used to love talking about it, and he was actually doing that and it was just working it out within ourselves. And because he had no sort of ideals about it, it was a lot more – he was a lot more thoughtful of me as well which is why it is very different.

(young woman, aged 21, ESW, middle class)

What is strikingly lacking in most of the women's accounts of first intercourse is this sense of either partner being 'thoughtful of me'.

These young women's varied accounts of their experiences of 'first sex' indicate their strategies for managing masculinity. Heterosexual intercourse is not only differently experienced by men and women: it is socially different. For a young man, achieving intercourse is an empowering moment of symbolic and physical importance, whereby through a physical performance, his identity as a man and, therefore, a competent sexual actor is confirmed. The passage from inexperience for the young woman is far more ambiguous and contradictory. Despite various possibilities for (re-)claiming it, first intercourse is not really her moment. Yet she has an important role to play in 'being heterosexual', through her part in constituting heterosexuality through intercourse, and managing the interaction. It is only through access to her body that the boy can achieve manhood. Through her participation in his performance she is inducted to the world of heterosexual sexuality, where she must learn to play by the masculine rules of the game, or take the consequences of resistance.

Within this game, her sexual identity, subjectivity and desire are silent. To succeed as a woman, and to be rewarded, she must become proficient in supporting and satisfying masculine values and needs. Negotiation of the rules of the game is not merely a matter for the woman and her sexual partner: reward and sanction are rather held by the wider peer group, and exercised through social mechanisms such as 'reputation' (Holland *et al.* 1996a).

How was it for you?

Young people's accounts of their first sexual experiences go some way towards making the process of achieving heterosexual sexual identities visible, and offer some insight into the constitution of heterosexuality as masculinity. Making heterosexuality visible is difficult, since its power as 'the natural order of things' hinders both its actors and the social theorist in extricating contested meanings from the apparent certainties of first intercourse. Young people are all in the same boat, in that heterosexuality turns out to be masculinity only thinly disguised, but from a feminist perspective they are not in the same boat, in that heterosexuality could be otherwise.

It is clear from both the young men's and young women's accounts that within the privacy of individual relationships, the rules of male domination can be negotiated and disrupted. Levels of experience and inexperience can be matched creatively to enable equitable explorations of pleasure and bodies. Yet these private reorderings remain exceptions to the rules of heterosexuality and dependent on particular configurations of partner and timing. It is yet to be seen whether such alternative heterosexualities will be valued by the outside world and protected by the social mechanisms that police early sexual relationships.

The social and sexual worlds of adolescents continue to be highly gendered. The two worlds of adolescent masculinity and femininity come together at the moment of 'first sex' in a way that powerfully confirms respective positions of agency and object, of doing sex and of being done to. These meanings and positions are difficult to escape, despite the self-awareness and resistance expressed by many of our respondents. So many of the strategies employed by the young women to escape objectification are all too easily incorporated within the larger scheme of things. Rushing into sex may leave you disappointed, taking the lead can make you a 'slag', and giving way too easily can call into question your claims to virginity. Unless heterosexuality itself is recognised and resisted, the only potential positions of female power appear to be negative and disembodied: either by saying 'no' or by ridiculing her partner's performance.

It is possible that a key to female empowerment may lie in resisting the institutionalisation of intercourse as *the* sexual act. It is this social construction of intercourse that locks together the languages and practices of male agent and female object, the fear and bravado of male performance and the absence of female sexual agency. Lucy Bland's observation, that the identification of 'sex' with heterosexual intercourse may have hindered the possibilities of our thinking on sexuality (Bland 1994), could also offer some optimism for the future possibilities of reworking the languages and practices of being heterosexual.

Notes

1 This chapter is based on the work of two research projects. The Women, Risk and AIDS Project was staffed by the authors, Sue Sharpe (author and research consultant) and Sue Scott (University of Stirling), working collectively. It was financed by a two-year grant from the ESRC. It also received grants from Goldsmiths' College Research Fund and the Department of Health. Valuable assistance was given by Jane Preston, Polly Radcliffe and Janet Ransom. WRAP used purposive samples to interview in depth 150 young women aged 16–21, stratified by class and ethnicity, in London and Manchester between 1988 and 1990. The Men, Risk and AIDS Project was staffed by the authors, Sue Sharpe and Tim Rhodes, and was given a grant by the Leverhulme Trust for a study of 50 young men (also stratified by age, class and ethnicity) in London 1991–2, and for comparison of the two studies. Information on publications from these studies is obtainable from The Tufnell Press, 47 Dalmeny Rd, London N7 0DY, and in Holland *et al.* (1996b).
2 A large-scale UK sample survey asked respondents about their age at first heterosexual intercourse (defined as first 'sexual intercourse with someone of the opposite sex' after age 13) (Johnson *et al.* 1994: 69–109). 'The data for first heterosexual intercourse show a pattern of decreasing age at occurrence, together with an increase in the proportions reporting experience before the age of 16 and some convergence in the behaviour of men and women over time' (p. 106).
3 We have deliberately focused on gender relations rather than other social divisions, as these are central to intimate heterosexual relations. But this does not mean that we take gender to be isolated from other social divisions (for example, class, sexual orientation, ethnicity) (Holland 1992); nor does it mean that we take men's power over women to be undifferentiated (Holland *et al.* 1994b).
4 Since sexuality cannot be taken as fixed and universal, our generalisations are limited, and definitions need to be qualified . Our analysis should apply fairly generally to English-speaking cultures and to much of Europe, but the nature and extent of variation, across time, cultures and social divisions is not established.
5 We do not have space here to develop and qualify this contentious claim but have argued the point elsewhere (Holland *et al.* 1994a; Ramazanoglu 1995).
6 In exploring these issues we are not considering here cases where young women have been forcibly penetrated by men, or have their first experiences of intercourse under direct social or physical pressure. We have discussed pressured sex in Holland *et al.* (1992a).
7 See for example Fine (1988); Bowie and Ford (1989); Ford and Morgan (1989); Thompson (1990), Lees (1993).
8 'ESW' indicates 'English/Scottish/Welsh', which was used in our purposive sample as a category of ethnic origin.

10

Collusion, collaboration and confession: on moving beyond the heterosexuality debate

Carol Smart

It's been very nice to lose my phobia about cocks. Our culture's phallic mythology has given the male sex organ so much highly charged significance that anything powerful is a phallic symbol.

(Califia 1994: 188)

It has, I think, been slowly dawning on feminists that we have been inadvertently inflating male power by colluding with a long-standing cultural presumption in Western societies that power and the phallus are fundamentally intertwined and that, at the more mundane bodily level, this power is about penises. Moreover, in feminist work we have built on this presumption to create a powerful critique of heterosexuality and heterosexual practices, because a defining feature of heterosexuality is presumed (in both orthodox and feminist writing) to be penetration. Since it is too often assumed that penetration is about the penis/vagina 'interface', heterosexuality has been construed as submission to the phallic power of the owners of the penises. In this logic there are a lot of presumptions that more recent theories on sexuality (especially queer theory) have started to challenge. In as much as these new theories have started to allow for the reconceptualisation of sexualities, I am interested in whether they allow for any rethinking of *hetero*sexuality. Can we extract discussions of heterosexuality from the framework constructed by feminisms[1] in the 1970s, or must we simply reassert that all heterosexual sex is oppression? Before I turn to this issue, however, I want to reconsider the old question of the phallic penis and its power.

The overinflated penis

Let me start with an anecdote. I have been teaching a course on sexuality/ies for some years now. When I come to Freud I inevitably give my students the (in)famous quotation so critically cited by Millett:

> [Little girls] notice the penis of a brother or playmate, strikingly visible and of large proportions, at once recognise it as the superior counter-part of their own small and inconspicuous organ, and from that time forward fall a victim to envy for the penis.
>
> (Freud, quoted in Millett 1972: 181)

At this point they usually fall about laughing, or at least the women do. I have usually chided them that their laughter is inappropriate because, follow-ing Mitchell's (1974) interpretations of Freud, I explain that what the little girl finds awesome is the power and privilege which accompanies masculin-ity and which are symbolised in the phallus/penis. At this point they stop laughing. But I now wonder what I have done to successive cohorts of stu-dents in suppressing this mirth about the supposedly awesome penis. To what extent have I disqualified a counterdiscourse in order to insist that it is in this fragile organ that power resides? Have I also unintentionally bolstered an essentialist notion of masculine supremacy amongst my male students? This is possible, I suppose, although most have always managed to look uncom-fortable rather than complacent or emboldened. In fact, it was a highly per-ceptive male student who said to me, several years before the idea became current, that feminist work seems to assume that men have phalluses rather than penises.

Has feminist work managed to collude with Freud and the psychoanalytic school in general by collapsing the phallus into the penis and in construing almost all power as phallic?

The problem of psychoanalysis

> At this stage the contrast between the sexes is not stated in terms of 'male' or 'female' but of 'possessing a penis' or 'castrated'.
>
> (Freud, quoted in Mitchell 1974: 87)

> After a woman has become aware of the wound to her narcissism, she develops, like a scar, a sense of inferiority.
>
> (Freud, quoted in Mitchell 1974: 99)

The girl's Oedipus complex is much simpler than that of the small bearer of the penis.

(Freud, quoted in Mitchell: 98)

These quotations from Freud very clearly demonstrate the core, even holy, place of the penis in psychoanalytical thinking. Indeed, even the male child merely becomes the bearer of the penis and all children are presented with one of two subject positions; that which possesses the penis and that which is castrated. Not only is this a very narrow world but it places maleness, psychically and physiologically, at its centre. In 1969 Kate Millett first offered a trenchant critique of Freud; her argument requires little elaboration here. She challenged Freud's phallocentrism and made his core ideas appear self-interested and plainly silly. None the less she recognised the real power that psychoanalysis has had to affect the lives of women adversely. But in 1974 Juliet Mitchell offered another reading. In a critical appreciation of Freudian texts, she argued that Freud's references to the penis should not be treated so literally. Contextualising Freud historically and culturally, she argued that he offered a metaphor of the development of femininity under a rigidly patriarchal psychic system. She argued that Freud could therefore be understood to be explaining patriarchy rather than condoning it, even though he might never have seen his work in this light. Mitchell both sociologised Freud and brought psychoanalysis into feminism. She infused a social meaning into the penis so that it ceased to be a simple biological organ with psychic connotations, and became a biological organ replete with distilled social meanings about the historical and cultural positions of men and women. In Mitchell's reading, the girl child 'sees' the penis and recognises gendered social and political power. The girl child is thus already an adept (albeit unconscious) reader of complex cultural signs. In this reading Mitchell broke the link between biology (which is so often assumed to be immutable) and power and offers instead a symbol of social power (which is not immutable) which has been overlaid on the object of the penis. Mitchell's reading is therefore a much more hopeful reading for a feminist audience in that she transcends the apparent biological determinism of orthodox Freudianism that would always have the bearers of the penises empowered.

It is, I think, for this reason that Mitchell's account became so compelling. She allowed feminism, which had been highly sociological until that time, to admit to the unconscious mind and to acknowledge ambivalence and difference. But perhaps, in another way, it was a pity that she was so successful. Kate Millett had buried Freud for feminism, but Mitchell resurrected him. In resurrecting him she reinvigorated the idea of phallic power. Thus, although Mitchell had split the symbolic phallus from the biological penis, it was still the bearers of the penises who had this phallic power. The phallus kept collapsing back into the penis and only men had these. The radical break that she made could not, therefore, really be sustained without an accompanying radical reconceptualisation of biology and bodies of the sort provided by Butler (1993a). The having of a penis remained the unchallenged, self-evident foundation of phallic power. In the 1970s we were still trapped within the same circle of meanings initiated by Freud. But worse, Freud had ceased to be a figure of fun and the phallus remained awesome in place of the increasingly untenable 'strikingly visible' and well-proportioned penis.

Although the way in which Mitchell's work has been interpreted is not her responsibility, we can now see that challenging biological determinism could not be easily achieved by merely translating the biological organ into a psychic symbol. Precisely because the organ itself was unchallenged, the psychic symbol could merely rest on it. Mitchell's work avoided an engagement with the penis by directing the gaze to the unconscious/symbolic meaning of it. But she was doing this at a time when feminisms in Western cultures were still mostly grounded in unproblematised biologically based notions of gender difference. In a sense her work came too soon. Thus she unintentionally contributed to making the problems faced by feminists greater (at the conceptual level) because, whilst the penis was a small thing, the phallus was huge and omnipresent.

Of course, this tendency to see male power everywhere can hardly be simply 'credited' to Mitchell. Other feminists were doing this in a much more overt way because in the 1970s feminism was concerned to expose this power and raise awareness about its many forms, rather than focusing on the wider range of questions which preoccupy us today. So I am not trying to identify Mitchell as a villain diverting the path of 'true' feminism, but I am suggesting that *Psychoanalysis and Feminism* kept alive a linkage between the penis and male power even if it was Mitchell's precise objective to break with this biological reductionism.

From the penis to penetration and the enactment of phallic power

For Freud, as is well known, women's resistance to penetration and any signs that they preferred clitoral to vaginal stimulation, was a sign of their failure to adjust to mature femininity. This was a failure to submit to the status of inferiority as well as a failure to recognise that the only true route to finding one's own (substitute) penis was through pregnancy and childbirth. For Freud the 'normal' woman gave up ideas about her own independence and submerged herself in motherhood to find what compensations she could for not having been born male. Perhaps the key difference between Freud and some later feminists, both of whom recognised this same sexual system that insisted on women's inferiority and treated men as the normative standard, was that whilst he urged women to succumb, they urged women to resist (i.e. de Beauvoir 1974; Mackinnon 1987; Jeffreys 1990). Their broad comprehension of the sexual system as based on the subjugation of the feminine/woman was not at variance, but they arrived at completely different solutions.

For both Freud and many feminists, penetration was a crucial part of this process of subjection and for both, this sexual subjection was of far greater significance than a mere sexual practice confined to the bedroom. It was seen as a defining element of the whole of women's lives. For Freud, women had to put up with this limitation; for feminists like Jeffreys the solution was to opt out of heterosexuality, the core defining element of which is sexual intercourse. There is an 'all-or-nothingness' to these two positions. Freud's women were required to face their feminine destiny or remain immature. Jeffreys's women must renounce their heterosexual desires or remain oppressed. She states: 'The question we have to ask ourselves is whether we want our freedom or whether we want to retain heterosexual desire. Feminists will choose freedom' (Jeffreys 1990: 314).

For Freud there was no alternative because of the power of anatomy as destiny. Quite simply boys have penises, girls do not. All else flows from this basic fact. Jeffreys refutes this kind of biological reductionism in that she allows that male supremacy can be overcome, but for her there seem to be no half-way measures: only a total abandonment of heterosexual desire and, possibly, practice can shake the edifice.

The question therefore that I wish to explore is why some feminists see penetration and heterosex as such a defining element of oppression and why this act has come to symbolise all the harm that may be done to women as women. Why is it, once again, that the penis becomes the symbol of such awesome power?

In *Anticlimax* Jeffreys (1990) constructs a powerful critique of sexology (in its various forms) since the 1950s. She offers an alternative reading of these teachings on sex and of the rise of sex therapy. Her core argument is that most of these developments – that were aimed at eroticising the wife in order to make marriage more enjoyable – merely made it more enjoyable for husbands and thus enhanced his power in an already unequal power relationship. Her argument is compelling; her critique of the work of authors like Alex Comfort reveals the sexism hidden in an apparently liberal/liberated approach to heterosexuality. She points out that women were subtly and not so subtly pressured into a specific form of sexual practice, the parameters of which were framed by dominant ideas of male sexual satisfaction. She is equally critical of some early feminist work in this sexual liberationist mould. Although she recognises the power of the 'discovery' of the clitoris and clitoral orgasm for women, Jeffreys argues that this too became largely hijacked into a method of making women more eager and accepting of heterosex. These early feminists, therefore, simply confirmed male power. She states:

> It was, and is, very important for women to feel that they have a right to their own bodies, to look at them, to feel them and to care for their

health and pleasures. But the ideas and practice of these feminists were locked into a sexual revolution agenda that was not premised upon women's interests, but on the maintenance of male supremacy.

(Jeffreys 1990: 236)

Following this critique, Jeffreys moves on to provide a specific revolutionary feminist position on heterosexuality. This position was first outlined in an important paper written by the Leeds Revolutionary Feminist Group (1981) in 1979 of which Jeffreys was a member. Citing this key document, she argues that 'it is specifically through sexuality that the fundamental oppression, that of men over women, is maintained' (Jeffreys 1990: 291). Then, quoting from Canadian radical feminist work, Jeffreys argues that 'from heterosexuality flow all other oppressions' (p. 297). Thus it is suggested that all systems of domination and subordination flow from this primal construction of eroticised sexual difference. And it is, of course, penetration that constitutes the defining act of this heterosexual system. We are thus back to the problem of the bearers of the penises even though feminisms need not rely on, and indeed often refute, biological determinism as the basis of analysis.[2] The point is that within some feminist theorising, penetration can have only one meaning under patriarchy (Dworkin 1987; MacKinnon 1987; Jeffreys 1990). It always signifies gender subordination, precisely as it did for Freud.

Is it possible, however, that penetration can have meanings other than being the eternal primal moment of women's subordination, even where gender inequalities exist? And is it possible that heterosexuality might also be seen as less awesome, omnipotent and overdetermining? Can we, on the one hand, deflate the phallus discursively (rather than surgically) and, on the other, deconstruct this mythic status of unitary, transhistorical heterosexuality and start to talk of heterosexualities and diverse and competing meanings associated with and deriving from these heterosexualities?

Changing meanings: penetration

Speaking of penetration, Dworkin has said,

What does it mean to be the person who needs to have this done to her: who needs to be needed as an object; who needs to be entered; who needs to be occupied; who needs to be wanted more than she needs integrity or freedom or equality? . . . The brilliance of objectification as a strategy of dominance is that it gets the woman to take the initiative in her own degradation . . . It is the best system of colonialization on earth.

(Dworkin 1987: 142)

Thus her definition of penetration is that it is a form of occupation and/or colonisation. Whilst there is patriarchy all intercourse is really rape. It is, as the quotation suggests, the antithesis of integrity, freedom and equality and it is degrading. The woman to whom this happens or, worse, who actively participates, gives up her selfhood and her humanity; she also becomes, as far as Dworkin is concerned, a collaborator: 'Collaboration by women with men to keep women civilly and sexually inferior has been one of the hallmarks of female subordination; we are ashamed when Freud noticed it, but it is true' (p. 142).

Obviously Dworkin's analysis of penetration arises directly from her understanding of it as the expression of men's enduring hatred of women. Her emphasis on hatred rather than, for example, institutional power or the more nebulous notion of gender inequality gives rise to an intense concentration on this specific act as distilling every aspect of male power and the dehumanisation of women. Thus she seems to offer a fixed, once-and-for-all meaning of penetration precisely because this hatred seems so omnipresent, all-encompassing and historically and culturally undifferentiated. Yet she is critical of those who would see biology as what drives heterosexuality. Rather she argues that men continue to *choose* to hate women. But it is clear from this that only with a complete social revolution can penetration take on any other meanings. This position is significantly different from that put forward by Kitzinger and Wilkinson (1994a) who, it seems to me, offer a more fully contextualised reading of penetration and heterosexuality:

> We have also been surprised by the extent to which our focus on heterosexuality has been characterised as 'essentialist' or even 'biologist' . . . In our writing we have repeatedly emphasised that lesbianism, bisexuality and heterosexuality are *not* fixed, essential (let alone biologically determined!) identities . . . Any particular sexual identity carries a *range* of political meanings: there is no *one* lesbian identity; no one 'heterosexual' identity to serve as its illusory polar opposite; nor any single 'bisexual' identity.
>
> (p. 332; emphasis in original)

What is suggested here is that there can be multiple meanings (although not any old random meanings) attached to different sexualities at the same time. Thus heterosexuality and penetration does not have to mean, for example, the rape and dehumanisation of all women, even though it may mean this in certain contexts or at certain moments.

In the debates over penetration and heterosex, first in the 1970s and then again in the early 1990s, it is perhaps hardly surprising that there has been so much anger on both sides. Moreover, it seems that the framework that dominated the early debate (collaborators versus lesbian separatists) was so powerful that it was widely assumed that when Wilkinson and Kitzinger (1993) reopened the debate they merely wanted to retrace these same painful but unresolved arguments. Indeed, initially many contributors to their edited collection *Heterosexuality: a Feminism and Psychology Reader* fell in line according to this old, harmful dichotomy. It was as if there were really only two available positions; one which seemed to gloat over the mistakes of heterosexual women and one which seemed to apologise for being heterosexual. I stress 'seemed' because, although this reading was available, as more contributors have joined the debate (especially those who were perhaps not personally involved in the 1970s debates) other interpretations and understandings are emerging. There seems, therefore, to be two levels to the current debate. One could be characterised as the working out of old angers, or the return of the repressed, and the other could be seen as a fresh attempt to create discursive heterosexualities (and bisexualities) open to the same constructive scrutinies as have been lesbian and gay sexualities. (Of course, it is entirely possible that both levels can appear in a single contribution to the debate.)

The return of the repressed

It has been a main element of much feminist writing that heterosexuality is about the eroticisation of power difference. On the one hand, it is argued that it demonstrates a real problem of masculinity that men get aroused by women's vulnerability; on the other, it is argued that this eroticisation both disguises and naturalises social inequalities. I find I cannot disagree with this analysis as far as it goes. If we look at the discursive construction of masculinity in sexological writings there is clear evidence of encouragement to men to pursue, to take, to possess the reticent, nervous woman. As Jeffreys has pointed out, even when the sexologists were encouraging women to be more forthcoming and initiatory in the 1970s, they were warned never to demand as this would turn men off: 'We notice that women must not demand sexual servicing from men lest the men feel threatened, but they must initiate sexual servicing of the men' (Jeffreys 1990: 119).

We also know that women who break these codes of sexual behaviour have been punished as prostitutes, nymphomaniacs or as slags. But more recently we have also become more aware of the extent to which men too are punished for failing to live up to these codes. Hall (1991), Seidler (1991) and others have discussed the hidden anxieties of masculinity. This growing deconstruction of masculinity has begun to suggest that it is not so monolithic. It also suggests that – allowing for gendered power imbalances and structural inequalities – patriarchal power regulates men as well as women.

The idea that heterosexuality naturalises social inequalities is also powerful. Similar ideas have been used in explaining racial oppressions, in particular the use of sociobiological ideas on racial difference and intelligence. To seek to explain a social phenomenon in relation to 'nature' is extremely powerful in a culture so deeply imbued with popularised ideas deriving from the biological and natural sciences. But it is precisely the case that this naturalisation occurs in a range of areas and that social inequalities have been masked by theories of genetic difference, hormonal difference, chromosomal difference, difference in brain size or different hemispherical dominance and so on, which reveals that it is a general strategy applied to questions of class and 'race' and not one peculiar to the workings of heterosexuality. Laqueur (1990), for example, has documented the role of the new medical sciences after the eighteenth century in the construction of 'natural' inequalities between the sexes. He shows how the female sex became discursively constructed as vulnerable to sickness, mental impairment and general instability. Emily Martin (1989) has developed this theme in a more contemporary context, pointing out how modern medicine, and gynaecology in particular, continuously reconstructs the female body as a site of failure and impairment. Both authors seek to show that what is presented as natural is highly ideological and culturally specific. Feminism has done the same thing for heterosexuality, arguing that ideas about men's naturally hydraulic sexuality which must have release are little more than excuses for rape, prostitution and sexual abuse. Ideas about women's sexual passivity have been challenged on the same grounds, namely that such biologically reductive ideas ignore the enforced conditions surrounding much of women's participation in heterosex.

The question is, however, whether this recognition of the strategy of naturalisation means that women's only choices are to opt out or to accept the dominant ideology? In other areas, such as medicine, the tendency has been to suggest that women can resist these discursive constructions of womanhood, albeit with difficulty. But Dworkin and Jeffreys seem to suggest only one strategy, that of abandoning heterosexual desire and practice (at least in the present). The revival of this old 'solution' in recent texts on heterosexuality – as well as the unhelpful rhetoric of war, treachery and violence associated with the term 'collaborators' which both Dworkin and Jeffreys use – has regenerated an old anger. Heterosexual feminists now appear to be on the defensive; they feel attacked and vulnerable. Wilkinson and Kitzinger have similarly reported that they have been subjected to abuse by heterosexual women in a way which seems similar to the abuse Jeffreys feels that the Leeds Revolutionary Feminists experienced in 1979. Both 'sides' feel abused and there has therefore been a retrenchment behind the old barricades.

Wendy Hollway (1993) was one of the heterosexual feminists who tried to take issue with the way in which the renewed debate seemed to be framed. Although she has written quite extensively on heterosexuality, particularly in relation to questions of power and anxiety, her main line of argument in this specific exchange was to refocus on heterosexual pleasure. Hollway argued that the framing of the heterosexuality debate by Wilkinson and

Kitzinger meant that only the pains and problems of heterosexuality could be voiced. Indeed, I too have argued elsewhere that the only legitimate voice for heterosexual feminists has been the voice of suffering (Smart 1996). Hollway therefore sought to offer an alternative perspective on hetero-sexuality by focusing on pleasure. In so doing, however, she was in turn criti-cised for apparently forgetting the structural inequalities which frame the heterosexual act. At the same time Wilkinson and Kitzinger were subjected to the criticism that they focused only on the harms of heterosexuality and ignored similar harm within lesbianism. At this point it might have seemed that the repressed really had returned: radical feminists were blamed for ignoring positive aspects of heterosexual women's sexuality and heterosexual feminists were blamed for talking about pleasure in the face of systems of sexual exploitation and abuse. The old retrenched positions re-emerged and threatened to swamp emergent nuances and new intonations. We therefore need to decide whether to consign the whole debate back to the silence of a sort of feminist collective unconscious, or whether to build constructively on some of the new voices.

Speaking heterosexualities

I have recently been struck by how, at this time of recognition of diversities and differences, heterosexuality is always presented as a unitary concept. Yet in writings on lesbian and gay sexualities and identities we can see the growing acknowledgement of difference. Contested as these different iden-tities might be, we find appreciations of differences between, for example, butch/femme and lesbian nation, between lipstick lesbians and dykes, between queer, bisexual and homosexual, between gay macho, camp and transvestite. The recognition of these differences (whether of styles, politics or preferences) does not, as far as I can see, undermine the idea that lesbians, gay men and bisexual men and women, are institutionally discriminated against and often personally oppressed and abused by heterosexuals. But it does cast doubt on the happy heterosexist assumption that all lesbians or all gay men are a single type who came to their sexuality identity/preference through a unicausal route (for example Oedipal problems, powerful mothers, weak fathers, etc.).

Writings from lesbians, gays and, more recently, bisexual women and men, have done much to undermine what Foucault (1981) identified as the medico-legal construction of the homosexual as a species or type to whom certain (limited and unpopular) characteristics could be attached. Yet we still do not seem to have grasped that heterosexuality may be many things, even if at times we need to collectivise this diversity (for example when recognising heterosexual privilege and its naturalisation).

One reason why we have avoided thinking in terms of heterosexuali*ties* is undoubtedly that this pluralisation might appear as if it were trying to evade the accusation of 'holding' institutional power. It might seem that, if we acknowledge heterosexuali*ties*, heterosexuals as a 'class' cannot be held responsible for heterosexism and homophobia and the range of harms addressed to 'other' sexualities. In this desire to hang on to a unitary hetero-sexuality in order to reveal who holds power, we should be aware that pre-cisely the same conceptual/political struggles have been waged in related areas. Marxists argued against the inclusion of gender difference as a cat-egory on the grounds that it would dilute the class struggle. Activists in the field of racism argued that all non-whites should be classified as black in order that the division of power in racist societies should be clear. Feminists used to argue that the only division of significance was the gender division and that class and race were subsidiary to this and should not be organising categories. But these moves to create a unity have had their tensions as well as their successes. I need not repeat these debates here as they have been thoroughly aired elsewhere (see Butler 1990a; Harding 1991; Sawicki 1992). Suffice it to say that there are now available different modes of conceptual-ising class, 'race', gender and sex categories which do not necessarily col-lapse into a presumption that we are all equal and that no one can exercise more power than anyone else. We are also turning a more critical gaze towards the reproduction of difference by problematising those who do exer-cise more power. Thus we now have critical studies of masculinities and also a slow but growing recognition that white is an ethnic status – not a natural given – which is a norm against which the Other must be judged. We need a similar move in the field of heterosexuality/ies.

Katz (1995) has begun such a move. He has argued that the concept of heterosexuality and the identity of the heterosexual is largely a twentieth-century creation. He writes:

> In the United States, in the 1890s, the 'sexual instinct' was generally identified as a *procreative* desire of men and women. But that repro-ductive ideal was beginning to be challenged, quietly but insistently, in practice and theory, by a new *different-sex pleasure* ethic. According to that radically new standard, the 'sexual instinct' referred to men's and women's erotic desire for each other, *irrespective of its procreative potential* . . . Under the old procreative standard, the new term *hetero-sexual* did not, at first, always signify the normal and good.
>
> (Katz 1995: 19; emphasis in original)

He goes on to argue that the term 'heterosexual', when it was first used by sexologists, inevitably referred to a perversion. This perversion was identi-fied as sexual lust for its own sake, rather than sex for procreation. The idea that sex might simply give or be about pleasure was one of the newly identi-fied pathologies that late Victorian doctors were so keen to typologise. Katz suggests that it is Freud who turned heterosexuality from a perversion into what has become taken as the normal. Freud's theory of heterosexuality made this orientation 'normal' and not simply 'natural'. This is an important distinction according to Katz, because nature and the natural were not necessarily seen as moral, nor capable of self-reflection. Freud's heterosexual was a moral, self-reflexive being who had achieved normality. The aim of bodily pleasure was normalised and it is clear that Freud did not imagine that the sole goal of heterosex – for men anyway – was anything other than pleasure. This new normality resided in the achievement of different-sex desire: 'A different-sex erotic ideal was slipped silently into modern consciousness, constructed as the dominant term of the dominant sexual ideology, the norm we all know without ever thinking much about it' (p. 67).

Katz goes on to argue that the later sexologists continued this trend until after the 1920s, when the heterosexual became a public figure who could openly acknowledge pleasure in sex. Although I have some doubts about whether this figure was a woman, Katz does point out how the rise of the newly heterosexualised woman at that time undermined women's romantic friendships and made it much harder for women to live together and show affection for one another. He points to a growing suspicion of the threat of lesbianism which was a new development. In this respect his argument is very close to that of Jeffreys, who stresses that heterosexuality, as a system, works actively against female bonding and insists that women only commit themselves to men.

But Katz and Jeffreys would part company over his argument that it is lesbian feminist discourse which constitutes heterosexuality as a monolithic and political institution. He suggests that it is this work which has tended to depict heterosexuality as timeless and ahistorical, and thus as more fixed than it is. Katz's strategy, arising from his historical analysis, is to try to destabilise heterosexuality by challenging the binary divide of heterosex and homosex. So he does not support the call for all women to become lesbian (or all men to become gay), but rather points to the immense diversity of lifestyles which are already occurring in the US, and how rigid identities are being challenged. In this shift, bisexuals are of course vital to the redefinition of people as merely fitting into the two categories of hetero- and homosexual. As more bisexual men and women begin to claim a distinct sexual identity and refuse to be treated as sitting on the fence or as lapsed homosexuals, it becomes harder to sustain the idea that there are only two sexual orientations.

Katz's arguments are not without their problems. His distinction between different-sex acts as procreation and different-sex sexuality as pleasure allows us to see important historical shifts and to see the rise of certain modern meanings attached to forms of sexuality. But he leaves untouched how this modern heterosexuality might be mapped on to older ideas of natural, procreative sex and how such ideas coexist with more recent ideas on pleasure and normality. One cannot escape the fact that in England, at least, sodomy used to be a hanging offence whereas sex between men and women never has been (even at its most abusive and violent). It is important to historicise our concepts, but it is problematic if our history always starts in the late nineteenth century.

At least Katz has started the process of historicising heterosexuality. He has also provided a way into the slippery terrain of heterosexual identity. For a long time we have recognised heterosexuality as the silent signifier, the invisible inferential framework within which other sexualities are subordinated. But the pervasive normality of heterosexuality has meant that heterosexual identity has remained formless except in those moments of proclaiming its superiority against the rise of counterclaims by gay and lesbian movements. As heterosexuality has become threatened, it has started to congeal into an identity – albeit a most offensive one. But there is more to heterosexual identity than this. I want to suggest that, although we should now start to talk of heterosexual identities, until relatively recently a unitary identity was in fact available through the persuasiveness of psychoanalytic explanations of sexual development. Freud gave the heterosexual an identity by emphasising feeling rather than acts (Katz 1995: 66) and by linking the emergence of heterosexuality with the emergence of a moral conscience. The process of becoming heterosexual was, for Freud, a process of becoming a fully social, gendered, moral actor. We have already seen that he thought that the rigours of the Oedipal struggle were less for girls, and that girls therefore became less fully developed as moral and human actors; but we have tended to link this with an understanding of *gender* difference rather than seeing it in relation to heterosexual identity (Mitchell 1974). Although the homosexual had become a perverse type prior to the impact of Freud's writing in the English-speaking world, it was Freud's work that gave shape to the heterosexual. Not only did he newly confirm the superiority of masculinity over femininity (just as medical science had in the nineteenth century) but gave all the most desirable characteristics to the normal heterosexual. The early successful resolution of the Oedipal struggle confirmed a later effortless superiority to heterosexual identity. Freud gave us a metaphor which gave form to a formlessness. He also created the context in which male heterosexuality, once achieved, need never be questioned (he was always less certain about women). After Freud, heterosexuality *per se* really ceased to be an intellectual problem,[3] and sexologists mainly focused on improving the techniques of heterosexuality rather than seeking to explain it (Bejin 1986) or, of course, on 'curing' the perversions. Heterosexual identity is therefore akin to a white colonial identity. It entails an effortless superiority, a moral rectitude, a defeat of the emotional and the neurotic by the power of unconscious struggle and, of course, the certain knowledge of masculine superiority.

Little happened to challenge this effortless superiority until the rise of gay movements and lesbian feminisms. Certainly the so-called sexual revolution of the 1960s did not do this, even if it did achieve other important changes. But, broadly speaking, heterosexuals were not discomforted by the sexual liberation movement in the way they have been more recently by direct challenges to their unconscious self-legitimacy. The question that we now must face is whether we can both fragment this hegemonic identity and yet retain a politics and pleasure in more fragmented heterosexualities.

Pleasure and politics

Segal (1994) has offered us a contemporary exploration of straight sex, an appreciation of the place of pleasure and a grounded politics. *Straight Sex* is a debate about heterosexuality which, unlike Katz's work, is specifically interested in women's position in relation to sexuality. Segal is searching for both a theory of and a politics of women's (hetero-)sexuality. She wants to allow both for the element of pleasure in heterosexual practices and for a much more woman-centred heterosexuality, but she also problematises the assumption that there are simple and clear dichotomies of sexual categories. Equally, she seeks to situate this in the context of material realities facing women in Britain in the 1990s. Hence she points to a constant tension between the attraction of the potentially subversive politics of the new consumerism around sexual choice and what she sees as the lack of economic choice facing many women (but most especially poor, young working-class women) for whom heterosexuality might still mean pregnancy, financial dependence and abusive relationships. Moreover, Segal draws to our attention the shifts in welfare policy and rhetoric which seek to reduce the limited independence women might have had living on State benefits by increasing the pressure on them to become dependent on individual men. As she says, 'With such values becoming only ever more pervasive today, women's pursuit of their own autonomy and pleasure is going to require a lot more than the choices opened up to them by market consumerism' (Segal 1994: 308–9).

It is at this point that one might anticipate that Segal would suggest shelving issues of heterosexuality until there have been improvements to the material conditions of women's lives. Questions of poverty and pleasure sit uneasily together; there seems to be a moral imperative to choose the former over the latter, and almost a distaste with considering the latter at all.

However, Segal takes a different route. She argues that the (re)discovery of pleasure in our bodies can be personally empowering and that 'sexual pleasure is far too significant in our lives and culture of women not to be seeking to express our agency through it' (pp. 313–14). In some ways Segal is arguing, implicitly, that feminist work on sexuality has come to be over-preoccupied with 'internal' arguments over the significance of penetration and the flight from heterosexuality. She suspects that this has alienated young women from feminism (see Frith 1994) and that the feminist old guard is left increasingly speaking to itself. But this has also meant that feminism in Britain has effectively ignored the growing legitimacy of the anti-sex moral majority. For example, sex education, officially at least, has retreated further into a homophobic procreative-dominant model of sex as responsibility. It is hard to imagine sex educators today daring to speak openly of pleasure and joy, or of discussing the benefits of young women learning to masturbate so that they know their own bodies before they experiment with another person. Children may be taught about safety but it is increasingly difficult to treat sex as a source of empowerment rather than as a source of danger. It is these sorts of developments that Segal feels are escaping feminist attention because of the impasse that has been reached in feminist theorising about (hetero-)sexuality.

Segal is therefore arguing that an emphasis on pleasure is not simply a hedonistic retreat but a source of resistance to negative and punitive discourses which are in the ascendancy. She declares herself in favour of a politics of sexual liberation, which is a controversial stance not only because of the radical feminist dismissal of these ideas, but because of Foucault's claim that there is no such thing as sexual liberation, as sexuality always resides in a field of power relations. However, Segal's attempt to direct the discussion back to issues of sexual liberation may not be idealistic nor based on the idea that sex resides outside the social. Rather she seems to be linking a politics of sexuality both to an institutional politics (of welfare rights, etc.) and to the concept of agency and personal empowerment. It is crucial to Segal's argument that these elements of structure and agency are linked because a focus on personal pleasure is hardly radical or ethical in itself. But she gives a subversive status back to pleasure by pointing out that there is again a strong movement to deny women pleasure and bodily autonomy and empowerment, as well as a desire to push them back into domesticity and orthodox heterosexual relationships. She encourages us to see that pleasure is not a hedonistic abandonment of moral or political values; it is actually on the same side of the struggle, along with anti-poverty and other social movements, against the new conservatism. In this way Segal takes on board some of the assertions made under the rubric of queer theory but, unlike authors such as Califia (1994), she does not appear to isolate sex and sexuality from questions of class and 'race', poverty and traditional politics.

So can we now begin to speak differently about heterosexualities? Rather than speaking of heterosexuality as all bad or all good, can we differentiate between oppressive and empowering heterosexualities, between muted and flagrant heterosexualities, between masculine heterosexualities and feminine, or even feminist, heterosexualities? In *Heterosexuality: a Feminism and Psychology Reader* (Wilkinson and Kitzinger 1993), a number of the women who had been invited to write about their experiences as heterosexual feminists disputed this appellation as too simplistic. A few quotations make this point tellingly:

> The label 'heterosexual' as usually applied doesn't really encompass these complexities of love, respect, anger and sensuality. Rather, I think of myself as a women-identified person who, because of a decision to

enter into a long-term affectional and sexual relationship with a man, is situated in a largely heterosexual social context.

(Crawford 1993: 43)

[A]lthough I have lived monogamously with a man I love for over 26 years, I am not now and never have been a 'heterosexual'. But neither have I ever been either a 'lesbian' or a 'bisexual'. What I am – and have been for as long as I can remember – is someone whose gender and sexuality have just never seemed to mesh very well with the available cultural categories.

(Bem 1993: 50)

Why address me so categorically as a heterosexual? Why was anyone so sure? Because I am married: Or because my husband seems 'straight'? Is it about my hairdo or my shoes or the things I have said, or not said?

(Gergen 1993: 62)

The cynical response to these careful remarks was to assume that these heterosexual women were in 'denial'. I find that in reading and rereading these remarks that what these women are expressing is both an ambivalent relationship to institutional or traditional heterosexuality and a fluid identity which refuses to be trapped by a crudely defined notion of heterosexual identity. I suggest that we need to build on these insights rather than dismiss them as justifications or excuses. These women were saying that they had no commitment to orthodox heterosexuality; we have surely known for a long time that many women who would never see themselves as lesbian or bisexual have had precisely this kind of ambiguity about orthodox heterosexuality. This ambiguity has taken many forms. Even Freud could not 'fix' women into heterosexuality the way he could men with his theory of the Oedipal struggle. More mundanely, we have accounts and personal tales of women's withdrawal from a male-defined heterosexuality and a refusal of penetration (even if other forms of sensual gratification were welcomed). Why else did the sexologists from the 1920s onwards set out to persuade women to keep having sexual intercourse with their husbands if it were not that many women were disinclined to continue the practice? We can now perhaps see that these women wanted a different type of heterosexuality. On the other hand there are women who enjoy penetration and who might not feel fully satisfied without it. Does this mean that their sexuality is male defined, or that they know what they like?

We know about the appalling abuse some women experience in heterosexual relationships, but we still know virtually nothing about how women in non-abusive relationships are negotiating their sexuality. Even if we were to ask, we know that the language available to describe sexuality is rigid and preformed in discourses of sexology, the tabloid media, sex education, the moral right and so on. The feminists who wrote of 'being' heterosexual in *Heterosexuality* were clearly struggling to find words and ways of expressing experiences which did not fit with preconceived ideas, including pre-conceived feminist ideas. Out of their struggle perhaps we can see hetero-sexualit*ies* emerging; perhaps also a new language which avoids terms like collusion, collaboration and even confession. We can certainly see radically different heterosexual identities emerging in which these women are far from being the dupes of patriarchy, are far from homophobic, are far from accept-ing male sexual dominance, and are far from seeking their own missing penises as Freud would have us do. Some of them also seem to be having a good time even if they feel they should do so quietly. But until we can start to find this new way of speaking of heterosexualities and allowing ourselves to appreciate differences of meaning and experience, feminist theories of sexuality will remain strangely repressed on a most important aspect of the lives of many women.

Notes

1 In this essay I shall try to avoid labelling and categorising feminisms. I appreciate that this is both controversial and difficult. Some might also find it objectionable because categories such as radical feminism are adhered to as a matter of real politi-cal affiliation and of pride. So I am not trying to ignore these differences out of an ignorance of their significance. But in this essay these differences are not the focus of my concern. I want to avoid the trap of appearing to define a whole category of feminist thought by reference to one or two authors because this merely invites the accusation that one misrepresents the whole. I do refer to revolutionary feminism at one stage, but this is essential because I am referring to the work of the Leeds Revolutionary Feminist Group. I may also label women 'feminist' where they have expressly labelled themselves but I am not trying to use any author as a represen-tative of a 'tendency'. There is also another reason for trying to avoid these cat-egories as much as possible. It is part of my argument that any discussion of heterosexuality seems to invoke old hostilities and rather worn-out debates. I suggest we need to go beyond a rerun of the old debates; in order to do this it helps if 'sides' are not labelled now as they were in former times as this just seems to invite old antagonisms back into the discussion.

2 I would suggest that the old argument that radical feminists were biological reduc-tionists is fallacious. Not because radical feminism was not, but because all femin-isms were until Judith Butler made us think much more clearly about these issues. Even so, I am not at all sure that many of us can avoid biologistic thinking since it is so much a part of common-sense and everyday speech that the mere invoking of the concept 'woman' invites a presumption of the foundational position of biology.

3 I realise that this is a contentious point and that post-Freudians did go on to argue about exactly how the child became heterosexual and whether it was the penis of the father or the breast of the mother that was most important. But the point that I am trying to make is that is that whilst psychoanalysis recognised that hetero-sexuality was achieved and not simply a biological given, they did not go on to problematise this final state as something which could, for example, be improved upon or which could be broadened out to recapture an infantile state of bisexu-ality. Heterosexuality was 'reinstated' as the norm and there it remained.

References

Abbott, P. and Wallace, C. (1989) The family, in P. Brown and R. Sparks (eds) *Beyond Thatcherism: Social Policy, Politics and Society*. Milton Keynes: Open University Press.

Abbott, S. and Love, B. (1972) *Sappho was a Right-On Woman*. New York: Stein and Day.

Adams, P. (1989) Of female bondage, in T. Brennan (ed.) *Between Feminism and Psychoanalysis*. London: Routledge.

Adkins, L. (1995) *Gendered Work: Sexuality, Family and the Labour Market*. Buckingham: Open University Press.

Allen, K.R. and Demo, D.H. (1995) The families of lesbians and gay men: a new frontier in family research, *Journal of Marriage and the Family*, 57: 111–27.

Anderson, R. (ed.) (1992) *Clinical Lectures on Klein and Bion*. London: Routledge.

Arendt, H. (1958) *The Human Condition*. Chicago: University of Chicago Press.

Austin, P. (1992) Femme-ininism, in J. Nestle (ed.) *The Persistent Desire: A Fem/Butch Reader*. Boston, MA: Alyson Publications.

Baker, P. (1994) Under pressure: what the media is doing to men, *Cosmopolitan*, November: 129–32.

Banks, A. and Gartrell, N.K. (1995) Hormones and sexual orientation: a questionable link, *Journal of Homosexuality*, 28(3/4): 247–68.

Bartky, S. (1988) Foucault, femininity, and the modernization of patriarchial power, in I. Diamond and L. Quinby (eds) *Feminism and Foucault: Reflections on Resistance*. Boston, MA: Northeastern University Press.

Bartky, S. (1990) *Femininity and Domination*. New York: Routledge.

Bartky, S.L. (1993) Hypatia unbound: a confession, in S. Wilkinson and C. Kitzinger (eds) *Heterosexuality: a Feminism and Psychology Reader*. London: Sage.

Beam, J. (ed.) (1986) *In the Life: a Black Gay Anthology*. Boston, MA: Alyson Publications.

Bejin, A. (1986) The decline of the psycho-analyst and the rise of the sexologist, in P. Aries and A. Bejin (eds) *Western Sexuality*. Oxford: Blackwell.

Bell, V. (1993) *Interrogating Incest: Feminism, Foucault and the Law*. London: Routledge.

Bem, S.L. (1993) On the inadequacy of our sexual categories: a personal perspective, in S. Wilkinson and C. Kitzinger (eds) *Heterosexuality: a Feminism and Psychology Reader*. London: Sage.

Beneke, T. (1989) Men on rape, in M.S. Kimmel and M.A. Messner (eds) *Men's Lives*. New York: Macmillan.

Benhabib, S. (1992) *Situating the Self*. Cambridge: Polity.

Benjamin, J. (1984) Master and slave: the fantasy of erotic domination, in A. Snitow, C. Standell and S. Thompson (eds) *Desire: the Politics of Sexuality*. London: Virago.

Benjamin, J. (1990) *The Bonds of Love*. London: Virago.

Benjamin, J. (1995) Sameness and difference: toward an 'over-inclusive' theory of gender development, in A. Elliott and S. Frosh (eds) *Psychoanalysis in Contexts: Paths between Theory and Modern Culture*. London: Routledge.

Berk, S.F. (1985) *The Gender Factory: the Apportionment of Work in American Households*. London: Plenum Press.

Berlant, L. and Freeman, E. (1993) Queer nationality, in M. Warner (ed.) *Fear of a Queer Planet: Queer Politics and Social Theory*. Minneapolis: University of Minnesota Press.

Bersani, L. (1987) Is the rectum a grave?, *October*, 43, winter: 217.

Berthoud, R. (ed.) (1985) *Challenges to Social Policy*. Aldershot: Gower.

Berube, A. and Escoffier, J. (1991) Queer/Nation, *Out/Look: National Lesbian and Gay Quarterly*, 11: 13–15.

Bev Jo (1984) For women who call themselves lesbians – are you thinking of getting pregnant?, in S. Lucia-Hoagland and J. Penelope (eds) *For Lesbians Only*. London: Onlywomen Press.

Birke, L. (1992) In pursuit of difference: scientific studies of women and men, in G. Kirkup and L. Smith Keller (eds) *Inventing Women: Science, Technology and Gender*. London: Polity/Open University.

Bland, L. (1994) Heterosexuality, feminism and the *Freewoman* journal in the early twentieth century. Paper presented to the British Sociological Association Annual Conference, Preston. Forthcoming (1996) as: The shock of the *Freewoman* journal: feminists speaking on heterosexuality in early 20C England, in J. Weeks and J. Holland (eds) *Sexual Cultures: Communities, Values and Intimacy*. London: Macmillan.

Blumstein, P. and Schwartz, P. (1983) *American Couples: Money, Work, Sex*. New York: Pocket Books.

Bornstein, K. (1994a) *Gender Outlaws: On Men, Women and the Rest of Us*. London: Routledge.

Bornstein, K. (1994b) Interview, in *Deneuve*, 4: 5.

Bowie, C. and Ford, N. (1989) Sexual behaviour of young people and the risk of HIV infection, *Journal of Epidemiology and Community Health*, 43(1): 61–5.

Brah, A. (1988) Extended review, *British Journal of Sociology of Education*, 9(1): 115–21.

Braidotti, R. (1991) *Patterns of Dissonance: a Study of Women in Contemporary Philosophy*. Cambridge: Polity Press.

Brennan, T. (ed.) (1989) *Between Feminism and Psychoanalysis*. London: Routledge.

Brennan, T. (1993) *History after Lacan*. London: Routledge.

Britton, R. (1992) The oedipus situation and the depressive position, in R. Anderson (ed.) *Clinical Lectures on Klein and Bion*. London: Routledge.

Britton, R. (1993) The missing link: parental sexuality in the oedipus complex, in D. Breen (ed.) *The Gender Conundrum*. London: Routledge.

Brod, H. (ed.) (1987) *The Making of Masculinities: the New Men's Studies*. Boston, MA: Allen and Unwin.

Brod, H. (1990) Pornography and the alienation of male sexuality, in J. Hearn and D. Morgan (eds) *Men, Masculinities and Social Theory*. London: Unwin Hyman.

Bryan, B., Dadzie, S. and Scafe, S. (1985) *The Heart of the Race*. London: Virago.

Butler, J. (1982) Lesbian S & M: the politics of dis-illusion, in R. Linden, D. Pagano, D. Russell and S. Leigh Star (eds) *Against Sadomasochism*. San Francisco: Frog in the Well Press.

Butler, J. (1990a) *Gender Trouble: Feminism and the Subversion of Identity*. New York: Routledge.

Butler, J. (1990b) Gender trouble, feminist theory and psychoanalytic discourse, in L. Nicholson (ed.) *Feminism/Postmodernism*. New York: Routledge.

Butler, J. (1991) Imitation and gender insubordination, in D. Fuss (ed.) *Inside/Out: Lesbian Theories, Gay Theories*. London: Routledge.

Butler, J. (1993a) *Bodies that Matter: on the Discursive Limits of 'Sex'*. London: Routledge.

Butler, J. (1993b) Critically queer, *GLQ: a Journal of Lesbian and Gay Studies*, 1(1): 17–32.

Byne, W. (1995) Science and belief: psychobiological research on sexual orientation, *Journal of Homosexuality*, 28(3/4): 303–44.

Caldwell, M.A. and Peplan, L.A. (1984) The balance of power in lesbian relationships, *Sex Roles*, 10: 587–600.

Califia, P. (1981) Feminism and sadomasochism, *Heresies*, 12: 30–4.

Califia, P. (1994) *Public Sex*. Pittsburgh, PA: Cleis Press.

Calkin, J. (1994) The third sex, *The Age*, Melbourne, Australia, 10 September.

Cameron, D. (1993) Telling it like it wasn't: how radical feminism became history, *Trouble and Strife*, 27: 11–15.

Cameron, D. and Frazer, E. (1987) *The Lust to Kill*. Cambridge: Polity Press.

Campbell, B. (1980) Feminist sexual politics, *Feminist Review*, 5: 1–18.

Canaan, J.E. and Griffin, C. (1990) The new men's studies: part of the problem or part of the solution?, in J. Hearn and D. Morgan (eds) *Men, Masculinities and Social Theory*. London: Unwin Hyman.

Caprio, F. (1954) *Female Homosexuality: a Psychodynamic Study of Lesbianism*. New York: Citadel Press.

Capron, D. (1994) A review of 1992, *Population Trends*, 75: 1–9.

Carabine, J. (1992a) Constructing women: women's sexuality and social policy, *Critical Social Policy*, 34: 23–37.

Carabine, J. (1992b) 'Constructing women: women's sexuality and social policy', unpublished Ph.D. thesis. University of Sheffield.

Carabine, J. and Richardson, D. (1995) Redefining social policy: sexuality and social policy. Paper presented to Social Policy Association Annual Conference, Sheffield Hallam University, Sheffield.

Carrigan, T., Connell, R.W. and Lee, J. (1985) Toward a new sociology of masculinity, *Theory and Society*, 14: 551–604.

Case, S.-E. (1993) Toward a butch-femme aesthetic, in H. Abelove *et al.* (eds) *The Lesbian and Gay Studies Reader*. London: Routledge.

Cavin, S. (1985) *Lesbian Origins*. San Francisco: ism Press.

Chapman, R. and Rutherford, J. (1988) *Male Order: Unwrapping Masculinity*. London: Lawrence and Wishart.

Cheal, D. (1991) *Family and the State of Theory*. Toronto: University of Toronto Press.

Chesler, P. (1978) *About Men*. London: The Women's Press.

Chodorow, N. (1978) *The Reproduction of Mothering: Psychoanalysis and the Sociology of Gender*. Berkeley: University of California Press.

Chodorow, N. (1992) *Feminism and Psychoanalytic Theory*. London: Yale University Press.

Chodorow, N. (1994) *Femininities, Masculinities, Sexualities: Freud and Beyond*. London: Free Association Books.

Christian, H. (1994) *The Making of Anti-Sexist Men*. London: Routledge.

Clark, David (ed.) (1991) *Marriage, Domestic Life and Social Change*. London: Routledge.

Clark, David and Haldane, D. (1990) *Wedlocked?* Cambridge: Polity Press.

Cline, S. (1993) *Women, Celibacy and Passion*. London: Andre Deutsch.

CLIT Collective (1974) CLIT Statement No.2, in S. Lucia-Hoagland and J. Penelope (eds) *For Lesbians Only: a Separatist Anthology*. London: Onlywomen Press.

Cockburn, C. (1991) *In the Way of Women: Men's Resistance to Sex Equality in Organizations*. London: Macmillan.

Collins, P.H. (1990) *Black Feminist Thought: Knowledge, Consciousness and the Politics of Empowerment*. London: HarperCollins.

Connell, R.W. (1987) *Gender and Power: Society, the Person and Sexual Politics*. Cambridge: Polity Press.

Connell, R.W. (1995) *Masculinities: Knowledge, Power and Social Change*. Cambridge: Polity Press.

Contratto, S. (1987) Father presence in women's psychological development, in G.M. Platt, J. Rabow and M. Goldman (eds) *Advances in Psychoanalytic Sociology*. Malabar, FL: Krieger.

Cooper, D. (1995) *Power in Struggle: Feminism, Sexuality and the State*. Buckingham: Open University Press.

Cooper, J. (1991) Births outside marriage: recent trends and associated demographic and social changes, *Population Trends*, 63: 8–18.

Cornwall, A. and Lindisfarne, N. (eds) (1994) *Dislocating Masculinity: Comparative Ethnographies*. London: Routledge.

Cosis Brown, H. (1992) Lesbian, the state and social work practice, in M. Langan and L. Day (eds) *Women, Oppression and Social Work: Issues in Anti-Discriminatory Practice*. London: Routledge.

Coward, R. (1984) *Female Desire: Women's Sexuality Today*. London: Collins/Paladin.

Craib, I. (1987) Masculinity and male dominance, *Sociological Review*, 34(4): 721–43.

Craig, S. (ed.) (1992) *Men, Masculinity and the Media*. London: Sage.

Crawford, M. (1993) Identity, 'passing' and subversion, in S. Wilkinson and C.

Kitzinger (eds) *Heterosexuality: a Feminism and Psychology Reader*. London: Sage.

Crimp, D. (1991) Jacket note to E.K. Sedgwick *Epistemology of the Closet*. London: Harvester Wheatsheaf.

Dale, J. and Foster, P. (1986) *Feminists and State Welfare*. London: Routledge, Kegan and Paul.

Davis, A. (1982) *Women, Race and Class*. London: The Women's Press.

Davy, K. (1993) Fe/male impersonation: the discourse of camp, in M. Meyer (ed.) *The Politics and Poetics of Camp*. London: Routledge.

de Beauvoir, S. (1974) *The Second Sex*. Harmondsworth: Penguin.

Delphy, C. (1977) *The Main Enemy: a Materialist Analysis of Women's Oppression*. London: Women's Research and Resources Centre.

Delphy, C. (1984) *Close to Home: a Materialist Analysis of Women's Oppression*. London: Hutchinson.

Delphy, C. (1992) Mothers' Union?, *Trouble and Strife*, 24: 12–19.

Delphy, C. (1993) Rethinking sex and gender, *Women's Studies International Forum*, 16(1): 1–9.

Delphy, C. (1994) Changing women in a changing Europe: is 'difference' the future for feminism?, *Women's Studies International Forum*, 17(2/3): 18–27.

Delphy, C. and Leonard, D. (1992) *Familiar Exploitation: a New Analysis of Marriage in Contemporary Western Societies*. Cambridge: Polity.

d'Emilio, J. (1984) Capitalism and gay identity, in A. Snitow, C. Stansell and S. Thompson (eds) *Desire: the Politics of Sexuality*. London: Virago.

d'Emilio, J. and Freedman, E.B. (1988) *Intimate Matters: a History of Sexuality in America*. New York: Harper Row.

Dominelli, L. (1991) *Women across Continents: Feminist Comparative Social Policy*. Hemel Hempstead: Harvester Wheatsheaf.

Douglas, C.A. (1990) *Love and Politics: Radical Feminist and Lesbian Theories*. San Francisco: ism Press.

Driver, E. and Droisen, A. (eds) (1989) *Child Sexual Abuse: Feminist Perspectives*. London: Macmillan.

Dunne, G. (1992) Difference at work: perceptions of work from a non-heterosexual perspective, in H. Hinds, A. Phoenix and J. Stacey (eds) *Working Out: New Directions for Women's Studies*. London: Falmer Press.

Dworkin, A. (1981) *Pornography: Men Possessing Women*. London: Women's Press.

Dworkin, A. (1987) *Intercourse*. London: Secker and Warburg.

Easthope, A. (1990) *What a Man's Gotta Do: the Masculine Myth in Popular Culture*. London: Unwin Hyman.

Edwards, T. (1994) *Erotics and Politics: Gay Male Sexuality, Masculinity and Feminism*. London: Routledge.

Eichenbaum, L. and Orbach, S. (1982) *Outside In . . . Inside Out*. Harmondsworth: Penguin.

Eisenstein, H. (1991) *Gender Shock: Practising Feminism on Two Continents*. Sydney: Allen and Unwin.

Elliott, A. (1992) *Social Theory and Psychoanalysis in Transition*. Oxford: Blackwell.

Ernst, S. (1987) Can a Daughter be a Woman?, in S. Ernst and M. Maguire (eds) (1987) *Living with the Sphinx: Papers from the Women's Therapy Centre*. London: The Women's Press.

Evans, D.T. (1993) *Sexual Citizenship: the Material Construction of Sexualities*. London: Routledge.

Evans, M. (1994) Desire incarnate: review of Judith Butler's *Bodies that Matter, Times Higher Education Supplement*, 18 February.

Faderman, L. (1981) *Surpassing the Love of Men: Romantic Friendship and Love Between Women from the Renaissance to the Present*. London: Junction Books.

Fine, M. (1988) Sexuality, schooling, and adolescent females: the missing discourse of desire, *Harvard Educational Review*, 58(1): 29–53.

Flax, J. (1993) *Disputed Subjects: Essays on Psychoanalysis, Politics and Philosophy*. London: Routledge.

Ford, N. and Morgan, K. (1989) Heterosexual lifestyles of young people in an English city, *Journal of Population and Social Studies*, 1(2): 167–85.

Foster, P. (1991) Well women clinics – a serious challenge to mainstream health care?, in M. Maclean and D. Groves (eds) *Women's Issues in Social Policy*. London: Routledge.

Foucault, M. (1972) *The Archaeology of Knowledge* (trans. A.M. Sheridan-Smith). London: Tavistock. (First published in French 1969)

Foucault, M. (1979) *Discipline and Punish* (trans. A.M. Sheridan-Smith). London: Penguin. (First published in French 1975)

Foucault, M. (1980) Truth and power, in C. Gordon (ed.) *Michel Foucault: Power/Knowledge*. Brighton: Harvester.

Foucault, M. (1981) *The History of Sexuality: Vol. 1*. Harmondsworth: Pelican Books.

Foucault, M. (1990) *The History of Sexuality. Volume 1: an Introduction* (trans. R. Hurley). New York: Vintage Books. (First published in French 1976)

Fraser, N. (1989) *Unruly Practices: Power, Discourse and Gender in Contemporary Social Theory*. Cambridge: Polity Press.

Friedman, S. and Sarah, E. (eds) (1982) *On the Problem of Men: Two Feminist Conferences*. London:The Women's Press.

Frith, H. (1994) Turning us off, *Feminism and Psychology*, 4(2): 315–16.

Frosh, S. (1987) *The Politics of Psychoanalysis*. London: Macmillan.

Frosh, S. (1994) *Sexual Difference: Masculinity and Psychoanalysis*. London: Routledge.

Frye, M. (1977) Some reflections on separatism and power, in H. Abelove *et al.* (eds) *The Lesbian and Gay Studies Reader*. New York: Routledge.

Frye, M. (1983) *The Politics of Reality: Essays in Feminist Theory*. Trumansburg, NY: The Crossing Press.

Frye, M. (1992) *Willful Virgin: Essays in Feminism*. Freedom, CA: The Crossing Press.

Fuss, D. (1990) *Essentially Speaking: Feminism, Nature and Difference*. London: Routledge.

Fuss, D. (ed.) (1991a) *Inside/Out: Lesbian Theories, Gay Theories*. New York: Routledge.

Fuss, D. (1991b) 'Inside/Out', in D. Fuss (ed.) *Inside/Out: Lesbian Theories, Gay Theories*. New York: Routledge.

Fuss, D. (1993) Freud's fallen women: identification, desire, and 'A case of homosexuality in a woman', in M. Warner (ed.) *Fear of a Queer Planet: Queer Politics and Social Theory*. Minneapolis: University of Minnesota Press.

Gagnon, J. and Simon, W. (1974) *Sexual Conduct*. London: Hutchinson.

Gallop, J. (1982) *Feminism and Psychoanalysis: the Daughter's Seduction*. London: Macmillan.

Garber, M. (1993) *Vested Interests: Crossdressing and Cultural Anxiety*. London: Penguin.

Gatens, M. (1991) A critique of the sex/gender distinction, in S. Gunew (ed.) *A Reader in Feminist Knowledge*. London: Routledge.

Gates, H.L. Jr. (1993) The black man's burden, in M. Warner (ed.) *Fear of a Queer Planet: Queer Politics and Social Theory*. Minneapolis: University of Minnesota Press.

Geltmaker, T. (1992) The queer nation acts up: health care, politics, and sexual diversity in the county of angels, *Environment and Planning D: Society and Space*, 10: 609–50.

Gergen, M. (1993) Unbundling our binaries – genders, sexualities, desires, in S. Wilkinson and C. Kitzinger (eds) *Heterosexuality: a Feminism and Psychology Reader*. London: Sage.

Giddens, A. (1992) *The Transformation of Intimacy: Sexuality, Love and Eroticism in Modern Societies*. Cambridge: Polity Press.

Ginsburg, N. (1992) *Divisions of Welfare: a Critical Introduction to Comparative Social Policy*. London: Sage.

Goetz, J. (1987) Interrupting homophobia, *Achilles Heel*, 8: 5–7.

Goldsby, J. (1993) Queen for 307 days: looking b(l)ack at Vanessa Williams and the sex wars, in A. Stein (ed.) *Sisters, Sexperts, Queers: Beyond the Lesbian Nation*. New York: Plume.

Gorna, R. (1992) Delightful visions: from anti-porn to eroticizing safer sex, in L. Segal and M. McIntosh (eds) *Sex Exposed: Sexuality and the Pornography Debate*. London: Virago.

Graham, H. (1993) *Hardship and Health in Women's Lives*. London: Harvester Wheatsheaf.

Gregson, N. and Lowe, M. (1993) Renegotiating the domestic division of labour? A study of dual career households in north east and south east England, *Sociological Review*, 41: 475–505.

Griggers, C. (1993) Lesbian bodies in the age of (post)mechanical reproduction, in L. Doan (ed.) *The Lesbian Postmodern*. New York: Columbia University Press.

Guillaumin, C. (1981) The practice of power and belief in nature. Part 1: The appropriation of women, *Feminist Issues*, 1(2): 3–28.

Halberstam, J. (1994) F2M: the making of female masculinity, in L. Doan (ed.) *The Lesbian Postmodern*. New York: Columbia University Press.

Hall, L. A. (1991) *Hidden Anxieties*. Cambridge: Polity Press.

Hallet, C. (ed.) (1995) *Women and Social Policy*. Basingstoke: Macmillan.

Ham, C. (1992) *Health Policy in Britain* (3rd edition). Basingstoke: Macmillan.

Hanmer, J. (1990) Men, power and the exploitation of women, in J. Hearn and D. Morgan (eds) *Men, Masculinities and Social Theory*. London: Unwin Hyman.

Hanmer, J. and Maynard, M. (eds) (1987) *Women, Violence and Social Control*. London: Macmillan.

Harding, S. (1991) *Whose Science? Whose Knowledge?* Ithaca, NY: Cornell University Press.

Harper, P.B. (1993) Eloquence and epitaph: black nationalism and the homophobic impulse in responses to the death of Max Robinson, in M. Warner (ed.) *Fear of a Queer Planet: Queer Politics and Social Theory*. Minneapolis: University of Minnesota Press.

Harris, O. (1984) Households as natural units, in K. Young, C. Wolkowitz and R. McCullagh (eds) *Of Marriage and the Market: Women's Subordination Internationally and its Lessons* (2nd edition). London: Routledge.

Hayes, C. and Wright, A. (1989) Preparations for change in north west Hertfordshire, in M. Pye, M. Kapila, G. Buckley and D. Cunningham (eds) *Responding to the AIDS Challenge: a Comparative Study of Local AIDS Programmes in the UK*. Harlow: Longman.

Hayes, S. (1994) Coming over all queer, *New Statesman/Society*, 16 September.

Hearn, J. (1987) Changing men's studies, *Achilles Heel*, 8: 19–22.

Hearn, J. (1992) *Men in the Public Eye*. London: Routledge.

Hearn, J. and Morgan, D. (eds) (1990) *Men, Masculinities and Social Theory*. London: Unwin Hyman.

Hearn, J., Sheppard, D.L., Tancred-Sheriff, P. and Burrell, G. (1989) *The Sexuality of Organization*. London: Sage.

Heath, S. (1982) *The Sexual Fix*. London: Hutchinson.

Hemmings, C. (1993) Resituating the bisexual body, in J. Bristow and A.R. Wilson (eds) *Activating Theory: Lesbian, Gay, Bisexual Politics*. London: Lawrence and Wishart.

Hemmings, S. (1986) Overdose of doctors, in S. O'Sullivan (ed.) *Women's Health: a Spare Rib Reader*. London: Pandora.

Hewitt, M. (1992) *Welfare Ideology and Need: Developing Perspectives on the Welfare State*. Brighton: Harvester Wheatsheaf.

Heyn, D. (1992) *The Erotic Silence of Married Women*. London: Bloomsbury.

Hinshelwood, R.D. (1991) *A Dictionary of Kleinian Thought*. London: Free Association Books.

Hochschild, A. (1989) *The Second Shift: Working Parents and the Revolution at Home*. London: Piatkus.

Holland, J. (1992) *The Sexual Knowledge and Practice of Young Women in the Context of HIV/AIDS with particular reference to different ethnic groups*. Report for the Department of Health. London: Department of Health.

Holland, J., Ramazanoglu, C., Sharpe, S. and Thomson, R. (1992a) Pleasure, pressure and power: some contradictions of gendered sexuality, *Sociological Review*, 40(4): 645–74.

Holland, J., Ramazanoglu, C., Scott, S., Sharpe, S. and Thomson, R. (1992b) Pressure, resistance, empowerment: young women and the negotiation of safer sex, in P. Aggleton, P. Davies and G. Hart (eds) *AIDS: Rights, Risk and Reason*. London: Falmer Press.

Holland, J., Ramazanoglu, C., Sharpe, S. and Thomson, R. (1994a) Power and desire: the embodiment of female sexuality, *Feminist Review*, 46: 22–38.

Holland, J., Ramazanoglu, C., Sharpe, S. and Thomson, R. (1994b) Achieving masculine sexuality: young men's strategies for managing vulnerability, in L. Doyal, J. Naidoo and T. Wilton (eds) *AIDS: Setting a Feminist Agenda*. London: Taylor and Francis.

Holland, J., Ramazanoglu, C., Scott, S. and Thomson, R. (1994c) Desire, risk and control: the body as a site of contestation, in L. Doyal, J. Naidoo and T. Wilton (eds) *AIDS: Setting a Feminist Agenda*. London: Taylor and Francis.

Holland, J., Ramazanoglu, C., Sharpe, S. and Thomson, R. (1996a) Reputations: journeying into gendered power relations, in J. Weeks and J. Holland (eds) *Sexual Cultures: Communities, Values and Intimacy*. London: Macmillan.

Holland, J., Ramazanoglu, C., Sharpe, S. and Thomson, R. (1996b) *The Male in the Head: Heterosexuality, Gender and Power*. London: The Tufnell Press.

Hollibaugh, A. (1989) Desire for the future: radical hope in passion and pleasure, in C. Vance (ed.) *Pleasure and Danger: Exploring Female Sexuality*. London: Pandora.

Hollway W. (1984a) Gender difference and the production of subjectivity, in J. Henriques *et al. Changing the Subject*. London: Methuen.

Hollway, W. (1984b) Women's power in heterosexual sex, *Women's Studies International Forum*, 7(1): 63–8.

Hollway, W. (1989) *Subjectivity and Method in Psychology: Gender, Meaning and Science*. London: Sage.

Hollway, W. (1993) Theorizing heterosexuality: a response, *Feminism and Psychology*, 3(3): 412–17.

Hollway, W. (1995a) A second bite at the heterosexual cherry, *Feminism and Psychology*, 5(1): 126–30.

Hollway, W. (1995b) Feminist discourses and women's heterosexual desire, in S. Wilkinson and C. Kitzinger (eds) *Feminism and Discourse*. London: Sage.

Hollway, W. (forthcoming) The Maternal Bed, in W. Hollway and B. Featherstone (eds) *Subject Mother/Subject Child: Mothering and Ambivalence*. London: Routledge.

hooks, b. (1989) *Talking Back: Thinking Feminist-Thinking Black*. London: Sheba.

Irigaray, L. (1974) *Speculum of the Other Woman* (trans. G.C. Gill). Ithaca, NY: Cornell University Press.

Jackson, D. (1993) Letters page, *Body Politic*, 2: 7.

Jackson, M. (1987) 'Facts of life' or the eroticization of women's oppression? Sexology and the social construction heterosexuality, in P. Caplan (ed.) *The Cultural Construction of Sexuality*. London: Tavistock.

Jackson, M. (1994) *The Real Facts of Life: Feminism and the Politics of Sexuality c1850–1940*. London: Taylor and Francis.

Jackson, S. (1978a) The social context of rape, *Women's Studies International Quarterly*, 1(1): 27–38.

Jackson, S. (1978b) How to make babies: sexism and sex education, *Women's Studies International Quarterly*, 1(4): 341–52.

Jackson, S. (1982a) *Childhood and Sexuality*. Oxford: Blackwell.

Jackson, S. (1982b) Masculinity, femininity and sexuality, in S. Friedman and E. Sarah (eds) *On the Problem of Men*. London: The Women's Press.

Jackson, S. (1992) The amazing deconstructing woman: the perils of postmodern feminism, *Trouble and Strife*, 25: 25–31.

Jackson, S. (1993a) Even sociologists fall in love: an exploration in the sociology of emotions, *Sociology*, 27(2): 201–20.

Jackson, S. (1993b) Love and romance as objects of feminist knowledge, in M. Kennedy, C. Lubelska, and V. Walsh (eds) *Making Connections: Women's Studies, Women's Movements, Women's Lives*. London: Taylor and Francis.

Jackson, S. (1994) Heterosexuality as a problem for feminist theory. Paper presented to 'Sexualities in Social Context', British Sociological Association Conference, Preston.

Jackson, S. (1995) Heterosexuality, power and pleasure, *Feminism and Psychology*, 5(1): 131–5.

Jackson, S. (1996) Heterosexuality as a problem for feminist theory, in L. Adkins and V. Merchant (eds) *Sexualising the Social: Power and the Organisation of Sexuality*. London: Macmillan.

Jardine, A. and Smith, P. (eds) (1987) *Men in Feminism*. London: Methuen.

Jefferson, A. (1994) Theorizing masculine subjectivity, in T. Newburn and E. Stanko (eds) *Just Boys Doing Business: Men, Masculinity and Crime*. London: Routledge.

Jeffreys, S. (1985) *The Spinster and her Enemies*. London: Pandora.

Jeffreys, S. (1989) Butch and femme, now and then, in Lesbian History Group (eds) *Not a Passing Phase*. London: The Women's Press.

Jeffreys, S. (1990) *Anticlimax: a Feminist Perspective on the Sexual Revolution*. London: The Women's Press.

Jeffreys, S. (1994) *The Lesbian Heresy: a Feminist Perspective on the Lesbian Sexual Revolution*. London: The Women's Press.

Johnson, J. (1973) *Lesbian Nation: The Feminist Solution*. New York: Touchstone.

Johnson, M. (1988) *Strong Mothers, Weak Wives: the Search for Gender Equality*. Berkeley: University of California Press.

Johnson, M. (1989) Feminism and the theories of Talcott Parsons, in R.A. Wallace (ed.) *Feminism and Sociological Theory*. London: Sage.

Jukes, A. (1993) *Why Men Hate Women*. London: Free Association.

Kanneh, K. (1993) Sisters under the skin: a politics of heterosexuality, in S. Wilkinson and C. Kitzinger (eds) *Heterosexuality: a Feminism and Psychology Reader*. London: Sage.

Kaplan G. and Rogers, L. (1990) The definition of male and female: biological reductionism and the sanctions of normality, in S. Gunew (ed.) *Feminist Knowledge: Critique and Construct*. London: Routledge.

Kappeler, S. (1986) *The Pornography of Representation*. Cambridge: Polity Press.

Katz, J.N. (1995) *The Invention of Heterosexuality*. New York: Dutton.

Kelly, L. (1988) *Surviving Sexual Violence*. Cambridge: Polity Press.

Kennedy, E.L. and Davis, M.D. (1993) *Boots of Leather, Slippers of Gold: The History of a Lesbian Community*. New York: Routledge.

Kimmel, M. (1987) *Changing Men: New Directions in Research on Men and Masculinity*. Newbury Park, California: Sage.

Kimmel, M. (1988) The Gender Blender, *Guardian*, 29 September: 20.

Kinsman, G. (1995) Men loving men: the challenge of gay liberation, in M.S. Kimmel and M.A. Messner (eds) *Men's Lives* (3rd edition). Needham Heights, MA: Allyn and Bacon.

Kitzinger, C. (1994) Problematizing pleasure: radical feminist deconstructions of sexuality and power, in H.L. Radtke and H.J. Stam (eds) *Power/Gender: Social Relations in Theory and Practice*. London: Sage.

Kitzinger, C. and Wilkinson, S. (1993a) The precariousness of heterosexual feminist identities, in M. Kennedy, C. Lubleska and V. Walsh (eds) *Making Connections: Women's Studies, Women's Movements, Women's Lives*. London: Taylor and Francis.

Kitzinger, C. and Wilkinson, S. (1993b) Theorizing heterosexuality, in S. Wilkinson and C. Kitzinger (eds) *Heterosexuality: a Feminism and Psychology Reader.* London: Sage.

Kitzinger, C. and Wilkinson, S. (1994a) Re-viewing heterosexuality, *Feminism and Psychology*, 4(2): 330–6.

Kitzinger, C. and Wilkinson, S. (1994b) Virgins and queers: rehabilitating hetero-sexuality?, *Gender and Society,* 8(3): 444–63.

Koedt, A. (1972) The myth of the vaginal orgasm, in A. Koedt (ed.) *Radical Feminism.* New York: Quadrangle.

Koestenbaum, W. (1991) Jacket note to E.K. Sedgwick *Epistemology of the Closet.* London: Harvester Wheatsheaf.

Kotz, L. (1993) Anything But Idyllic: Lesbian Filmmaking In The 1980s And 1990s, in A. Stein (ed.) *Sisters, Sexperts, Queers: Beyond the Lesbian Nation.* New York: Plume.

Lacan, J. and L'Ecole Freudienne (1982) *Feminine Sexuality* (ed. J. Mitchell, trans. J. Rose). London: Macmillan.

Lamos, C. (1994) The postmodern lesbian position: on our backs, in L. Doan (ed.) *The Lesbian Postmodern.* New York: Columbia University Press.

Land, H. (1991) Time to care, in M. Maclean and D. Groves (eds) *Women's Issues in Social Policy.* London: Routledge.

Laqueur, T. (1990) *Making Sex.* Boston, MA: Harvard University Press.

Larkin, J. and Popaleni, K. (1994) Heterosexual courtship violence and sexual harass-ment: the private and public control of young women, *Feminism and Psychology*, 4(2): 213–27.

Layder, D. (1994) *Understanding Social Theory.* London: Sage.

Leeds Revolutionary Feminist Group (1981) Political lesbianism: the case against heterosexuality', reprinted in Onlywomen Press (eds) (1981) *Love Your Enemy? The Debate Between Heterosexual Feminism and Political Lesbianism.* London: Onlywomen Press.

Lees, S. (1993) *Sugar and Spice: Sexuality and Adolescent Girls.* London: Penguin.

Lister, R. (1990) Women, economic dependency and citizenship, *Journal of Social Policy*, 19(4): 445–68.

Lothstein, L.M. (1983) *Female-to-male Transsexualism.* Boston, MA: Routledge and Kegan Paul.

Loulan, J. (1990) *The Lesbian Erotic Dance.* San Francisco: Spinsters.

Macey, D. (1995) On the subject of Lacan, in A. Elliott and S. Frosh (eds) *Psycho-analysis in Contexts: Paths between Theory and Modern Culture.* London: Rout-ledge.

Macintyre, S. (1976) 'Who wants babies?' The social construction of 'instincts', in D.L. Barker and S. Allen (eds) *Sexual Divisions and Society: Process and Change.* London: Tavistock.

MacKinnon, C. (1982) Feminism, Marxism, method and the state: an agenda for theory, *Signs*, 7(2): 515–44.

MacKinnon, C.A. (1987) *Feminism Unmodified: Discourses on Life and Law.* Cam-bridge, MA: Harvard University Press.

MacKinnon, C.A. (1989) *Towards a Feminist Theory of the State.* Cambridge, MA: Harvard University Press.

Maclean, M. and Groves, D. (eds) (1991) *Women's Issues in Social Policy.* London: Routledge.

Madge, N. and Brown, M. (1982) *Despite the Welfare State: a Report on the SSRC/ DHSS Programme of Research into Transmitted Deprivation.* London: Heineman.

Mansfield, P. and Collard, J. (1988) *The Beginning of the Rest of Your Life: A Portrait of Newly-Wed Marriage.* London: Macmillan.

Marshall, T.H. (1975) *Social Policy.* London: Hutchinson.

Marshall,T.H. (1977) *Class, Citizenship and Social Development.* Chicago: University of Chicago Press.

Martin, E. (1987) *The Woman in the Body.* Milton Keynes: Open University Press.

Martin, E. (1989) *The Woman in the Body.* Boston, MA: Beacon Press.

Marx, K. and Engels, F. (1970) *The German Ideology* (ed. C.J. Arthur). London: Lawrence and Wishart.

McIntosh, M. (1968) The homosexual role, in K. Plummer (ed.) *The Making of the Modern Homosexual.* London: Hutchinson.

McNay, L. (1992) *Foucault and Feminism: Power, Gender and Self.* Cambridge: Polity Press.

Mens Verhulst, J. van, Schreurs, K. and Woertman, L. (1993) *Daughtering and Mothering.* London: Routledge.

Mercer, K. and Julien, I. (1988) Race, sexual politics and black masculinity: a dossier, in R. Chapman and J. Rutherford (eds) *Male Order: Unwrapping Masculinity.* London: Lawrence and Wishart.

Metcalf, A. and Humphries, M. (1985) *The Sexuality of Men.* London: Pluto Press.

Middleton, P. (1992) *The Inward Gaze: Masculinity and Subjectivity in Modern Culture.* London: Routledge.

Mihalik, G.J. (1989) More than two: anthropological perspectives on gender, *Journal of Gay and Lesbian Psychotherapy*, 1(1): 105–18.

Millet, K. (1972) *Sexual Politics.* London: Abacus.

Mishra, R. (1981) *Society and Social Policy.* London: Macmillan.

Mitchell, J. (1974) *Psychoanalysis and Feminism.* London: Allen Lane.

Mitchell, J. (ed.) (1986) *The Selected Melanie Klein.* Harmondsworth: Penguin.

Mitchell, J. and Rose, J. (1982) *Feminine Sexuality – Jacques Lacan and the Ecole Freudienne.* London: Macmillan.

Modleski, T. (1984) *Loving with a Vengeance.* London: Methuen.

Molyneux, M. (1979) Beyond the domestic labour debate, *New Left Review*, 116: 3–27.

Moore, S. (1988) Getting a bit of the other – the pimps of postmodernism, in R. Chapman and J. Rutherford (eds) *Male Order: Unwrapping Masculinity.* London: Lawrence and Wishart.

Moraga, C. and Anzaldua, G. (eds) (1981) *This Bridge Called My Back: Writings By Radical Women of Color.* Watertown, MA: Persephone Press.

Morgan, D. (1992) *Discovering Men.* London: Routledge.

Morris, D. (1994) *The Naked Ape*, 2nd edn. (original edition 1967). London: Vintage.

Morris, L. (1985a) Renegotiation of the domestic division of labour in the context of male redundancy, in H. Newby (ed.) *Restructuring Capital.* London: Macmillan.

Morris, L. (1985b) Local social networks and domestic organisations: a study of redundant steel workers and their wives, *Sociological Review*, 33: 327–42.

Morris, L. (1990) *The Workings of the Household: a US-UK Comparison.* Cambridge: Polity Press.

Mort, F. (1994) Essentialism revisited? Identity politics and late twentieth-century discourses of homosexuality, in J. Weeks (ed.) *The Lesser Evil and the Greater Good: the Theory and Politics of Social Diversity*. London: Rivers Oram Press.

Nestle, J. (1987) *A Restricted Country*. London: Sheba.

Nestle, J. (1992) Flamboyance and fortitude: an introduction, in J. Nestle (ed.) *The Persistent Desire: a Femme/Butch Reader*. Boston, MA: Alyson.

Nichols, M. (1987) Lesbian sexuality: issues and developing theory, in Boston Lesbian Psychologies Collective (eds) *Lesbian Psychologies*. Chicago: University of Illinois Press.

Nicholson, L. J. (1984) Feminist theory: the private and the public, in C.C. Gould (ed.) *Beyond Domination: New Perspectives on Women and Philosophy*. Lanham, MD, USA: Rowman and Littlefield.

Nicholson, L. (1994) Interpreting gender, *Signs: Journal of Women in Culture and Society*, 20(11): 79–105.

O'Connor, M. and Ryan, J. (1994) *Wild Desires and Mistaken Identities: Lesbianism and Psychoanalysis*. London: Virago.

O'Connor, P. (1995) Understanding variation in marital sexual pleasure: an impossible task?, *Sociological Review*, 43: 342–62.

Oakley, A. (1984) *The Sociology of Housework* (2nd edition). Oxford: Blackwell.

Onlywomen Press (ed.) (1981) *Love Your Enemy: The Debate Between Heterosexual Feminism and Political Lesbianism*. London: Onlywomen Press.

OPCS (1993) *Marriage and divorce statistics, 1991*. London: HMSO.

Orr, D. (1995) Say Grace, *Guardian Weekend*, London: 22 July.

Parker, R. (1995) *Torn in Two: The Experience of Maternal Ambivalence*. London: Virago.

Parsons, T. and Bales, R. (1955) *Family, Socialization and Interaction Process*. Glencoe, IL: Free Press.

Pateman, C. (1988) *The Sexual Contract*. Cambridge: Polity Press.

Patton C. (1985a) *Sex and Germs: The Politics of AIDS*. Boston, MA: South End Press.

Patton C. (1985b) Heterosexual AIDS panic: a queer paradigm, *Gay Community News*, 9 February, pp.6–8.

Patton, C. (1993) Tremble, hetero swine!', in M.Warner (ed.) *Fear of a Queer Planet: Queer Politics and Social Theory*. Minneapolis: University of Minnesota Press.

Penelope, J. (1992) *Call Me Lesbian: Lesbian Lives, Lesbian Theory*. Freedom, CA: The Crossing Press.

Penelope, J. (ed.) (1994) *Out of the Class Closet: Lesbians Speak*. Freedom, CA: The Crossing Press.

Person, E.S. (1989) *Love and Fateful Encounters: The Power of Romantic Passion*. London: Bloomsbury.

Pleck, J. H. (1987) The theory of male sex-role identity: its rise and fall, 1936 to the present, in H. Brod (ed.) *The Making of Masculinities: the New Men's Studies*. Boston, MA: Allen and Unwin.

Plummer, K. (1975) *Sexual Stigma: an Interactionist Account*. London: Routledge and Kegan Paul.

Plummer, K. (1992) Speaking its name: inventing a lesbian and gay studies, in K. Plummer (ed.) *Modern Homosexualities: Fragments of Lesbian and Gay Experience*. London: Routledge.

Plummer, K. (1995a) Sociology under the sign of homosexuality. Paper presented at 'The Future of Lesbian and Gay Studies' conference, Homostudies Department, University of Utrecht, Netherlands, 3–5 July.

Plummer, K. (1995b) *Telling Sexual Stories: Power, Change and Social Worlds.* London: Routledge.

Polity Press (1994) *The Polity Reader in Gender Studies.* Cambridge: Polity Press.

Popenoe, D. (1988) *Disturbing the Nest: Family Change and Decline in Modern Societies.* New York: Aldine de Gruyter.

Popenoe, D. (1993) American family decline, 1960–1990: a review and appraisal, *Journal of Marriage and the Family*, 55: 527–55.

Population Trends 77 (1994) Table 7: Population: age, sex and marital status: 45.

Prendergast, S. (1995) With gender on my mind: menstruation and embodiment at adolescence, in J. Holland and M. Blair (with S. Sheldon) (eds) *Debates and Issues in Feminist Research and Pedagogy.* Clevedon: Multilingual Matters in association with the Open University.

Radicalesbians (1970) The woman-identified woman, in A. Koedt, E. Levine and A. Rapone (eds) *Radical Feminism.* New York: Quadrangle Books.

Radway, J. (1987) *Reading the Romance.* London: Verso.

Ramazanoglu, C. (ed.) (1993) *Up Against Foucault: Explorations of some tensions between Foucault and feminism.* London: Routledge.

Ramazanoglu, C. (1994) Theorising heterosexuality: a response to Wendy Hollway, *Feminism and Psychology*, 4(2): 320–1.

Ramazanoglu, C. (1995) Back to basics: heterosexuality, biology and why men stay on top, in M. Maynard and J. Purvis (eds) *(Hetero)sexual Politics.* London: Taylor and Francis.

Ramazanoglu, C. and Holland, J. (1993) Women's sexuality and men's appropriation of desire, in C. Ramazanoglu (ed.) *Up Against Foucault: Explorations of some tensions between Foucault and feminism.* London: Routledge.

Ramos, J. (ed.) (1987) *Compañeras: Latina Lesbians: an anthology.* New York: Latina Lesbian History Project.

Raymond, J.G. (1986) *A Passion for Friends.* Boston, MA: Beacon.

Raymond, J.G. (1994) *The Transsexual Empire*, 2nd edn. New York: Teachers College Press.

Reinhold, S. (1994) Through the parliamentary looking glass: 'real' and 'pretend' families in contemporary British politics, *Feminist Review*, 48: 61–79.

Rich, A. (1980) Compulsory heterosexuality and lesbian existence, *Signs*, 5(4): 631–60.

Rich, A. (1983) Compulsory heterosexuality and lesbian existence, in E. Abel and E.K. Abel (eds) *The Signs Reader: Women, Gender and Scholarship.* London: University of Chicago Press.

Richardson, D. (1992) Constructing lesbian sexualities, in K. Plummer (ed.) *Modern Homosexualities.* London: Routledge.

Richardson, D. (1993) Sexuality and male dominance, in D. Richardson and V. Robinson (eds) *Introducing Women's Studies: Feminist Theory and Practice.* London: Macmillan.

Richardson, D. (1996) 'Misguided, dangerous and wrong': On the maligning of radical feminism', in D. Bell and R. Klein (eds) *Radically Speaking.* Melbourne: Spinifex Press.

Richardson, D. (forthcoming) Social Theory, Social Change and Sexuality. London: Routledge.

Richardson, D. and Robinson, V. (1994) Theorizing women's studies, gender studies and masculinity: the politics of naming, *European Journal of Women's Studies*, 1(1): 11–27.

Riley, D. (1988) '*Am I that Name?' Feminism and the Category of 'Women' in History*. London: Macmillan.

Robinson, V. (1993a) Heterosexuality: beginnings and connections, in S. Wilkinson and C. Kitzinger (eds) *Heterosexuality: a Feminism and Psychology Reader*. London: Sage.

Robinson, V. (1993b) Introducing women's studies, in D. Richardson and V. Robinson (eds) *Introducing Women's Studies: Feminist Theory and Practice*. London: Macmillan.

Robinson, V. and Richardson, D. (1994) Publishing feminism: redefining the women's studies discourse, *Journal of Gender Studies*, 3(1): 87–94.

Roscoe, W. (ed.) (1992) *Living the Spirit: a Gay American Indian Anthology*. NY, USA: St. Martin's Press.

Roseneil, S. and Mann, K. (1994) Some mothers do 'ave 'em: gender and the underclass debate, *Journal of Gender Studies*, 3, 3: 315–29.

Rowland, R. (1993) Radical feminist heterosexuality: the personal and the political, in S. Wilkinson and C. Kitzinger (eds) *Heterosexuality: a Feminism and Psychology Reader*. London: Sage.

Rubin, G. (1975) The traffic in women, in R. Reiter (ed.) *Toward an Anthropology of Women*. New York: Monthly Review Press.

Rubin, G. (1984) Thinking sex: notes for a radical theory of the politics of sexuality, in C. Vance (ed.) *Pleasure and Danger: Exploring Female Sexuality*. London: Pandora.

Rubin, G. (1992) Of catamites and kings: reflections on butch, gender, and boundaries, in J. Nestle (ed.) *The Persistent Desire*. Boston, MA: Alyson Publications.

Ruse, M. (1980) *Homosexuality: A Philosophical Inquiry*. Oxford: Basil Blackwell.

Russell, D.E.H. (ed.) (1989) *Exploring Nuclear Phallacies*. New York: Pergamon.

Rustin, M. (1991) *The Good Society and the Inner World*. London: Verso.

Rutherford, J. (1992) *Men's Silences: Predicaments in Masculinity*. London: Routledge.

Rycroft, C. (1972) *A Critical Dictionary of Psychoanalysis*. Harmondsworth: Penguin.

Sawicki, J. (1992) *Disciplining Foucault*. London: Routledge.

Scruton, R. (1986) *Sexual Desire: a Philosophical Investigation*. London: Weidenfeld and Nicolson.

Scully, D. (1990) *Understanding Sexual Violence*. London: Unwin Hyman.

Sedgwick, E.K. (1985) *Between Men: English Literature and Male Homosocial Desire*. New York: Columbia University Press.

Sedgwick, E.K. (1990) *Epistemology of the Closet*. Berkeley: University of California Press.

Segal, H. (1979) *Klein*. London: Fontana/Collins.

Segal, L. (1990) *Slow Motion: Changing Masculinities, Changing Men*. London: Virago.

Segal, L. (1994) *Straight Sex: the Politics of Pleasure*. London: Virago.

Seidler, V.J. (1989) *Rediscovering Masculinity: Reason, Language and Sexuality*. London: Routledge.

Seidler, V. (1991) *Recreating Sexual Politics*. London: Routledge.

Seidler, V.J. (ed.) (1992) *Men, Sex and Relationships: Writings from Achilles Heel*. London: Routledge.

Seidler, V.J. (1994) *Unreasonable Men: Masculinity and Social Theory*. London: Routledge.

Seidman, S. (1992) *Embattled Eros: Sexual Politics and Ethics in Contemporary America*. New York: Routledge.

Shotter, J. (1993) Psychology and citizenship: identity and belonging, in B.S. Turner (ed.) *Citizenship and Social Theory*. London: Sage.

Smart, C. (1992) Disruptive bodies and unruly sex: the regulation of reproduction and sexuality in the nineteenth century, in C. Smart (ed.) *Regulating Womanhood: Historical Essays on Marriage, Motherhood and Sexuality*. London: Routledge.

Smart, C. (1996) Desperately seeking post-heterosexual woman, in J. Holland and L. Adkins (eds) *Sex, Sensibility and the Gendered Body*. London: Macmillan.

Smyth, C. (1992) *Lesbians Talk Queer Notions*. London: Scarlet Press.

Søndergaard, D.M. (1993) *Feminism and Psychology*, 3(3): 395–6.

Stacey, J. and Thorne, B. (1985) The missing feminist revolution in sociology, *Social Problems*, 32(4): 301–16.

Stanley, L. (1992) *Is there a Lesbian Epistemology?* Manchester: Manchester University Sociology Department, Feminist Praxis Monograph 34.

Staples R. (1995) Stereotypes of black male sexuality: the facts behind the myths, in M.S. Kimmel and M.A. Messner (eds) *Men's Lives* (3rd edition). Needham Heights, MA: Allyn and Bacon.

Stein, A. (ed.) (1993) *Sisters, Sexperts, Queers. Beyond the Lesbian Nation*. New York: Plume.

Steinman, C. (1992) Gaze out of bounds: men watching men on television, in S. Craig (ed.) *Men, Masculinity and the Media*. London: Sage.

Stoller, R. (1985) *Observing the Erotic Imagination*. New Haven, CT: Yale University Press.

Stoltenberg, J. (1989) *Refusing to be a Man: Essays on Sex and Justice*. New York: Meridan.

Stone, S. (1991) The *Empire* strikes back: a posttranssexual manifesto, in J. Epstein and K. Straub (eds) *Body Guards: the Cultural Politics of Gender Ambiguity*. London: Routledge.

Swindells, J. (1993) A straight outing, *Trouble and Strife*, 26: 40–4.

Taylor, H. (1989) *Scarlett's Women: Gone with the Wind and its Female Fans*. London: Virago.

Thompson, D. (1994) Retaining the radical challenge: a reply to Wendy Hollway, *Feminism and Psychology*, 4(2): 326–9.

Thompson, S. (1990) Putting a big thing into a little hole: teenage girls' accounts of sexual initiation, *Journal of Sex Research*, 27(3): 341–61.

Thomson, R. (1994) Moral rhetoric and public pragmatism: the recent politics of sex education, *Feminist Review*, 48:40–61.

Torton Beck, E. (ed.) (1982) *Nice Jewish Girls: a Lesbian Anthology*. Boston, MA: Beacon Press.

Trouble and Strife Collective (1983) Editorial, *Trouble and Strife*, 1: 2–3.

Tucker S. (1995) *Fighting Words: An Open Letter to Queers and Radicals*. London: Cassell.

Turner, B.S. (1993) *Citizenship and Social Theory*. London: Sage.

US Bureau of the Census (1991) *Statistical Abstract of the United States: 1991* (111th edition). Washington, DC: US Government Printing Office.

VanEvery, J. (1991/2) Who is 'the family'? The assumptions of British social policy, *Critical Social Policy*, 33: 62–75.

VanEvery, J. (1995a) *Heterosexual Women Changing the Family: Refusing to be a Wife*! London: Taylor and Francis.

VanEvery, J. (1995b) Heterosexuality, heterosex and heterosexual privilege, *Feminism and Psychology*, 5(1): 140–4.

VanEvery, J. (1996) Sinking into his arms . . . arms in his sink: heterosexuality and feminism revisited, in L. Adkins, J. Holland, V. Merchant and J. Weeks (eds) *Sexualizing the Social: Power and the Organization of Sexuality*. London: Macmillan.

Walby, S. (1990) *Theorizing Patriarchy*. Oxford: Blackwell.

Walby, S. (1994) Is Citizenship Gendered?, *Sociology*, 28(2): 379–95.

Walker, A. (1983) Social policy, social administration and the social construction of social policy, in M. Looney, D. Boswell and J. Clark (eds) *Social Policy and Social Welfare*. Milton Keynes: Open University Press.

Ward, A., Gregory, J. and Yuval-Davis, N. (eds) (1992) *Women and Citizenship in Europe*. Stoke-on-Trent: Trentham Books.

Warner, M. (ed.) (1993) *Fear of a Queer Planet: Queer Politics and Social Theory*. Minneapolis: University of Minnesota Press.

Watney, S. (1987) *Policing Desire: Pornography, AIDS and the Media*. London: Methuen.

Weedon, C. (1987) *Feminist Practice and Poststructuralist Theory*. Oxford: Blackwell.

Weeks, J. (1981) *Sex, Politics and Society*. London: Longman.

Weeks, J. (1985) *Sexuality and its Discontents*. London: Routledge and Kegan Paul.

Weeks, J. (1986) *Sexuality*. London: Ellis Horwood/Tavistock Publications.

Weeks, J. (1990) *Sex, Politics and Society* (2nd edition). London: Longman.

West, C. and Zimmerman, D.H. (1987) Doing gender, *Gender and Society*, 1(2): 125–51.

Weston, K. (1993) Parenting in the age of AIDS, in A. Stein (ed.) *Sisters, Sexperts, Queers: Beyond the Lesbian Nation*. New York: Plume.

Westwood, S. (1984) *All Day, Every Day*. London: Pluto Press.

Wiegman, R. (1994) Introduction: mapping the lesbian postmodern, in L. Doan (ed.) *The Lesbian Postmodern*. New York: Columbia University Press.

Wilkinson, S. and Kitzinger, C. (eds) (1993) *Heterosexuality: a Feminism and Psychology Reader*. London: Sage.

Wilkinson, S. and Kitzinger, C. (1994) Dire straits? Contemporary rehabilitations of heterosexuality, in G. Griffin, M. Hester, S. Rai and S. Roseneil (eds) *Stirring It: Challenges for Feminism*. London: Taylor and Francis.

Williams, E. and Rose, G. (1995) Elaine Williams talks to Gillian Rose: keep your mind in hell and despair not, *Times Higher Education Supplement*, 14 April: 15, 17.

Williams, F. (1989) *Social Policy: A Critical Introduction*. Cambridge: Polity Press.

Wilson, E. (1993) Is transgression transgressive?, in J. Bristow and A. Wilson (eds) *Activating Theory: Lesbian, Gay, Bisexual Politics*. London: Lawrence and Wishart.

Wilton, T. (1992) *Antibody Politic: AIDS and Society.* Cheltenham: New Clarion Press.

Wilton, T. (1993a) Queer subjects: lesbians, heterosexual women and the academy, in M. Kennedy, C. Lubelska and V. Walsh (eds) *Making Connections: Women's Studies, Women's Movements, Women's Lives.* London: Taylor and Francis.

Wilton, T. (1993b) Sisterhood in the service of patriarchy: heterosexual women's friendships and male power, in S. Wilkinson and C. Kitzinger (eds) *Heterosexuality: a Feminism and Psychology Reader.* London: Sage.

Wilton, T. (1994) Feminism and the erotics of health promotion, in L. Doyal *et al.* (eds) *AIDS: Setting a Feminist Agenda.* London: Taylor and Francis.

Wilton, T. (forthcoming) *En/gendering AIDS: Sex, Texts, Epidemic.*

Wittig, M. (1981) One is not born woman, *Feminist Issues,*1(2): 47–54.

Wittig, M. (1992) *The Straight Mind and Other Essays.* Brighton: Harvester Wheatsheaf.

Wolfenden Report (1957) *Report of the Committee on Homosexual Offences and Prostitution.* London: HMSO.

Woods, C. (1995) *State of the Queer Nation: A Critique of Gay and Lesbian Politics in 1990s Britain.* London: Cassell.

World in Action (1993) *Children Having Children.* Granada TV, October.

Yanagisako, S. and Delaney, C. (eds) (1995a) *Naturalizing Power: Essays in Feminist Cultural Analysis.* London: Routledge.

Yanagisako, S. and Delaney, C. (1995b) Naturalizing power, in S. Yanagisako and C. Delaney (eds) *Naturalizing Power: Essays in Feminist Cultural Analysis.* London: Routledge.

Young, A. (1993) The authority of the name, in S. Wilkinson and S. Kitzinger (eds) *Heterosexuality: a Feminism and Psychology Reader.* London: Sage.

Zimmerman, B. (1992) *The Safe Sea of Women: Lesbian Fiction 1969–1989,* London: Onlywomen Press.

Zita, J.N. (1992) The male lesbian and the postmodern body, *Hypatia,* 7(4): 106–27.

Zita, J.N. (1994) Gay and lesbian studies: yet another unhappy marriage?, in L. Garber (ed.) *Tilting the Tower: Lesbians Teaching Queer Subjects.* New York: Routledge.

Index

UNDERSTANDING MASCULINITIES
SOCIAL RELATIONS AND CULTURAL ARENAS

Máirtín Mac an Ghaill (ed.)

Masculinity is gaining increasing popular and academic interest. At one level, football hooligans, absent fathers, 'Essex man' and 'new men' are regular media presences. At the same time, masculinity is the subject of increasingly sophisticated theoretical discussion, and there are a wide range of accounts of what masculinity means.

Understanding Masculinities is the first introductory text to examine the range of different theoretical and methodological approaches to the understanding of masculinity. It brings together overviews of the key theoretical debates with new empirical material, focusing on different social and cultural arenas, and the wide range of masculinities which exist. It discusses education, unemployment, sport, sexuality, HIV, and black masculinities. *Understanding Masculinities* critically explores the gendered and sexual dynamics of these masculinities, challenging and transforming our conventional assumptions.

Understanding Masculinities will be important reading for undergraduate and masters students of sociology, women's studies, gender and psychology. It will also be of interest to anyone concerned with broadening their understanding of masculinity.

Contents
Introduction – Part I: Social relations of masculinities – Hard rulers – 'Feckless fathers' – Masculinities and families – Schooling masculinities – 'Men' at 'work' – Men, masculinity and the challenge of long-term unemployment – Part 2: Cultural arenas of masculinities – Freedom – Masculinity, power and identity – 'One thing leads to another' – Sporting masculinities – Are you sitting comfortably? Men's storytelling, masculinities, prison culture and violence – From 'little boy' to 'the complete destroyer' – 'Empowering men to disempower themselves' – Part 3: Critical evaluations of masculinities – White fright – Reading black masculinities – Is masculinity dead? – Index.

Contributors
Joyce E. Canaan, David Collinson, Nigel Edley, Christine Griffin, Christian Haywood, Jeff Hearn, Christine Heward, Tony Jefferson, Richard Johnson, Máirtín Mac an Ghaill, David Marriott, Andrew Parker, Peter Redman, Richard Thurston, Sallie Westwood, Margaret Wetherell, Sara Willott.

240pp   0 335 19460 5 (Paperback)   0 335 19461 3 (Hardback)

POWER IN STRUGGLE
FEMINISM, SEXUALITY AND THE STATE

Davina Cooper

What is power? And how are social change strategies shaped by the ways in which we conceptualize it? Drawing on feminist, poststructuralist, and marxist theory, Davina Cooper develops an innovative framework for understanding power relations within fields as diverse as queer activism, municipal politics, and the regulation of lesbian reproduction. *Power in Struggle* explores the relationship between power, sexuality, and the state and, in the process, provides a radical rethinking of these concepts and their interactions. The book concludes with an important and original discussion of how an ethics of empowerment can inform political strategy.

Special features

- brings together central aspects of current radical, political theory in an innovative way
- offers a new way of conceptualizing the state, power and sexuality

Contents

Introduction – Beyond domination?: productive and relational power – The politics of sex: metaphorical strategies and the (re)construction of desire – Multiple identities: sexuality and the state in struggle – Penetration on the defensive: regulating lesbian reproduction – Access without power: gay activism and the boundaries of governance. Beyond resistance: political strategy and counter-hegemony – Afterword – Bibliography – Index.

192pp   0 335 19211 4 (Paperback)   0 335 19212 2 (Hardback)

DISARMING PATRIARCHY
FEMINISM AND POLITICAL ACTION AT GREENHAM

Sasha Roseneil

'To disarm patriarchy, to resist and transform relations of male domination and female subordination, must be the ultimate goal of feminism. The question of how this is to be done is, therefore, one of feminism's central concerns, and is also my subject here. This book is about how, at one historically specific moment, in one particular place in the world, women acted together to confront patriarchy and to challenge militarism.'

(from the Introduction)

In *Disarming Patriarchy*, Sasha Roseneil examines the ways in which feminists can resist and transform relations of male domination and female subordination. It is an important contribution to the debates which surround feminism, politics, identity, sexuality and militarism. It is also about one of the most momentous social movements of the twentieth century, a movement which galvanized into action hundreds of thousands of women, confronting patriarchal ideas and challenging the foundations of militarism. *Disarming Patriarchy* is the first in-depth sociological study of the Greenham Common Women's Peace Camp, and is an important contribution to the understanding of women's agency and feminist politics, and to the analysis of contemporary social movements.

Disarming Patriarchy is important reading for students of women's studies, sociology, politics and international relations and for everyone interested in our recent social history.

Contents

240pp   0 335 19057 X (Paperback)   0 335 19058 8 (Hardback)